20-Minute

Learning

Connection

by Douglas B. Reeves, Ph.D.

Simon & Schuster
New York - London - Singapore - Sydney - Toronto

Kaplan Publishing
Published by Simon & Schuster, Inc.
1230 Avenue of the Americas
New York, NY 10020

For bulk sales to schools, colleges, and universities, please contact:
Order Department, Simon & Schuster, Inc.,
100 Front Street, Riverside, NJ 08075
Phone: (800) 223-2336 Fax: (800) 943-9831.

Kaplan® is a registered trademark of Kaplan, Inc.

Designed by Richard Oriolo

Manufactured in the United States of America

January 2002
10 9 8 7 6 5 4 3 2 1

Library of Congress Cataloging-in Publication-Data

ISBN: 0-7432-1183-9
ISSN:

Contents

Acknowledgements

In my discipline of statistics, we learn about *a priori* and *a posteriori* probabilities. There is a lesson in such study. My *a priori* obligations include a debt of thanks to the grandfather I never knew, Sherman Vester Reeves, but whose 1906 teaching license I found in my father's office. Teachers in Green Forest, Arkansas at the dawn of the 20th century had their test scores on their teaching licenses. If one were to search for the genesis of high academic standards, the search might profitably begin in Carroll County. My grandmother, Laura Anderson Johnson, was a teacher and superintendent of schools. My mother, Julie Reeves, taught as a volunteer for decades, with her only compensation being the love and admiration of her students. My father, J.B. Reeves, devoted his last years of his life to the professorate, but those who knew him would argue that from his time as a field artilleryman in World War II until his last breath, he was a teacher to generations.

My *a posteriori* obligations are to my children, whose enthusiasm, love, and kind words are the lights of my life. Having said those nice things, I offer this plea: If you see four children laughing uproariously in the education section of your local bookstore as they point at this book, their names are Brooks, Alexander, Julia, and James. Please tell them to behave themselves and return to the self-improvement aisle where they belong.

Between the past and future lies the present, in which I wrote this volume. Maureen McMahon of Simon & Schuster is walking evidence of Stephen King's maxim that, "to write is human; to edit, divine." Rudy Robles provided encyclopedic knowledge of state standards and synthesized his knowledge in a manner so clear and concise that he will never find employment in Washington, D.C. Lori Duggan Gold provided a steady stream of connections to reporters and policy analysts who helped me distinguish the rhetorical chaff from the intellectual wheat. Abby Remer's creative and thoughtful voice preserved an emphasis on art, music, beauty, and enjoyment in a world in which standards are stereotyped as sterile and dull.

Special thanks are due to the hundreds of parents, teachers, and school leaders who took the time to participate in focus groups and personal interviews as part of my research for this book. I am particularly indebted to Charles Sodergren, a retired principal and teacher, whose extensive comments and perspectives as a parent, grandparent, and career educator were very helpful.

For reassurance at just the right time, challenge when I needed it, and love when I least deserved it, I am always indebted to Shelley Sackett. This mother, lawyer, teacher, and wonderful spouse makes books worth writing and life worth living.

dr
Swampscott, Massachusetts

How to Get the Most Out of This Book

Here is the most important test question you will ever have:

A parent's best strategy to promote school success is to:

a) *Terrorize* children by threatening them with failure and loss of promotion to the next grade.

b) *Humiliate* children by comparing them to other kids with better scores.

c) *Exhaust* children by engaging in frantic last-minute test preparation.

d) *Build, nurture, and empower* children by giving them the skills to be confident and capable learners.

If the last choice appeals to you more than the first three alternatives, then this book is written for you. You will learn not only how to help your child meet academic standards and succeed on tests, but more importantly, you will learn how to help your child become a confident, capable, and empowered learner.

a busy parent

How Can You Make a Difference in Just 20 Minutes a Day?

Although we have not met, I believe I have a good idea of who you are and why you selected this book. You are a busy parent. Whether you work at home, at an office, or on the road, you manage multiple priorities and face many demands on your time. You want to be more involved in your children's education, but some days it seems as if the time required by your other responsibilities leaves little time for a focus on your child's schoolwork. You read the report cards and newsletters and often look at your child's schoolwork, some of which may be on your refrigerator door. You attend parent meetings and school events whenever you can. You read with your child, though not as much as you did during the preschool years. You have heard about academic standards and know that some of the tests required by the state and school district are very important, and you have a nagging feeling that your child should be better prepared. But at the end of a long day, you really don't feel like adding the role of substitute teacher to your long and growing list of duties. Am I getting close to your reality?

Practical Advice for Busy Parents

Your busy lifestyle is the norm, not the exception. Less than a third of children attending school today come from a home of the 1950s' television stereotype with a stay-at-home mother whose principal role is the management of family and nurturing of children. Far more typical is a case in which both parents are working outside the home or there is only one parent in the household, and that person must work to support the family. Even the parents who have chosen to stay at home and make the raising of children their primary goal have a far different routine than Donna Reed and her television counterparts. The caricature of the stay-at-home parent has given way to parents who are active in political, cultural, and social causes and for whom school activities are one of many other pursuits. The fact that these parents earn no money outside the home does not indicate that they are not working. These parents are subject to the same exhaustion, burn-out, and frustration as parents who rise at 5:30 every morning, get children ready for school, work a full day and more, and return home in the evening to potentially overwhelming demands for help from their children.

Here is the good news: If you can devote 20 minutes each day to helping your children succeed in school, you can make a profound difference in the intellectual development and emotional growth of your child. If you like the ideas put forth here, you may find that the amount of time you spend building confident, capable, and empowered children will be worth more than 20 minutes a day. But make no mistake: Twenty minutes a day, focused on the right questions and the most effective activities, can make a huge difference in the lives of your children and their success in school. We are not talking about aimless discussions and unproductive questions such as the exchange known to every parent:

"What did you do in school today?"
"Nothing."

Rather, we offer practical advice for kids and parents. Throughout this book you will find checklists, activities, even letters to school officials that have been written for you. While no one, least of all authors, can take the place of parents, we can save you some time and make your role in supporting school success somewhat less stressful and time consuming.

The path to student success is not without some challenges. Therefore, we will address the requirements for making some reasonable trade-offs and minor changes in family routine. Fair warning: This will involve a little less television and a little more reading. It will involve moving a few chairs and creating the space and time for an effective home learning environment. But our goal is joyful learning, not joyless boot camp. Even as an exceptionally busy parent, you can make 20 minutes into a powerful learning experience if you will commit to three principles:

First, be yourself. Find activities that you genuinely enjoy and with which you can model the creative energy that comes from intellectual engagement with your child. This book contains a wonderful variety of activities that directly support essential knowledge and skills for your child. Although the activities are arranged in the same order as the state standards, you need not go through them in that sequence. Find activities that are engaging, exciting, interesting, and fun for both you and your child.

The second principle that will make your 20 minutes most valuable is that you are supportive. Remember the last time you learned a new skill? Perhaps it was a computer program, a foreign language, or a musical instrument. No matter how talented and brilliant you are, learning new things takes some time and patience. No matter how motivated you are, learning requires some perseverance and emotional resilience. Some of the academic requirements for children in school today are as challenging for them as they were for you when you were struggling with and eventually acquiring complex skills. If you can recall the need for patience, understanding, and clarity during your own difficult learning experiences, then assume that those needs apply in exponentially large proportions for your child. An important part of your support is the clarity of your expectations. Two of the most important intellectual skills you will build with your child are reflection and self-evaluation. You will build those skills by regularly asking your child to revise and improve work, whether it is a letter to a relative or a recipe for dinner. Performing these activities will be most valuable if you encourage your child to take a moment to reflect and ask, "What did I learn and how can I do this better next time?"

Third, it is important that you are consistent. Find a regular time, perhaps immediately before or after your evening meal, for your 20-Minute Learning Connection. During this time, the television is off and the telephone answering machine is on. You are giving your children the gift that they need, indeed crave, more than anything else in the world: your undivided attention. The focus that you provide during these 20-minute activities will model the concentration and diligence that you associate with learning.

What Are Standards and Will They Last?

Academic standards have been the single most important movement in education in the last fifty years. Standards—simple statements of what students should know and be able to do—will continue long after every other contemporary educational fad has expired. While teachers and parents are weary of the "flavor of the month" educational reforms that come and go with the phases of the moon, standards have two qualities that guarantee their success: fairness and effectiveness.

Because so many educational movements have come and gone, it is reasonable to wonder whether standards will follow "new math" into oblivion. The enduring nature of standards rests with the fact that standards are the key to fairness, and fairness is a value that is timeless. Lots of trends come and go in education, but the simple requirement—that teachers, students, and parents should understand what students are expected to know and be able to do—is an enduring element of education both in the U.S. and abroad. Every state, and virtually every industrialized nation in the world, has some form of academic standards. The actual content of the standards varies, with some sets of standards emphasizing certain academic areas more than others. But the central idea of standards is consistent from Peoria to Paris, from Florida to Florence, from Los Angeles to London: School should not be an impenetrable mystery, and students have a right to know what is expected of them. Fairness will not go out of style.

Rather than exposing children to a demoralizing environment in which lucky students understand what makes the teacher happy and the unlucky just "don't get it," standards-based schools offer a clear set of expectations. With standards, students, teachers, and parents have the opportunity to know and understand what is expected of every student. Children have an innate sense of fairness. They understand that clarity is better than ambiguity and that consistency is superior to uncertainty.

The second essential quality of standards is that they are effective. When they are properly implemented, school standards have an impact on test designers, curriculum creators, teachers, and school leaders, as well as students. Far from transforming schools into joyless boot camps, effective school leaders use academic standards to make connections to the arts, extracurricular activities, and every other element of school life.

Thus standards are related not only to academic success but also to the emotional and intellectual welfare of children. Our desire is to help build confident, capable, and empowered learners. This means much more than drilling students in math and spelling facts (though that is still not a bad idea), and more than asking children to read aloud after dinner (though that is a wonderful family practice). Children become confident, capable, and empowered not only when they know the right answer on a test, but when they have the emotional resilience to persist in learning difficult concepts and when they persevere in the face of challenging, ambiguous, or seemingly impossible test items. Real student empowerment rests not in the futile effort to memorize the answer to every conceivable test question, but on the realistic prospect of developing strategies that can be used on every test in school, in college, and in the world of work and life beyond school.

empowered learners

Connections: Music, Art, Physical Education, and More

Although this book focuses on the most commonly tested academic standards—mathematics, language arts, social studies, and science—it is important to note that other areas of the school curriculum remain vitally important for your child's intellectual growth and development. Evidence from a number of research studies is consistent: Students who participate in the arts, physical education, and extracurricular activities consistently demonstrate superior academic and social skills. Thus, our focus on academic standards is not intended to diminish other athletic, artistic, and extracurricular activities that enrich the lives of children. In fact, many of the activities in this book combine academic and artistic, or academic and athletic skills.

Stress and Anxiety

Perhaps the most important message for parents is this: Stress and anxiety are communicable diseases. Children are not born with stress about school, homework, and tests; they *learn* that debilitating stress and anxiety are a part of school. Perhaps these destructive lessons are learned from schoolmates and teachers, but it is far more likely that such lessons are learned at home. No parent intentionally creates anxiety and stress for a child, but our conversations about school—particularly our discussions of tests—can have such an effect. This is very likely a reflection of the parents' own attitude toward school and testing. Take a few minutes to think about your own experiences and the stress and anxiety you experienced as a student. Most parents can objectively recognize that their school experiences had some good and bad elements. We are far more likely, however, to recall and transmit the parts of school that had the strongest emotional impact, and strong emotional impact in school is quite likely to be negative. The embarrassment over a failed exam, the humiliation as other students laughed, the feeling of despair and rejection when a teacher expressed disappointment—these memories linger far more than a hundred "smiley faces" that we routinely received on schoolwork. Thus, it is the parent, and no one but the parent, who adds balance and clarity to the school experience. The two essential ways in which effective parents add this balance include constructive and accurate discussions about school and the creation of learning opportunities that occur outside of school. The activities in this book are designed to support schoolwork and they will also develop students who are confident and capable. These activities have value not only because they are related to educational standards, but also because they will help to create a learning environment in your home. They will help you model the love of learning that every child must have and which every parent can nurture.

only a parent

The Most Important Teacher: You

The enormity of the task ahead can be daunting. After all, a parent might ask, "Shouldn't schools be doing this?" It's a fair question. In some cases, the schools can and should do more. But there is one thing that even the best schools with unlimited resources and brilliant teachers cannot do: They cannot be parents. Parents are the most important teachers any child can ever have. This doesn't mean that parents must be experts in every subject or masters of teaching techniques. But only a parent can give a child the ability to say words such as:

"I know that my mom and dad are proud of me."

"I mess up sometimes, but it's okay, because I know I can learn from my mistakes."

"I didn't do as well as I wanted to, but I know how to get better next time."

Only a parent can provide the emotional security and strength of character that build a child who is confident, capable, and empowered. Unfortunately, some parents substitute their own academic expertise for emotional resilience. Every time there is the "nuclear-powered science fair project" obviously done by a parent, the emotional consequence is not pride, but the absolute conviction by the child that "I'm not good enough to do this on my own." The activities in this book will show you how to create a learning environment in which you and your child learn together, make mistakes together, laugh together, and maintain a love of learning amidst all the chaos of daily life, as your child develops independence and confidence.

If You Don't Have Time for the Whole Book

A few readers are thinking, "I can't read the whole book—where do I start?" Although every page is here for a purpose, we recognize the limits of time and the need to focus on the essentials. Therefore, if your time is limited and you want the maximum value in the minimum time, we suggest that you focus on three areas. Start with Chapter 2 for the "why" of standards, then proceed to Chapter 5 for the "how" of standards. Then find an activity from the section starting on page 145 that you and your child will enjoy. Finish with a review of the appendices, where you can find additional resources that are directly relevant to your particular needs. Not every reader will be interested in the sections for students with special needs nor will everyone find the chapter on home schooling essential. We include those chapters because they represent significant and growing areas in education.

Learning Activities

At the end of this book you will find a variety of learning activities. You will find that these ideas have value, not only because they are directly related to the academic standards of your state, but also because they help to build the necessary thinking, reasoning, and communication skills your child needs in any school in any state. These activities will help you make family learning time a regular part of your routine.

A Special Note for Parents of Children with Special Needs

More than ten percent of students in school have a disability that influences their success in school. These disabilities range from differences in the way that they process information to profound physical and neurological challenges. These students are protected by a variety of federal and state statutes, the Individuals with Disabilities Education Act (IDEA) being the most significant legislation in this area. Parents of these students are often alarmed when a school official states that academic standards must apply to "all" students, sometimes adding sarcastically, "What is it about the word 'all' you don't understand?" Chapter 9 is devoted entirely to students with special needs. The bottom line, however, is the clear legal mandate that the individual needs of students must be taken into consideration in all matters involving standards, testing, and curriculum. Standards have great merit for schools, but there is danger in linking legitimate educational standards to the "standardization" of policies for students for whom the law clearly requires attention to individual needs.

It has been said that education is the "new civil right." This is true for students with special needs as well as disadvantaged families. The individualization of standards and testing requirements for students with special needs is not merely a nice thing to do; it is a legal requirement. Chapter 9 and the appendices provide sample letters and checklists for parents of students with special needs to ensure that you are empowered to protect the rights of your child and serve as an advocate on his behalf.

What about Changes in Standards and Tests?

Finally, the subject of standards and testing is changing on a daily basis. As this book goes to press, legislatures throughout the nation are being challenged to change tests and reformulate standards. The only thing that is certain is that tests and standards will continue to change. To help you keep up to date on the latest changes in standards and assessment for your state, we have created an Internet website with current information on the latest changes in standards and tests for your state. Just go to www.kaptest.com/crusadeintheclassroom and click on the name of your state for the latest updates on standards and assessment in your area. You will also find links to the state education department for your state where you can find the latest information on policy and procedures for education in your state.

The prospect of changes in standards, however, must not obscure this essential fact: While individual standards and particular testing policies may change, the fundamentals of standards are here to stay. Standards will endure because they are the most fair and effective way to educate children. While change may be a certainty in our world, it is also certain that the educational system will not retreat to the age of mystery in which a "standard" was whatever captured the interest of a teacher and "proficiency" varied from one classroom to another. Fads may come and go, but the imperatives of fairness and effectiveness will never vanish from the educational landscape.

communication

A Dose of Reality

My children are in public schools, including elementary, middle, and high school. My travels to schools throughout the world place me in contact with teachers, school leaders, and parents, hundreds of whom contributed ideas for this book. Each year I speak and listen to more than a hundred audiences, and thus far have worked in 49 states as well as Africa, Asia, and Europe. Whether these conversations take place in the United States or abroad, whether in an economically advantaged setting or a financially depressed area, there are remarkably common themes that I hear from parents, teachers, and school leaders. The number one issue is always communication. Parents want to hear more specific and more frequent information from the school; teachers want to have more immediate feedback from parents. Parents want to be welcomed into the classroom and insist that the individual needs and characteristics of their children be taken into account; educators and school leaders want parents to understand that today's schools are different from the classrooms of three decades ago. Most of all, parents do not wish to guess about the educational needs of their children. They want to know more than a list of subjects accompanied by a list of grades on a report card and demand to know what the expectations are and how their children can improve. This clarity and specificity is the essence of effective educational standards. I am also the beneficiary of a regular dose of blunt advice from Brooks, Alex, Julia, and James, children whose patience, love, and insight into educational matters are an unending source of inspiration and understanding. Thus, the following pages are not theoretical musings, but the result of daily contact with the real world of the reader.

Special Note to Academic and Professional Readers

Some teachers, school leaders, researchers, and professors may read the following pages and ask, "Where are the footnotes?" It is a fair question and it deserves a straight answer. This book is directed to a lay audience. In the interest of clarity, I have not provided the citations and footnotes that would normally accompany every allusion to research and each assertion of fact. For readers interested in my most recent writings directed toward a professional audience where the research is clearly cited, please consult the articles and book chapters that can be downloaded free of charge at www.edaccountability.org and www.makingstandardswork.com.

Chapter 1

Making the 20-Minute Learning Connection Work for You

The Power of 20 Minutes a Day

As important as the role of parent is, many parents have multiple roles, including spouse, worker, employer, neighbor, volunteer, and parent to other children. When asked to find 20 minutes a day for educational activities in an already crowded schedule, an exhausted parent might respond, "I've been up since 5:30 this morning and have four phone calls to make, dinner to cook, and after that comes Cub Scouts and choir practice. And you want me to do more to enrich my child's education? That's the school's responsibility. I'm doing the best I can!"

Both the fatigue and frustration are understandable, and the recommendations we offer to parents are not a retreat to the 1950s or an appeal only to parents with unlimited reserves of time and energy. There is great power in 20 minutes a day. This is not merely a convenient figure taken out of the air, but rather an amount of time that is both validated by research and supported by the practicalities of the busy lives of families. In one study of student achievement, those children who completed 20 minutes a day of independent reading outside of school were 60 percentile points higher than their counterparts who did no such reading. While reading an hour or more a day is wonderful, the greatest gain in achievement occurred from just 20 minutes a day.

What can you do in 20 minutes? This book is full of activities that are directly related to the academic standards of your state. But consider the routines that any family can create in just 20 minutes a day.

In 20 minutes you and your child can . . .

■ **Read aloud for fifteen minutes, and then describe what the story or news article was about for another five minutes.**

■ **Write a letter to a grandparent, friend, or relative.**

■ **Measure the ingredients for dinner.**

■ **Explore the factors affecting recent weather patterns and predict tomorrow's weather.**

■ **Draft and revise step-by-step instructions for the use of adult-defying devices such as VCRs and electronic games.**

■ **Plan an imaginary trip to an exotic location using maps, weather data, and transportation schedules.**

This chapter considers the practical details of creating the place and the time for your 20-Minute Learning Connection. The habits you develop and the time you invest in making a learning connection with your child can fundamentally change the way you talk about school and, more importantly, the way your child thinks about learning. You can move away from conversations that are unproductive and threatening to discussions that are focused on interesting and engaging activities. You can move away from an inspection of the backpack and the dreary march through the daily homework toward learning for the sheer joy of spending time together, developing new skills, and contemplating new ideas. Of course, the 20-Minute Learning Connection does not replace homework any more than it will avoid death and taxes. But these moments will give your child the skills, enthusiasm, and knowledge to make homework and other academic challenges more accessible.

opportunity for reflection

"What Did You Do in School Today?"

Most parents have had the following unproductive conversation:

"What did you do in school today?" Nothin.

"Why did you get that grade?" I dunno.

The antidote to this conversational dead-end is not browbeating the child until, after parental cross-examination, the child confesses some activity during the school day. Rather, we must re-frame the conversation about school. Let us begin by asking different questions. Here are some conversation starters that are quite different from "What did you do in school today?"

"What did you learn in school today?"

"What happened in school today that was scary?"

"What happened today that made you happy?"

"What happened today that made you sad?"

"What happened today that made you feel great?"

By shifting the conversation from a narrative of news events to a focus on the child's own feelings, there is the opportunity for reflection and personal engagement. Without asking these sorts of emotionally relevant questions, parents risk waiting until they read a bad report card or receive an alarming call from school before learning about significant problems.

The Power of Expectations

In a famous series of experiments in the early 1960s, two different groups of teachers were given students who were similar with regard to prior learning and demographic characteristics. One group, however, was described to their teachers as the "smart" group, while the other was described as "slow." A year later, both groups of students were measured on a variety of academic and intelligence tests. Despite the similarity of these two groups, the teachers and their widely varying expectations had an enormous impact on student performance, with the students living up to—and down to—the expectations of their teachers. Parental expectations are even more profound in their influence on student achievement. There is a fine line between parental pressure and expectations, and the difference is not always clear. We all know of the parents who "expect" their child to become a doctor or lawyer, and any professional or educational decision short of the mark leaves the child feeling like a failure in the eyes of the parent. Far more common, however, is the reluctance of parents to articulate clear expectations of academic success. While most parents are quite clear in their expectations of behavior and integrity, the same parents are less clear about the "house rules" regarding reading, homework, and learning.

The older children get, the more ambiguous the academic expectations of parents become. While every kindergartner has a world of potential ahead, the impulse to rate, rank, sort, and label children is in full flower by late elementary school. The child with brilliant potential in first grade has, by the sixth grade, been determined to be someone who "just isn't a reader" or "just isn't very good at math." While many sixth graders can express ambitions to be a jet pilot, opera singer, astronaut, or brain surgeon, parents none too subtly scoff at such ambitions just a few years later. The skepticism is not always obvious, but the message is clear. Even the well-intentioned, "If that's what you want to do, then you will have to do a lot better in school" becomes "You've got to be kidding! You—a brain surgeon? Forget it." This destructive disapproval is a long emotional distance from the cheering parent on the sidelines at a basketball game assuring the twelve-year-old who makes one basket out of fifty, "I know you can do it!"

How do parents express their expectations for student success? Here are some positive practices you may wish to consider. Parents who expect their children to do well in school and in life value learning and model that value, just as parents who expect their children to have integrity and compassion model those values. In order to model a love of learning, parents should consider the following steps toward the creation of learning time and learning space in their home.

learning together

Time and Space for Your 20-Minute Learning Connection

Set aside a "learning time" of 20 minutes every day. Many families devote the time after dinner to this purpose. Among my fondest memories of childhood are the times after dinner when someone would ask a question, and the family would discuss the idea, read about it, and learn something new. These were not extended multi-hour discussions, but they were clearly opportunities to learn that were not related to the school day. The discussions, readings, and questions were the result of a love of learning and a passion for inquiry. There is another critical element to such discussions: They provide adults with an opportunity to take the views of children seriously. A child's day is full of reminders of the impotence of children compared to the power of adults. When a parent or other significant adult takes the time to listen, question, and learn together with a child, there is more than merely the acquisition of new information taking place. There is the development of a sense of value, the ability of children to take themselves seriously, and in time, to expect others to take them seriously as well. The time consistently devoted to learning and exploration should be appropriate to your family's lifestyle and it should be consistent. Many families identify one night a week in which other activities are not allowed to intrude and they play games, read, discuss, and enjoy one another's company. Other families take just 20 minutes after dinner. Still other families carve out time first thing in the morning before the busy day begins. Whatever time you establish, consistency will be important. It is important that you not allow the ideal to be the enemy of progress. In other words, even if ideally you would like to have a two-hour after-dinner discussion that is free of interruptions and unfettered by the activities of children and parents, such a vision should not stop you from making the best use of 20 minutes any time during the day.

Every home should have some "learning space" that is the family equivalent of a library. This space need not be a room devoted only to learning, for few family homes have libraries or studies. Rather, the learning space is instantly created by the way it is used. Your learning space might be the dinner table, a desk in the basement, or any place set aside that meets three conditions. First, it is relatively free of distractions. This means that when the learning space is being used, the television is turned off and a sibling is not practicing the trombone in the same area. Second, there is abundant light. Third, it is easily accessible. If the table in the kitchen or dining room is to be used as the learning place, then it becomes the learning place as soon as someone sits down and opens a book, begins to write, or otherwise starts learning. If it requires 15 minutes of clearing and setting up before learning can begin, then it is not sufficiently accessible. The learning place need not be formal or expensive, but it does need to be quiet, well lit, and easy to use.

Parents' Checklist:

❑ Create a "learning space" in your home that is quiet, well lit, and easily accessible.

❑ Identify 20 minutes of "learning time" for your family to stop their other activities and learn together. This might involve reading alone or aloud, asking questions, or investigating a puzzling problem. To start your journey, we have suggested a number of learning activities that are specifically linked to the academic standards of your state. You will find the list of standards and activities starting on page 145.

---

a learning space

Chapter 2

What Are Academic Standards and Why Do We Have Them?

Academic standards give every parent essential information about what children are expected to know and be able to do in school. Parents need not guess or speculate about the idiosyncratic preferences of teachers. More importantly, children need not worry about what it takes to succeed in school. With the proper implementation of academic standards, guesswork is replaced with clarity.

The Importance of Knowing the Rules

Any parent who has observed children playing games in the park or on the playground knows the following scenario well. Children are playing a game and a new child joins the fun. Within minutes, however, it is clear that something is wrong. Cries of "That's not fair!" fill the air. The sounds of playground glee are replaced by tears, anger, and the indignant wail, "I'm never playing this game again!" When the mess is sorted out, there are no villains, no cheaters, no schemers determined to deny the aggrieved party his due. Rather, the tears, anger, and resolution to play no more all stem from ambiguity about the rules. All parties to the dispute thought that they knew how the game was played, and all had strikingly different understandings of what the rules of the game were supposed to be. Our children know that it is impossible to play any game without knowing the rules. Without clear rules, our determined efforts are reduced to random guessing, and the errors that we make do not provide useful feedback to improve our performance, but only greater frustration, more anger, and a river of tears. Whether the game is a seemingly inconsequential contest in the park or a high-stakes test with important consequences for a child's future, it is impossible to play the game without knowing the rules.

clear rules

Standards: The Rules of the Game

Any discussion of games in the context of education invites cynicism. The careless use of this analogy might indicate that education, standards, and testing are nothing more than trivial games where strategy is elevated above moral, ethical, and educational issues. Nothing could be further from the truth. In fact, there are a number of elements of games that reflect not merely strategic considerations, but fundamental values, such as fairness. Thus, my reference to games in the context of educational standards is designed to force us to confront the fact that, while clarity and fairness are routine requirements in games ranging from the playground to professional sports, the necessity for clarity and fairness applies no less to every important endeavor, including education. While these values may have trivial implications in a game, they are at the very heart of understanding why standards are so essential. Standards provide students with clear, unambiguous statements of what is required of them. In other words, standards are the rules of the game in school.

As I stated before, academic standards are statements of what students should know and be able to do. Although there are, to be sure, numerous examples of standards that are poorly worded, vague, over-reaching, unrealistic, and otherwise unhelpful, we must consider the alternative. Without standards, what would students have? They would be left with the mystery, guesswork, and ambiguity that prevail in the absence of rules.

Whenever I ask grandparents and experienced parents to tell me about the lessons they have learned about effective parenting, I find a theme in their advice. "You have to be consistent," they counsel. "Don't confuse sympathy and understanding with weakness. You have to be clear." For added emphasis, they warn, "You won't always make the right decisions, but children must know that they can count on you, and that requires consistency and dependability." There is wisdom in the words of these elders. Because perfection in parenting is not an option available to most of us, we are left with making the best of our imperfection. One way to reduce the risk of the mistakes that we inevitably make is clarity and consistency. This certainly does not guarantee the popularity or even the rectitude of our decisions about parental discipline, but clarity and consistency certainly will increase the probability that our children perceive us as fair, predictable, and dependable.

In contexts as diverse as child discipline and playground games, the role of standards is clear. Rules are necessary for motivation and fairness. Why is the role of standards so controversial in education? The value of clarity, consistency, and fairness is clear in the context of discipline and games. When the third-grade soccer championship or the sixth-grade music competition is on the line, few people doubt the necessity of standards, for the rules are the guarantor of fairness. Why does a football field always have 100 yards or a chessboard always have sixty-four squares? The answer is obvious: Without such clear and consistent rules, few people would be willing to play the game. Clarity and consistency are essential if people of any age are to be motivated sufficiently to engage in an activity. These standards are necessary in order for contests of any type, from the trivial to the most serious, to be regarded as fair. The fundamental rationale for educational standards is the same: a commitment to fairness.

The Old Way: Grading "On the Curve"

There are some people who are very upset with the standards movement and who have led angry demands for the abandonment of educational standards. They see standards as a device by which schools are rendered joyless boot camps and the needs of children are sacrificed to the needs of corporate employers. We should, therefore, consider where classrooms and schools would be if we had no standards. Recent history (and, unfortunately, many present-day schools) provides the answer. Without standards, we have the bell curve. You know that your child's school does not have a commitment to standards when you overhear the following conversation among children:

"How did you do on that assignment?"

"I didn't get the question right, but I was better than Steve!"

It is untrue that this school lacks standards. The standard is Steve, or any other child to whom another student can be favorably compared. No one knows what is really expected, because no one knows what Steve can do from one day to the next. But they do know this: If they can just beat Steve, then the teacher will have someone else on whom negative attention can be focused. Am I overstating the case? Consider the following authentic conversation from teachers in the schools I routinely visit:

"How do you evaluate students?"

"The best paper gets an A, the worst paper gets an F."

"How do you know what student work is acceptable?"

"I can't really tell you, but I know it when I see it."

Astonishingly, some parents embrace grading on the curve because it appears to foster the competitive spirit. After all, they reason, the cream rises to the top. It's a tough world out there, so my kids must get used to the competition. Ironically, grading on the curve does not produce the superior results and competitive spirit desired by parents. Rather, it creates the worst of both worlds because it discourages the competent student and fosters complacency in the incompetent student. The

"Steve Standard" provides justification to students who produce schoolwork that is incomplete, inaccurate, and disorganized but that is not quite as wretched as Steve's scrawl. With equally bad logic, the "Steve Standard" demoralizes the student who worked exceptionally hard to complete a wonderful assignment, but despite its exemplary quality, it was one footnote shy of the work submitted by Steve. Whether Steve is a wonderful student or a terrible student, the "Steve Standard" represents the shifting standards of grading on the curve. It is an inherently unfair and inaccurate way to evaluate students.

Some parents have a ready rejoinder: "But I don't want my child to be just 'good enough,' I want her to be the best. Only by comparing my child to other children can I be sure that she is meeting high standards." The subtext of this reasoning is the unrelenting counsel of successful business leaders of the past few decades who have insisted that business managers must be graded on the curve. This logic receives reinforcement from the sports world where there can be, after all, only a single champion. Because grading on the curve has proponents in business and athletics, it might be useful to use terminology that more accurately distinguishes a standards-based system from the alternative. Rather than call the competitive system "grading on the curve," we shall label it more accurately: mystery grading.

changing rules

The Worst Evaluation System: Mystery Grading

Imagine two children playing in the park. Lois challenges Robert to a ball game. With pleasure, Robert accepts the challenge, confident that he has played ball games successfully in the past. Lois then takes the ball and runs past an imaginary line and exclaims, "That's one point for me—I'm ahead!" Robert catches on quickly, takes the ball, and runs past the line happily. "You ran the wrong way!" Lois shouts. "That's another point for me—it's two to zero, my favor." Robert starts to pick up the ball, but Lois provides a quick elbow to his solar plexus, takes the ball, and runs past the line. "Three to zero," she says with a smile. Robert is upset, but under control. Confident that he now understands the game a bit better, he delivers a retaliatory blow to Lois and takes the ball, crossing the line with a smile of victory. "Foul!" Lois cries. "That's an automatic point for me—it's four to zero!" Robert is a bright child. How long do you think he will continue to play this game? It is a testimony to Robert's good grace and self-control that he has not been dispatched to the principal's office after having let his aggravation with Lois get the better of him. But despite his chivalry, this much is certain: Robert will not play this game again.

When the awarding of points is a mystery and when the rules of the game appear to shift with the winds, then children will not continue to play the game. When victory involves guessing and no amount of skill or prior information is of any value, then the game becomes an idle pursuit and not a purposeful enterprise.

Is this analogy exaggerated? Ask students why they received the grade they did. Sometimes you will receive a well-reasoned and clear answer. One student might say,

"The requirements of the assignment were this, but I actually did that. Therefore, I failed to meet the requirements and received a low grade. Having received this valuable feedback and recognizing the error of my ways, I shall return to my desk forthwith, revise this assignment, and resubmit it to my teacher."

If your child provides such a response, please return this book for a refund, proceed to the nearest radio station, and host a call-in show for perfect parents with perfect children in perfect schools. For most of us and for our children, grading remains mysterious. Even teachers who take the time to create clear and precise grading systems find that precision is an illusion, far clearer to the designer of the system than to the students who must perform under its mandates.

For the vast majority of students, grading remains a mystery dominated by the largely unknown personal preferences of the teacher. The student is placed in the role of the sorcerer's apprentice, weakly emulating the acts of the master, hoping that some of the magic will rub off. Systematic learning is impossible because teaching comes only from the inscrutable wisdom of the master teacher, and learning is a matter of fortunate insight rather than diligent work. It is no wonder that such a system is discouraging to the student who finds luck more important than skill. There is a better way. We can replace mystery with clarity. Students can replace guesswork with hard work. Parents can replace aimless searching with careful direction. In brief, we can have standards.

The Best Way: Know the Rules Before You Play the Game

The game played by Lois and Robert was unfair. The failure of fairness was not a result of the scheming of Lois, but rather the absence of rules. The fundamental requirement of fairness is the existence of clear and consistent rules—standards, if you will—that let the participants know what conduct is acceptable and what is not. We can only play the game when we know the rules.

This is hardly an alien notion to schools. During the first few hours of the first day of classes in most schools in the country, teachers discuss the importance of behavior, respect, and decorum in the classroom. Teachers do not display elaborate posters on classroom walls that contain the precise words of the Board of Education's disciplinary policy or the state criminal statutes. Rather, each teacher has a single piece of paper labelled "class rules," which lays out in simple and clear language the requirements of conduct for students. "Respect yourself and others," the rules typically begin. "Do not talk while others are speaking." "Raise your hand before speaking." "Be kind and help others." There is a long tradition of identifying the standards of behavior in classrooms with clarity and precision. These same qualities must be the goal of those desiring academic excellence.

clarity

What Standards Mean for Students

While the word "standards" conveys to some parents a threat of failure and an association with difficult academic tests, the actual implications of school standards are quite positive. In a standards-based school, students know what is expected and they routinely receive constructive feedback on how to improve their performance. The typical parent-child conversation after report cards are issued in a school without standards begins with the question, "How did you get that grade?" followed by the plaintive response, "I don't know." With standards, this unproductive conversation is replaced by these confident statements:

"I know what the teacher wants me to do."

"I know when I'm successful and when I am not."

"I know how to get better and I can do so tomorrow."

"I know what it takes to win and I know that I can be a winner."

"I can help someone else and still be a winner—I don't have to beat Steve to be a great student."

real achievement

What Standards Mean for Parents

I t is stunning for me to hear some parents bemoan the standards movement as a new educational fad when the requirement for fair and reasonable relationships among teaching, learning, curriculum, and assessment are as old as Socrates. Although our children may think their parents went to school in the Lyceum, we need not recall ancient Greece to consider our own examples of standards. Think of your favorite teacher or coach. Did that person patronize you with constant pats on the head or make your success a matter of mystery and luck? Or did that favorite coach or teacher let you know that whatever else had happened in your life, you would be a success if only you worked hard, followed the rules, and met the standards that the teacher clearly identified? These favorite teachers did not make learning easy, nor did they make learning impossible. Rather, our favorite teachers and coaches made learning challenging, fair, reasonable, and rewarding. This is the essence of standards-based teaching and learning.

Now that they are vividly called to mind, these influential teachers and coaches offer another interesting quality. Your success was not accomplished when you simply defeated another student, but when you met the standard articulated by the coach. Chances are, that standard included not only personal excellence, but also a willingness to help your teammates. While rivalries within teams are natural, the team that is beset by constant competition within the team is seldom able to deal with competition against other teams. In fact, your success was elevated by your willingness to help your colleagues. When you helped other students, you discovered an important truth: Not only did their performance improve, but your understanding of the same subject soared when you had the opportunity to help others master the subject. You found that helping other students was not an entirely altruistic act, but rather was the result of a collaborative process in which you both gave and received valuable lessons.

Academic standards imply a very different environment in school than many parents may have experienced. If your educational experience involved grading on the curve, frantic efforts to please a teacher, and a certain degree of mystery about the nature of your performance, then it is only natural that you might expect your own children to have a similar experience in school. If you have been successful in school and in life, you might initially prefer that your children attend a school that closely matches your own experiences when you were a student. Nevertheless, the case we have made for standards is based not upon personal history or popularity, but upon the fact that standards are fair and effective. Even if a standards-based approach to student achievement is not what you experienced as a child, please give it a chance. Your children will thrive in an environment in which the rules of the game are clear and their performance is rewarded based on real achievement rather than merely on a victory over a classmate.

What Standards Mean for Teachers and Schools

Standards offer clarity, fairness, and effectiveness, so teachers should universally rave about the use of academic standards. After all, if the case for standards is so overwhelming, why would any educational professional object? In fact, the reaction to standards by teachers and school administrators has been varied. Some teachers enthusiastically endorse the idea of standards and emphasize that it is hardly new. "What you call standards," they remark, "is what I have called 'good teaching' for about twenty-five years now."

But many other educators are wary. They have seen a number of educational fads come and go, and they reasonably wonder if this is just one more trend that will evaporate when something more popular comes along. In addition, some teachers resent the fact that standards were oversold when they were first introduced. Some proponents of standards let their enthusiasm surpass their judgment when they gushed, "Standards will make teaching easy!" Of course, nothing makes the difficult and complex job of teaching easy. Most of the objections to standards come from the failure of those who wrote the initial drafts of state standards to express their expectations with precision. Many standards swing from one extreme to the other, either describing curriculum content in excessive detail, or describing expectations of student performance in such broad generalities that teachers are left with little constructive guidance. Some teachers object that the standards are too difficult and too numerous. Considering all the other subjects that traditionally have been in the school curriculum, the additional layers of academic content seem to be too burdensome given the limited amount of time students spend in school. Finally, there are teachers who sincerely object to any outside interference in their classroom. Their rejoinder to standards or other intrusions is, "Just leave me alone and let me teach!" In their judgment, standards easily could become standardization, and such an approach to teaching fails to recognize the unique qualities of each individual student. Only the teacher, they argue, can make the subtle judgments required to identify what is appropriate for each child, and standards designed at the state or school district level fail to take into account the individual needs that are known only to the teacher.

Many parents have heard these arguments and have interpreted them as arguments against all academic standards. Every argument but the last one, however, is actually a persuasive case against poor standards, and the logical response is not the abandonment of standards, but the continuous improvement of them. Those people who make the final argument characterized as, "Just leave me alone and let me teach," will object to any standard. Improvements would not be sufficient, for even the most clear and constructive standard would represent an intrusion into their classroom and their curriculum.

Parents naturally appreciate a teacher who wishes to take into account the individual needs of their children. Moreover, most parents would object to any policy that appears to "standardize" their unique children. A balanced approach to standards might look something like this: The freedom and discretion of teachers are honored, respected, and encouraged, provided that this discretion takes place within a framework. That framework is one of academic excellence and equity in which all students have clear and fair guidelines and expectations. Educators have broad discretion to consider alternative strategies for teaching reading to a student who appears to be slow to catch on to phonics; the teacher does not have the discretion to say, "Considering his difficult upbringing and poor neighborhood, we really can't expect him to learn to read this year." Teachers can be creative and have wide latitude to collaborate with their colleagues to determine the best ways to improve mathematics skills, but they do not have the discretion to say (as I have actually heard a teacher and administrator claim),

"Well, those kids don't need algebra anyway." In a balanced approach to standards, there is neither micromanagement by school administrators, nor aimless anarchy among teachers. Standards need not dictate the day-to-day, minute-to-minute agenda for the classroom, but standards do establish the expectations of what all students should know and be able to do. When teachers have creative supplementary strategies to help students meet those expectations, that creativity is respected and rewarded. When, however, teachers make decisions that take students outside of the framework at the expense of meeting standards, then they have supplanted the needs of the child with the personal preferences of the teacher. That, in a school committed to excellence and equity, is not acceptable.

an effective classroom

What Standards Mean for Daily Life in School

The best way for students and teachers to succeed in school and to meet academic standards is a consistent emphasis on the thinking, reasoning, analysis, communication, and love of learning that characterizes any effective classroom. The frequent claim that the path to meeting standards lies in mindless drills, rather than analysis and thinking, is wrong. In extensive research from organizations as diverse as the Education Trust, the Center for Performance Assessment, and the National Science Foundation, the evidence is clear: Higher test scores on standards-based assessments are more likely to occur when students and teachers engage in critical thinking, extensive analysis, and frequent writing. The appropriate application of academic standards encourages an increase in thinking, reasoning, and communication by students.

To be sure, standards are the cause of some changes in schools, and those changes can be uncomfortable for the critics of standards. There are elementary classes that devote many hours of prime reading time to craft projects and preparation for performances, few of which are related to the improvement of student achievement. Some secondary teachers announce that next quarter will be devoted to current events "rather than standards," as if the possibility of relating contemporary political events to the study of history and government is impossible. There are many traditional projects that consume large chunks of time and the only thing that sustains these activities is their popularity, not their contribution to student learning. What is lost by the establishment of standards? Surely not thinking, reasoning, or even the fun of interactive and engaging activities in the classroom. What must be abandoned or modified, however, are the projects that have persisted year after year based only on the personal preference of the teacher and popularity with students and parents. Perhaps the least attractive feature of the standards movement is that it displaces popularity with effectiveness.

Does this mean that the kids can no longer carve pumpkins in October or dress up like Pilgrims in November? Certainly not. We know that hands-on activities and dramatic reenactments are splendid ways for students to learn. But some of these activities require close reexamination and detailed modification. If pumpkins are to be the theme for a few days, then much more than carving and candy must be the order of the day. There are wonderful classrooms in which students read about pumpkins, write about them, measure them, weigh them, compare them, and explore them. The traditional Thanksgiving drama, in which two students speak and many others look on in silence, can be replaced by an activity in which many students participate in writing the play based on their own reading and research. The speaking parts can be widely shared among all students, and the predominant feature of the activity is student learning rather than parent entertainment.

reasonable preparation

Won't Standards Result in Teaching to the Test?

Some teachers and parents have linked standards and testing to the point that any suggestion that standards are the basis of classroom instruction leads to the allegation that schools are "teaching to the test." It is true that there are examples around the nation in which some misguided administrators have encouraged a regimen of test drills and memorization rather than deep study, analysis, and reflection. It is also true that there are some schools that have curtailed traditional classroom activities and field trips, and a few people have blamed standards as the culprit that turned their schools into grim, academic factories.

The very phrase "teaching to the test" implies something unethical, as if teachers had sneaked into the State Department of Testing, secretly copied the test, and then conducted drills in class in which students memorized the answers by chanting, "Number 1 is C, number 2 is A, number 3 is B…" In fact, what most teachers have done is to use the freely available models of the practice tests to let students look at sample items in order to become more familiar with the format of the test. Moreover, thoughtful teachers also have reviewed their own curriculum and made appropriate revisions. "If my students need to know about graphs and tables for a test in March, and I was not going to address those skills until April, then it would be much more fair to my students if I changed my schedule to give them those skills before they take the test."

The contention that ethical teaching requires that testing must be a mystery must be challenged as absurd and unfair. Can you imagine students in a musical performance sitting down to discover that the music before them is completely unfamiliar? Can you imagine the football coach who refuses to use a football in practice or take students near an actual football field because practicing under such conditions would be "teaching to the test?"

The most appropriate way to discuss the relationship of classroom teaching to the tests students take is not "teaching to the test," but "teaching to the standard." Teachers cannot anticipate every single item on the test, but they can provide students with a fair opportunity to do well on any test. The opportunity for fairness is best provided when students have received curriculum and instruction based on the standards, and when the test designers have used those same standards as the basis for creating the tests. When the context is driving, music, or football, this would be called common sense. When the context is academic performance, it is not only common sense, but also fair and effective.

The Most Important Teacher Your Child Will Ever Have

When I was discussing this book with a teacher and grandparent in a border community where Spanish was the predominant language, she suggested a title for the Spanish-language edition of the book. "There's no doubt about it," she said. "Your title must be *Los Primeros Maestros*." This is a play on words, indicating that parents are not only the first teachers, but also the most important teachers that children will ever have. Her insight speaks volumes to parents of every culture, because we are all the first and most important teachers for our children.

Parents teach children so many things that they will never learn in school, including integrity, values, and respect for oneself and others. Parents also teach children about their interest in learning. This is not the same as their interest in school. Our children see through the ruse of the parent who berates a child over a poor grade in reading but never picks up a book for pleasure. Our children notice our inconsistency when we exclaim our disappointment in their writing abilities but fail ever to take pen in hand ourselves to write a letter. The most important lessons we teach are those with our actions and values, not our lectures.

Parents' Checklist:

❏ **Read the standards appropriate to your child's grade.**

❏ **Find one activity that you can complete in 20 minutes that will help your child achieve standards.**

❏ **Talk with your child's teacher about standards. If the teacher's attitude is negative, ask if the problem is the specific wording of the standards, or if the problem is any effort by the state to influence classroom activities. It is important for you to understand the teacher's commitment or aversion to standards.**

❏ **Find the exact dates of state tests for your child. Mark them on the calendar so that you can limit distractions and interruptions during that week.**

❏ **Ask your child about standards. "What do you think you have to do this year to be a great student?" Then listen carefully for the response. Standards only have meaning when children understand them. The response you receive will be your guide to future activities and discussions with teachers, school leaders, and your child.**

ask your child

Chapter 3

What Tests Tell You—and What They Don't

Tests are part of life. Babies take the Apgar test within moments of birth in the delivery room, and the results of that test can lead to essential and immediate medical intervention for the newborn child. Before formal schooling has begun, children routinely explore the world around them by experimenting with language and behavior. They "test" the world dominated by adults and older children and make instant observations about effective and ineffective strategies to meet their needs. When the young child is the one doing the testing and when the results of the test are immediately used to benefit the child, it is a remarkably effective way to learn about the world. In a few short years, however, the word "test" gains a very different meaning. It is no longer a way of learning and exploring, no longer a mechanism for gaining new knowledge and meeting the child's needs. Tests are soon associated with anxiety, demands for performance, and the prospect of failure. Three-year-old children take admissions tests for preschool and their older siblings are subjected to tests that will determine their acceptance or rejection by special programs in kindergarten. Within the minutes or hours that it takes to administer these tests, the path is set. Perhaps the child will bear the label of "gifted and talented" or "special needs" or, heaven forbid, "normal."

Because the tests purport to have scientific properties, the labels bestowed on children are rarely challenged. The purpose of this chapter is to confront the common acceptance of these labels by providing some background on what tests can and cannot tell parents about their children. Once you know that tests are merely snapshots of knowledge rather than definitive pronouncements about student ability, both you and your child can examine test results for what they are—a momentary record of achievement, not a certain prediction of future failure or success. Whether the test in question affects the labeling of a child, the acceptance into or rejection from a special program, or simply the awarding of a grade on a report card, the way that parents talk with children about tests reflects a philosophy that can be either discouraging or encouraging. Only through a deliberate effort to change the talk between parents and children into learning conversations will we make the transition away from test terror.

conquering anxiety

From Test Terror to Testing for Learning

Parents who have witnessed the transformation of testing from innocent exploration to childhood terror may express their dismay at how much inappropriate pressure is placed on children, not knowing that their own comments have already signaled the parents' anxieties to their children about the importance of tests. There are few more powerful psychological forces than the fear of disappointing a parent. Perhaps you can recall a time in which you would have preferred physical punishment to that look of dissatisfaction from a parent who sent the message, "I am disappointed in you." Few spankings could have been as painful. While no parent ever intends to send debilitating and terrorizing messages to children, we sometimes cannot help it. The stress and anxiety of every examination we have ever taken can subtly and unintentionally become the test terror we transmit to our children.

Constructive Skepticism for Tests

Fortunately, history is not destiny. Parents can fundamentally change their children's perceptions of testing. This cannot be accomplished by casually dismissing tests as unimportant. Our children see through that ruse, knowing that tests are indeed important, but that we are seeking to protect them. As surely as children know if they won or lost the soccer match in the supposedly "fun and scoreless" games that masquerade as noncompetitive exercises, children also know when tests are important, but their parents don't want to talk about them. If we are to liberate our children from test terror, we will do so not with patronizing tales about the irrelevance of tests, but with a philosophy toward testing that can best be described as "constructive skepticism."

Perhaps the best way to understand constructive skepticism for tests is to consider the opposite. Rather than engaging in rational analysis of the test, some students fall prey to analytical paralysis, when the test taker is convinced that failure, inadequacy, and stupidity are the inescapable diagnoses from an unsuccessful test attempt. "After all," these children reason, "either you know it or you don't, and I guess I just don't know it." The results of such analytical paralysis are predictable: anger, fear, and the studied avoidance of test taking opportunities in the future.

Constructive skepticism for tests is strikingly different. The child with constructive skepticism understands that every test is a game. Most of the rules of the game are clear, but the moves of the other side are not always obvious. Therefore, some strategy, some knowledge, and yes, some luck is involved in the successful completion of the game. Supplied with constructive skepticism for tests, children know that their success on a test is not necessarily the mark of genius, but of capable gamesmanship. When confronted with a test question that is unclear and ambiguous, the child with constructive skepticism does not conclude, "I'm a failure and I can't do this." Rather, this empowered test taker says, "I'm as smart as the person who wrote this test, but the right answer isn't very clear. Now I know that "B" is dumb and "D" is impossible, so I guess it's "A" or "C." I'm going to make a smart guess and move on, because this game is just about over..."

Constructive skepticism does not involve anger or the presumption of failure as the inescapable result when the right answer is not immediately clear. Rather, constructive skepticism provides students with the emotional resilience to persist even in the face of ambiguity and uncertainty. It is not just the intellectual ability to narrow the range of possible answers to a test question; it is the emotional ability to remain engaged in the game of test taking long after other students have given up on that test question and perhaps on the entire test. When students feel a sense of failure, they tend to generalize it: "I'm not only a failure on the soccer team; I can't do *anything* right! I can't read, I can't do math, and I can't kick the darn ball into the darn goal..." By contrast, the child with healthy skepticism for the test at hand possesses the emotional resilience to say, "Okay, so I can't remember what a rhombus is. Big deal. This question is asking about sides of a polygon, so that means that the answer has to have sides. So it can't be a circle and it can't be an ellipse—it must be either a trapezoid or a rhombus. I'll guess that it's a rhombus and move on to the next question."

At this point, the student with constructive skepticism is still in the game, engaged in the next question, convinced that thinking, reasoning, and skill are the keys to success. The student without this sort of resilience has given up, with pencil held limply in hand while the head rests on the desk waiting for the torture of this test to end. Whatever tests the future holds for your child, among the many valuable gifts you can provide is the gift of resilience—the ability for your child to remain engaged in a test or other difficult challenge, even when the questions are ambiguous and the answers are elusive.

Some readers may be uncomfortable referring to tests as games, especially when discussing tests with their children. "This is serious," they reason, "and references to gamesmanship trivialize tests, school, and education in general." This is a legitimate concern and it deserves a serious answer. The references to games in this chapter have three purposes, none of which trivializes tests or education. First, references to games help children recall experiences that have been successful and enjoyable. This is a more constructive basis for a conversation between parents and children than a stern lecture about the life-changing importance of a test and the associated risk of parental disappointment should the child not score sufficiently well. Feelings of trust, confidence, competence, and fun are the foundations of happy children and successful students, and parents do better when they nurture those feelings. Second, references to games involve strategy that both children and parents understand. Because tests are never perfect and answers are not always free of ambiguity, knowledge alone is insufficient. Strategy—thinking about the point of view of the test writer, eliminating wrong answers, and dealing with the uncertainty and ambiguity present in every test—is not only a great thinking skill for children, it is also the key to emotional resilience. Strategy—gamesmanship, if you will—is the bridge from "I don't know the answer so

I must be stupid" to "The right answer may not be obvious, but if I work on this I think I can figure it out." Third, I have observed that parents (with the exception of the stereotype of the abusive "Little League Dad") usually approach the performance of their children in games in a constructive and encouraging manner that builds confidence, success, and emotional resilience. When children play games, parents applaud, encourage, laugh, and console—all qualities sadly lacking in many discussions between parents and children when the subject is testing, homework, and school. In the final analysis, the references in this book to games have one central theme: Our children are more than the sum of their test scores, and the role of parents is not to cram every conceivable answer into the heads of their children, but to build healthy, happy, confident, capable, and empowered kids who know that they are loved and accepted by their parents.

emotional resilience

Tests Are Important, But . . .

It is national sport to ridicule school tests. After all, many people believe it is common knowledge that children are over-tested, that tests are irrelevant, that tests are political tools misused by critics of public education, and that tests fail to tell the complete and accurate story of student achievement. While each of these allegations may contain an element of truth, a fundamental fact remains: tests are an important and continuing part of life both during the early years of school and continuing into college, technical education, and the world of work. Moreover, students who have the intellectual and emotional ability to perform well on tests will find more open doors for educational and professional success. No doubt about it: Tests are important.

Success in test taking involves not only knowing the material, but also understanding the emotional foundations for successful test performance. Many readers can recall an instance in which they were intellectually prepared for a test and, as soon as the test administrator uttered the words "you may begin," their minds went blank. Terror replaced confidence and mystery replaced the clear organization of facts and concepts that the student possessed only moments before the test began. To make matters worse, we knew of students who had scarcely prepared for the same test, but who appeared to breeze through the examination. Our recollections of the power of panic make a profound case in favor of recognizing the importance of emotions in test success.

The Power of Emotions

While the prevalence of emotions over intellect may be perplexing to students, it is great news for parents. Although we may not always be able to provide the right answer on math or geography homework, every parent can provide extraordinarily powerful support for the emotional resilience and psychological endurance of their children. The power of emotions in test preparation is an essential element of parent support. This is why "Let me help you with your homework" is far less powerful than "You're a smart kid and I believe in you; I *know* that you can do this!" As parents, we want to help our children. It is only natural. It hurts to see them struggle. It would be instructive, however, to recall the first steps of our toddler. The parent cannot walk for the child, but can only hold out loving arms and offer earnest encouragement. "Come on, *you can do it!*" And they do. Our praise is genuine, enthusiastic, and encouraging. That praise, confidence, and encouragement set a standard in the minds of our children that is a difficult bar to reach in later years. "You can do it!" gives way to "Turn off the darn television and finish your homework!" "I believe in you" is replaced by "I just don't understand how you messed this up so badly." The emotional connection of parent and child has been replaced with one more layer of anxiety and stress.

Building Confident, Capable, and Empowered Children

Although few children enjoy tests, most children love games. They particularly enjoy games they can win. Think about it: Children's games, from Crazy Eights to Monopoly to a host of board and card games are typically a combination of knowledge, skill, strategy, and luck. Clever game designers know that part of maintaining the interest of children is the reasonable prospect of success. Parents help to build confident, capable, and empowered children every time they participate in an activity in which it is possible for children to succeed. This does not mean that parents deliberately lose and children win every time. Such games, children quickly learn, are boring and unrewarding. They know that the rewards that come too easily have little value. Part of building emotional resilience and persistence in the face of difficulty is the habit of trying again after a failure, full of confidence that success is a function of endurance, skill, and a little luck.

My youngest child, James, is on a basketball team. A 10-foot basketball hoop appears to be an insurmountable goal for a group of six- and seven-year-olds. During practice, the balls fly everywhere, it seems, but into the net. But once in a while—perhaps once every five to ten minutes—there is a "swish" of the ball through the net that keeps the enthusiasm of everyone in the room at a high level. There is a lesson here: We do not build capable, confident, and empowered children through the contrivance of easy tasks and low expectations. Whether the challenge is the ten-foot basket or two-digit subtraction, the prospect of success is what keeps the players engaged. They do not need the certainty of success every time, but they need to know precisely what the rules of the game are so that, when success comes, the delicious moment of victory can be savored for a moment before the players return to the game.

The game scenario has practical applications for how parents interact with children about homework and tests. Many parents tend to one of two extremes, in which one parent demands, "Go to your room and don't come out until all the homework is done!" and another parent hovers over the nervous student, correcting every error and focusing exclusively on every misstep. Can you imagine the same parents exploding with disappointment at every missed basket? Can you imagine these parents saying, after the ball goes into the basket, "Well, he made the shot, but he's no Michael Jordan!" On the contrary, these parents wait and wait, offering encouragement and perhaps a few sympathetic groans, and then they roar with approval and applause when a child—any child—makes a basket. When was the last time we roared with approval and applause for a homework assignment well done, a test question answered correctly, or a project completed on time? In some arenas, parental feedback is immediate, positive, and relevant to success. In other cases, parental feedback is infrequent, negative, and related to vague expectations of perfection that seem unreachable by the student.

The Confusion of Self-Esteem and Self-Confidence

Much has been written and said about self-esteem, with most of these words substituting rhetoric for evidence. The facts are clear: Self-esteem is important. When students, or for that matter, adults, feel a sense of self-worth, they tend to perform at higher levels. The issue is not whether self-esteem is important, but how this elusive quality is best achieved. Some parents believe that we build self-esteem through challenge and rigor, in the way that the movie stereotype of the Marine drill sergeants "build men" in boot camp through a mix of ridicule, shouting, and demands. Other parents, and an astonishing number of teachers, believe that we build self-esteem through constant affirmation of children, including reassurances that children are always great, wonderful, and terrific even when the children know that they are not always great, wonderful, and terrific. Both extremes are wrong. Parents must balance affirmation with honesty. We cannot tell a child that she made the basket when her own observation is to the contrary. It is equally unwise to tell a child that his performance is inadequate when the child just scored a point for his team.

Let us move the context from the playground to schoolwork. We should not tell the child that her paper is wonderful when she knows and we know that it is careless and inaccurate. We should not tell the child of her shortcomings because her paragraph of sixth grade work falls short of Hemingway. Honesty, rather than excessively high or low expectations, best serves children. We build self-esteem with clear, honest feedback, not with impossible challenges or improbable reassurances. "This was great and I'm really proud of you!" is as appropriate as "You are really getting good at this! With a little more work you're going to be even better. I know you can do it!"

While the distinction may appear subtle, the difference between self-esteem and self-efficacy is an important one. Esteem alone is not sufficient. Humans must not only feel a sense of worth, but they must also have the bone-deep conviction that their efforts make a difference. In other words, their self-esteem is the result of their genuine worth and effort, not merely awarded by someone out of sympathy for an incompetent child. Anyone who has listened attentively to the conversations of children about the important adults in their lives knows that children have a profound and insightful understanding of the difference between sympathy and confidence. The patronizing compliments of adults can be withdrawn, but the capacity that children have to make a difference in their own lives is enduring. Thus, it is not merely esteem that our children must develop and maintain, but efficacy. In the words of Dr. Jeff Howard, president of the Efficacy Institute, "Smart is something you get, not just something you are." When students believe that they have the capacity for improvement, they are far more resilient and persistent than when they depend on another person for compliments, assurances, and affirmation.

The Limits of Tests

As important as tests are, it is essential that parents and children understand what tests tell us and what they don't. The best any test can do is to report the performance of a student on a particular set of questions on a particular day. Just as a blood pressure test does not represent a complete physical and just as blood pressure is subject to change from one reading to the next, so also test results do not represent a complete analysis of student ability, and those results can change radically depending on testing conditions and student preparation.

The most meaningful tests report not only a score, but also how to get better. This is one of the most significant advantages of student self-evaluation. Rather than submitting work to an all-knowing teacher who then awards a grade, the student who engages in self-evaluation must understand the difference between acceptable and unacceptable work. Rather than communicating only a letter or numerical grade, the most effective tests challenge the complacent student and encourage the discouraged child. On letter-graded tests, the complacent student might receive an A or a B and receive the message, "I'm doing pretty well, so there isn't much else to learn." The discouraged student might receive a low grade and receive the message, "That's as well as I can do, so I guess I'm just not a very good student." The best tests not only evaluate, but educate students. These tests communicate to parents about the performance of their children and also provide specific information about what students know and where they need to improve. Supplied with these insights, parents can help their children improve. Of course, these ideal tests are rare in most schools. Parents receive a score, and that's it. Rather than attempt to draw conclusions from a score alone, parents need to be advocates for tests that educate. In addition, parents must be careful to avoid "over-interpreting" a test score or grade.

Consider the case of the child who brings home a "C" on a test. One parent's frame of reference might be that a C is acceptable, if not great work, so perhaps it's best not to make a big deal out of it, and another parent might exclaim, "You obviously didn't do your best work on this test—what went wrong?" Both conclusions are unhelpful and probably inaccurate. The focus of the parent-child conversation should not be on the evaluation, but rather on the learning that did and did not take place. Rather than begin the conversation with evaluative statements, we should reframe every discussion as a learning conversation. It is always wise to begin with something positive, such as, "You did a great job on number 17—I didn't know you knew all of that! Tell me more about it." Then we must do what is one of the most essential, and rare, activities of parents: We must listen. Parents and teachers routinely engage in the fantasy that because they are talking, children are learning. While there is value to talk from parents and teachers, conversations are far more constructive when they are informed by the child's point of view. Thus, we begin with what the child does know and the places on the test where the performance was satisfactory. After giving the child an opportunity to elaborate on the good parts of his performance, we can then ask, "What do you wish you had done differently on this test?" This opens the door to a discussion of the questions that were blank or answered incorrectly. You might learn that the child ran out of time. You might learn that the child had failed to study. You might learn that the child does not understand fundamental concepts necessary to performance on this test. But my experience suggests that it is far more likely that you will learn that the child knew the material, but failed to understand the instructions. You might learn, for example, that the child was so confident that the haste to display her knowledge got in the way of taking time to read the instructions. You might also learn that the instructions were unclear and that many reasonable test takers, including you, might have had the same misunderstanding as your child. And it is possible that you will learn that the response was correct after all and that the scoring of the test was wrong. None of these learning conversations will occur, however, if we respond to the grade on the test rather than the content of the test.

focus on learning

Report Cards and Learning Conversations

Just as learning conversations should prevail in our discussions of tests and homework, so should the communication between parent and child about report cards focus on learning rather than evaluation. This is difficult. As I write these words, I reflect on the times I have reacted in haste to report cards, with joy at the "A" and with disappointment at lower grades, and in neither case conducting a learning conversation with my children. Taking a deliberate break from our natural reactions toward evaluation rather than education requires intellectual and emotional discipline, and those qualities can be in short supply when any parent, including a professional educator, first sees a report card. But the skill can be learned. Consider the physician who looks at your test results and exclaims, "Oh boy, are *you* in trouble!" And with those words, orders you to "work harder in the future" and then quickly leaves the room. The bewilderment, fear, and rage that might be our natural reactions to such a confrontation with a preoccupied physician are not unlike the reactions of children to typical discussions of report cards with their parents. We expect the physician to stop, think, reflect, and then not only to offer the results of medical tests, but to engage in a conversation about how we can improve. If there is ambiguity or if the results indicate a problem, the wise physician might order additional tests or conduct additional examinations before coming to a hasty and potentially inaccurate conclusion. Even a physician who reports that a patient is in perfect health might be expected to offer analysis, insight, and discussion of how such excellent health can be maintained. We owe our children no less than the wise physicians owe their patients.

Inappropriate Uses of Test Scores

Just as we expect the wise physician to have a sound basis for drawing a conclusion, so must the wise parent and teacher have a reasonable body of evidence for the determinations they make about children. Incredibly, single tests are used inappropriately to make instant decisions on a routine basis. When this occurs, parents must become advocates not only for their children, but for the cause of accuracy in tests and the analysis of test results. By far the most common error made in the use of test scores is the overgeneralization about children, teachers, and schools. Based on a single test, a child can be denied promotion, a teacher's effectiveness can be questioned, or a school can be labeled as a failing institution. Worse yet are the life-changing decisions made based on a single test. Such decisions are typically associated with "high stakes" tests such as high school graduation examinations, but in fact many tests with significant consequences for children occur on a regular basis and do not have the label or the publicity associated with high stakes tests. Such important tests in which a few hours can make an enormous difference in the education and life of a child include the assessments used to label children as gifted or learning disabled, tests that grant or deny admission to special learning opportunities, and tests that claim to predict the ability, aptitude, or interests of children.

Parents should be deeply suspicious of tests that claim to draw conclusions about children, particularly when those conclusions are linked to words such as "intelligence" or "ability" or "aptitude." There is a sorry history of such tests stemming back to the early years of the twentieth century when the test results were appropriated by the eugenics movement to support their racist conclusions. With the jargon, statistics, and confidence of testing experts, the nation was assured of the scientific "proof" of the genetic inferiority of people of Irish, Italian, and Jewish descent, particularly if they came from southern or eastern Europe. These absurd conclusions were based on the low scores of recent immigrants taking the "Army Alpha" tests during the early days of World War I. Interestingly, the same populations displayed much higher scores a generation later as their language skills and familiarity with cultural references in the tests improved. Such changes prove that those tests did not measure anything like "intelligence" or "aptitude" because such qualities theoretically are not subject to change. If, however, the tests provide only a snapshot of the present knowledge of the test taker, then the results can change with the active decision of the test taker to improve. While the reader may find the racism of the test advocates of 1917 to be shocking and unacceptable, there is no logical distinction between the inappropriate conclusions based on a single test then and the overgeneralizations based on a single test for children in the early years of the twenty-first century.

Defenders of the use of tests for important decisions frequently refer to the objectivity, reliability, and validity that experts have claimed for these tests. Although this is not the forum for a professional discourse on the attributes of testing, there is one concept with which all parents should be familiar: validity. In lay terms, a test is valid when we test what we think we are testing. While this may seem simple on the face of it, the element of validity in testing is quite inconsistent. Consider the driving test we require in every state. Success on a multiple-choice test would not be a valid representation of driving ability. That is why every prospective driver must also get behind the wheel and demonstrate to the examiner some degree of proficiency in driving. Similarly, pilots do more than pass a multiple-choice exam; they must complete their flight examinations with an equal number of take-offs and landings. If the driving and pilot examinations result in the granting of licenses to unqualified applicants, the public safety is at risk. Conversely, if these examinations result in the denial of licenses to qualified applicants, it is not only inconvenient, but probably will result in litigation by the person to whom a license is denied. Such a reaction is possible because the test taker knows the impact of each test and is aware of the link between the test and an adverse decision.

While the requirement for validity is the same in every test, whether the subject is driving or kindergarten placement, the quality of testing is very different. We routinely make decisions about the educational opportunities for children based on test results, and in many cases the link between the test and the adverse decision is unclear or even secret. Counselors, teachers, and administrators give or deny students a variety of opportunities such as special reading groups or enrichment programs based on their performance on a single test. Worse yet, sometimes the decisions are based on tests that were taken during the prior school year.

The defenders of such decisions sometimes maintain that the students in special programs do better than the "average" and thus such tests must have been valid. In this context, validity becomes a self-fulfilling prophecy. A student does well on a test and then receives extra instruction from teachers who have high expectations. They come home to parents who have been told that their child is superior. If there is a challenge in school for such children, they assume that they can work harder, ask for help, and ultimately succeed. That is, after all, what smart kids, gifted kids, successful kids such as themselves would be expected to do. Of course, this combination of strategy, encouragement, expectations, persistence, and self-confidence would serve any student well. The converse is true. When a test indicates that a student has a poor math aptitude or is unlikely to become a good writer, then the subsequent expectations of teachers, parents, and the students themselves will assure that the negative prediction is accurate.

Does this mean that we should abandon all tests? Of course not. It is the use of the tests and the inappropriate interpretation of their results that should be reformed. The distinction that must be drawn is between tests as information and tests as prediction. Tarot cards provide information because the names of the cards are clear to any observer; few people outside of the Psychic Friends Network, however, would argue that the interpretation of the tarot cards can become transformed into accurate predictions. Consider other measurements in life. The bathroom scale may be mathematically accurate, but the next step—interpretation and prediction—can take one of two markedly different paths. A reading of 180 pounds can result in the inference, "I'd feel better if I lost ten pounds and I know just how to do it," or "I'm fat and stupid and ugly and can never change." The test was the same and the numbers were the same. The difference in the two responses involves interpretation and prediction.

Although parents may not always be able to influence the content or results of tests, we can make a profound impact on the interpretation of those tests and can fight the predictions that might be inaccurately made based upon those tests. The first challenge is in our own conversations about tests, focusing on learning and information rather than on evaluation, interpretation, and prediction. If parents fail to model learning conversations with children, they cannot influence the self-talk by children that inevitably occurs when parents are absent. Self-talk is powerful and, in the absence of strong logical challenges, can seem persuasive to anyone, particularly a child. Cognitive therapists challenge the illogical conclusions of their patients by helping them to identify the logical errors and destructive consequences of their self-talk. We do not need a therapist, however, to help our children think through why they believe as they do about their own successes and failures in school. If we listen, we might find thought patterns revealed in such self-talk as "I'm no good at math!" The source of such self-talk is rarely a scientific examination in which the algebra gene was found to be missing. Rather, there was some test, some conversation, some announcement of student proficiency in mathematics, and on that tenuous basis, an inappropriate conclusion was drawn. Sometimes the parent's first response is to offer assurances to the doubtful child such as, "Sure, you're good at math," or worse yet, "You think you were bad? I had trouble in math as well." It would be more constructive if we ask, "Why do you think that?" And then complete the conversation in a way that children can challenge their own conclusions. This might require some gentle inquiry and lots of listening by the parent. While the encouragement, love, and high expectations of parents are undeniably important, we must also develop the self-confidence of our children by giving them the skills to challenge their own negative images that stem from inappropriate interpretation and predictions of their past performance on tests.

Standards: The Path Toward More Fair and Meaningful Tests

Because the words "standards" and "testing" are frequently used in the same sentence, some people have associated bad tests and inappropriate usage of test information with the standards movement. In fact, the proper application of academic standards leads to tests that are more fair and educational than traditional tests that are shrouded in mystery. Standards-based tests are fundamentally different from traditional tests in that student performance is compared to a standard rather than to the performance of other students. An academic standard is a simple statement of what students are expected to know and be able to do. Because the standards are public documents, students need not guess about the expectations of teachers. Thus, with standards, tests are not a game of *Jeopardy* in which the student with the most encyclopedic memory of many disconnected facts is the winner. Rather, any student who meets the standard can be a winner. Student success in a standards-based environment is a matter of what you know, not who you beat.

Because standards-based tests reject the notion of comparing one student to another, the traditional bell-shaped curve is rejected as a method of analyzing student performance. When schools use the bell curve, they assume that there are a few students who perform significantly above the average, a few students who are significantly below the average, and the vast majority of students who are in the middle. The last group forms the "bell"—the large hump in the middle of the curve. Although the bell curve is widely used in statistics and has been a staple of educational evaluation for more than a century, there is just one thing wrong with it: It is an inaccurate way to describe student achievement. When educational evaluation is based on a comparison to the average—the middle of the bell curve—then we have another self-fulfilling prophecy. If the instrument used to evaluate children only allows for a few students who are very much above average, then the use of that instrument—not the nature of children being tested—establishes the proof of the bell curve.

Test designers have a clever way of avoiding any evidence that does not fit their theory. If, for example, all children get a particular question right, then some observers might be delighted at the obvious result of diligent work by teachers and students. But in a test dedicated to the bell curve, such a question is simply discarded. The "good" questions are those that clearly differentiate one student from another. Ironically, the technical term for such differentiation is "discrimination," a term whose connotation of unfairness might be more accurate than the statistical meaning of identifying differences among students.

There are some instances in which a bell curve approach to testing might make some sense. If there are scarce resources to be allocated—such as admission to a selective college or selection for a high-paying job—then some people argue that only a bell curve test can rank students from best to worst. This sounds great in theory. After all, isn't the ninety-eighth percentile always better than the ninety-six percentile? The answer is, not necessarily. In fact, on many tests, the difference between those two rankings might be the response on a very small number of questions and student mastery of those questions may or may not be related to success in the college or job under consideration. In fact, the difference between those two might be random or, at the very least, not relevant to the decision at hand. Consider other examinations, such as those for firefighter or jet pilot. In both cases, it is not sufficient for one candidate to beat another candidate. Any successful candidate applying for these positions must meet demanding physical and mental requirements. If no one meets those standards, the examiners do not say, "You can't carry someone out of a flaming building, but you're above the average of the other candidates, so we will accept you." Moreover, if there are several qualified candidates, the examiners do not say, "You are both highly qualified candidates, but Mary knew a little more about particle physics than Joe did, and therefore we will select Mary for the job." The candidates meet the standards or they don't, and if more people meet a standard than are needed to fill a vacancy, then the appropriate decision is not to resort to irrelevant information. In the context of education, the ultimate objectives should be accuracy and fairness. When schools use standards, teachers are liberated from the ancient and inaccurate practice of grading "on the curve" and instead can speak the truth: The student is proficient or not proficient compared to a standard, and a comparison to the work of other students is not relevant to my decision.

Standards are hardly a revolutionary approach to education. In fields as diverse as music and athletics, educators have long used standards. When a student wishes to play in the orchestra or participate on the basketball team, the requirement is not merely to beat other students, but rather to play scales, shoot baskets, or otherwise meet a standard that the conductor or coach has prescribed. The rules of the game are clear, and students need not guess about the height of the basket or the number of strings on a violin. Chapter 2 provides more detailed information about academic standards and what they mean for your child.

What about Talent and Intelligence?

Some readers are thinking, "Wait a minute! In the real world, everybody can't be a winner. Besides, there are some things that just can't be taught, and those things include talent and intelligence. You can't teach a golfer to be a Tiger Woods or a violinist to be Joshua Bell." This controversy about the relative impact of "born" traits versus taught skills has been at the center of educational debates since Plato. The Greek philosopher believed that there were "men of gold" who ruled over the "men of bronze." Not much has changed in the more than two thousand intervening years, as many people assume that "some kids have it and some don't."

Consider the example of musical talent, a quality many people assume is "born, not made." The Suzuki method of musical instruction has influenced literally millions of students and parents on every continent on the globe. As a result of the influence of Suzuki training, students without obvious genetic heritage of musicianship have found places in symphony orchestras throughout the world. Although the debate over talent and intelligence continues, those who discount the primacy of teaching and learning over inborn traits are deliberately indifferent to the evidence. There are surely cases of the most exceptional musicians, mathematicians, and athletes who may have some genetic predisposition toward their chosen careers. Nevertheless, the experience of the legions of students who have benefited from the Suzuki method make clear that the existence of exceptional talent and intelligence in a very few cases does not negate the general principle that talent and intelligence of the many can be nurtured, encouraged, and expanded. As Dr. Howard said, "Smart is something you get, not just something you are."

constructive conversations

Talking with Your Child about Standards and Tests

Children attribute an unusually high degree of credibility to what they hear at school, and thus the potentially negative conversations surrounding tests and standards that your child may encounter must be the subject of serious home discussion. Parents, not the local rumor mill, must determine the appropriate way for each child to react to standards and testing. This is not an issue on which the final parental word is, "Because I said so!" In our discussions with children, we must seek to equip them to stand on their own in the conflicts of the classroom and hallway. Thus, the following "point/counterpoint" dialogues are designed to suggest ways for you to talk constructively with your child about standards and tests.

"Those tests tell you how smart you are. If you don't do well, it means you're a dummy."

"Tests don't tell how smart you are, but tests do tell you a couple of things. They tell you what you have learned and they also tell you how good you are at figuring things out even

when the right answer isn't very clear. That's why it's a good idea to pay attention and study, and it's also a good idea to sit down with me and look at some of your old tests. If there is ever a test where you don't do well, we'll just work on it a little more. You're smart—and if you don't do well on a test, it just means we need to think through what happened and figure out how to do better. I know you can do it."

repeat positive

"If I don't do well on this test I'll be ruined! I won't get to go to the next grade with my friends. I just know I'm going to blow it!"

experiences

"It sounds as if you're pretty nervous about this test. Tell me how you're feeling about it right now. (Pause.) It's pretty scary, isn't it? Now, tell me how you felt when you did a great job in school. Remember that time when you got a perfect score on the math test and when you were so happy about your geography test? Tell me how you felt then. (Pause.) When you feel smart and good and happy, what did you do to make yourself feel that way? Let's make a list. Maybe we can discover the things that you have done when you felt smart and good and happy and we'll figure out how to do those things again now. If you do those same things, I know that you'll do a great job. And you know what? Even if your pencil breaks, the wind blows your test paper away, and the teacher turns into a green-eyed dragon and breathes fire on everybody's test, I'm going to love you anyway. Do we have a deal? Let's start making that list. . ."

"I can't possibly memorize all these things. My teacher said that the standards were impossible anyway and that no kids our age could do them. Mrs. Johnson said the same thing in the car on the way to school today. There's just nothing I can do. I give up!"

*"I don't know. I've heard a lot of people say that kids can't do things, like play soccer or go on the Internet or create plays and make up songs, and then the kids do a great job anyway. When you said that the standards were impossible, which standards were you talking about? (Pause.) Well, I haven't read them either, so do you want to look them up and see if they are really impossible or if you can do most of them after all? What's your best subject? Let's start there . . ."**

*The state standards for grades 6 through 8 are reprinted in the second part of this book.

"I don't want to meet the standards—I want to be me! All my teachers have said I was a great writer ever since first grade. Now they tell me that I can only write the same way, every time, with a beginning, middle, and end. I used to write funny stories with crazy characters and goofy conversations, but now they say I have to be more serious. I hate standards, and so does everybody else. I have a dumb assignment because the dumb standard says that I have to compare two different dumb things. It's just stupid, and I don't want to do it. I want to write my stories!"

"I love your creative stories, too. I've saved some of the ones that you've written in the past. They show me that you are an intelligent, creative, and passionate person. You really care about what you write. Did you know that there are other people, aside from me, who could be moved by your writing? Tell me about something that really makes you angry. It might be people hurting animals or each other. It might be about the environment. It might be something at school or in our community. It might even be something about me or that happens at our house. Take a minute and think about it, and tell me something that makes you angry and that you want to change. (Pause, and let the child think of several options—you might get a fairly long list from a middle school student.) That's great! This is something that makes you really angry and that you want to change. Now, here's what we're going to do. You're a great writer, and writers can change things with their ideas and words. Write a letter about this. You might write it to me, to the President, to your teacher, to the principal, to the newspaper, or to anyone who can make a difference on this matter that makes you so angry. Let's agree that your letter should be your very best work. That means that you'll probably need to make an outline first. Then you'll write a draft, then edit it for errors in spelling, grammar, and punctuation. Finally, you will write your final copy. Of course, if you want to write persuasively, you will have both passion and evidence, so make sure that you support your arguments with research and examples. Because this is your very best work, your letter will have a clear beginning, middle, and end. If your letter is to me, I promise that I'll write a personal response to you. If your letter is to anyone else, I promise that I'll mail it to the recipient. I'm really proud of you for caring so much about this. I can't wait to see your letter!"

Your Right to Know about Tests in Your Child's School

Testing need not be mysterious or filled with terror. In fact, federal law establishes a parent's right to know what tests their children are taking and what the tests are about. This right includes everything from the weekly spelling tests to psychological tests to diagnostic tests to high-stakes graduation tests. If tests are mysterious, it is because parents do not ask the right questions. A sample letter from a parent to school officials requesting access to test information appears on page 92.

Parents' Checklist:

☐ Ask questions about your child's day based on his feelings and emotions, rather than events.

☐ Find out what tests are given in your child's school and how they are used to make any decisions about your child. Enter each of these test dates on your family calendar so that you can help to provide encouragement and reduce anxiety for your child.

☐ Celebrate your child's school accomplishments with the same enthusiasm you found in her first steps or her latest victory in a game.

---

celebrate
accomplishments

Chapter 4

Parents' Questions about Standards and Tests

This chapter is the result of hundreds of encounters with parents in focus groups, interviews, casual conversations, and letters. My research included parents from a wide variety of economic, educational, and cultural backgrounds. Although the parents with whom I spoke frequently expressed the conviction that their concerns were unique, the themes of these conversations were remarkably consistent. Parents have heard many rumors about academic standards, and much of what they have heard is the cause of significant fear and apprehension. The most consistent and significant desire expressed by parents is for specific communication from teachers about what children need to know and be able to do. Parents want more than a report card and annual parent-teacher conference. Parents want to play a role beyond working at a table at the school carnival or operating the copy machine in the school office. Parents, in brief, want information that is accurate and relevant to their children.

Despite the differences among the parents interviewed for this chapter, all of them have one thing in common: They care deeply about the educational opportunities for their children. Whether the parent was a Harvard-educated attorney or a high school dropout, the message was the same: Parents want their children to have more opportunities than they had and they are willing to support schools that provide such opportunities. They also insist on fairness for their children and clear communication from schools. Parents detest jargon, slogans, patronizing speeches, memos, and notes that appear to diminish the importance of the family. At the same time, parents are leery of the implication that they are primarily responsible for the education of their children. Whether the subject of discussion was math homework, test preparation, or summer reading, many parents bristled at the notion that they were responsible for doing a job that the school was supposed to do. Finally, the parents with whom I spoke were deeply concerned about the impact of a single test on their child, and most parents saw more threats than opportunities in the high-stakes testing movement.

The questions and responses that follow are hardly exhaustive, but they represent a synthesis of the attitudes, feelings, beliefs, and concerns of parents throughout the nation. You might recognize some of your own questions in the dialogue that follows.

What Is the Fundamental Purpose of School in the Middle Grades—That Is, the Grades Between Elementary School and High School?"

Many parents are confused about the fundamental purpose of middle school. Is it to explore different subjects, or to build the self-esteem of adolescents during a particularly difficult time of life? Many professional educators and state policymakers have strong disagreements about the purpose of middle school. Over the past thirty years, considerable research has been devoted to the unique needs of adolescents and pre-adolescents. While reasonable people disagree on many of these points, my response to this question is as follows: First, the fundamental purpose of education in the middle years between elementary school and high school is to prepare students to enter high school with confidence and success. High school teachers are nearly unanimous in the belief that incoming students must have strong skills in reading, writing, mathematics, time management, organization, and personal discipline. Second, the desire for exploration of many different subjects is understandable, as adolescence is an inquisitive time of life. Nevertheless, if parents and educators must choose between exploration and the development of basic skills in reading, the latter should take precedence over the former. Third and most important, educational researchers and parents of more than one child are unanimous on one point: Children acquire information at different rates. Therefore, the curriculum of the middle grades should assume differentiation, not uniformity. Some students require one period a day to master seventh-grade reading skills, while other students need two or three periods. Students are not widgets in a factory to be moved about in a uniform manner, but individuals with needs that are variable. Effective schools provide a different schedule to meet the individual learning needs of different students, and parents should support the recognition, analysis, and curriculum changes that result from a recognition of different student needs.

reduce anxiety

What Should I Say to My Child about Standards and Tests?

This is a great opportunity to move your children away from test terror toward becoming confident and capable students. Start with a clear definition: *Standards are the things that you should know and be able to do.* Then identify some of the standards that your children are already meeting. Review just a few of the standards in this book and tell your child, "You are already doing this. You see, standards aren't always something new and extra that you must learn; you already know many of these things right now!"

It is difficult to have a discussion with your child about academic standards without also discussing the tests based on your state's standards. This conversation is about emotions, not just about facts. Some parents are tempted to say something like, "You'd better study hard or you'll flunk the test!" In fact, the primary emotion of fear is already overwhelming, and the role of the parent is not to add to that anxiety, but to reduce it. How can you reduce your child's anxiety? Avoid false reassurances such as, "It's no big deal!" or "I'm sure you'll do just fine, so don't worry about it." When, in the life of parents, has the statement "Don't worry about it" served as a useful reassurance? What children most need to know is that their parent has heard and understood their fears. It is better to say, "Yes, tests can be pretty scary. When you fear something, it's always better to talk about it than to pretend that it's no big deal. What is there on this list of standards, or what have you heard about the test that is the most scary for you?" The parent finally has the information that can take the conversation from a dialogue filled with fear to the realm of the confident and empowered child. You will know that you have succeeded in these conversations—don't expect the matter to be resolved with a single discussion—when your child starts saying things such as:

"I know what I'm supposed to do in school."

"If I don't know how to do something, I know that I can figure it out or I know where I can get some help."

"I may not get a perfect score on the test, but I know most of the things on there. And if I miss a few questions, it doesn't mean I'm stupid. I'll just continue to learn all I can and do my best."

These are the words of a confident and empowered child. Parents need not give their children illusions, as if the Test Fairy will come to their aid in time of need. Rather, parents must give their children facts: what the standards are, what the tests mean, and how children's own efforts will improve their ability to achieve standards and do well on tests.

Is This Just Another Fad?

You have probably heard of educational terms that sounded like fads, from "new math" to "whole language" to "learning styles" to "brain research" and a host of other labels that seem to dominate the discussion of educational matters from one year to the next. How do you know that the term "standards" is not just another passing fad? First, let's remember what standards are all about. The label is not important, but the essence of standards is vital. Standards are just about fairness. Because standards express what students should know and be able to do, and because standards-based schools expect teachers to give children the opportunity to meet those standards, there is nothing new or fancy at work here other than a simple commitment to fairness. Standards will not go "out of style" unless the desire of parents and teachers for fairness becomes a passing fad.

Who Sets the Standards?

In every state except Iowa, academic content standards are established by the state. In Iowa, every school district sets its own standards. Thus, some form of academic standards exists in every public school in the nation. Indeed, whether or not the term "standard" is used, most private and parochial schools also have a clear set of academic expectations for students.

One frequent misunderstanding is that "national standards" govern the content of the academic disciplines. In fact, a few groups such as the National Council for Teachers of Mathematics, National Council for Teachers of English, and other academic and professional organizations have offered suggested standards that frequently are used as resources by state departments of education and local school districts. There is not, however, a "Federal Department of Standards" in Washington, D.C. where busy bureaucrats wake up every morning plotting new ways to remove the local authority of school boards. There are no federally established academic standards imposed on schools. Although the federal government has broad authority with respect to protecting individual civil rights in school—particularly with regard to discrimination on the basis of ethnicity, gender, or disability—the federal role in curriculum is strictly advisory.

The evidence of state and local control over the curriculum is best revealed in the wide variation in the academic content standards of the states. Some states, such as New York and California, have very specific academic expectations, and those academic requirements are linked to curriculum documents and test objectives. Other states, by contrast, have academic requirements that are much more vague, leaving the discretion to select specific curriculum and test objectives to local school districts.

Despite the differences among state standards, there are some important commonalities. The most important distinguishing characteristic of standards-based schools is the comparison of students to a standard rather than to the average of other students. Many states blur this distinction in their testing policies. Rather than refer to the percentage of students who meet a standard, some state documents continue to make reference to "percentile" or other methods of ranking students. It will take some time before every state policy maker and administrator applies standards carefully and accurately.

Do Standards Place Too Much Emphasis on Academics?

Many parents expressed the concern that standards emphasize academic subjects to the exclusion of extracurricular activities, the arts, and simple fun in school. Some of these parents have heard alarming news stories (and more than a few unsubstantiated rumors) about schools that have been transformed into academic boot camps. In these dreary places, students do nothing except prepare for tests all day long. Work sheets and mock tests have replaced music and art. A number of popular writers have fanned the flames of this hysteria, fueled more by anecdote than by evidence.

It is true that when standards have been established with care, some traditional activities have been replaced by lessons with a greater academic orientation. This does not, however, imply the elimination of holiday celebrations and the systematic removal of fun from the school day. Students in standards-based schools will, for example, probably continue to discuss current events, enjoy physical activities, and participate in performing arts. It does not hurt the cause of student enjoyment, however, when students learn more about measurement and biology in their physical education classes, improve their mastery of fractions in their music classes, and otherwise incorporate academic relevance into fun activities. Indeed, the activities in this book make it clear that fun, engagement, and academic standards are not mutually exclusive.

Why Can't School Just Be Fun?

One of the frequent concerns expressed by parents I interviewed was the lament that school is no longer fun. Parents have heard tales of multi-hour homework assignments and children who complained that "Monday is the worst day of the week" because school was so terrifying. Some of these parents assumed that the appropriate reaction to the state of affairs must be a reduction of the academic expectations for their children. Parents should consider that it is entirely possible that the difficulties the students are facing arise because previous teachers did not have sufficiently high expectations of them. When everyone is focused on making school fun, the teacher who insists that students learn something is accused of being demanding and mean. This reinforces the notion that learning is burdensome and that school is dreadfully dull. The problem compounds itself in middle school, high school, and even in college, when the expectation of rigor is abandoned and students are viewed as "customers" who must be satisfied by credits that are easy, fun, and worthless.

What about the Basics—Reading, Writing, and Arithmetic?

Some parents are concerned that an emphasis on the higher order thinking skills included in many academic standards will reduce an emphasis on the "basics"—that is, skills in reading, writing, and arithmetic. In fact, there is not a contradiction between the requirement for higher order thinking and basic skills. Students cannot learn to master the challenge of mathematical problem solving if they do not have arithmetic skills. Moreover, students cannot respond to the challenge of critical thinking in social studies and science if they are unable to read their social studies and science textbooks or write a lab report.

The controversy over basic education has been particularly acute in mathematics. Partisans of pure "problem-solving" believe that an emphasis on mathematical concepts is essential, and that the dreary "drill and kill" of traditional worksheets must be discarded in favor of an emphasis on thinking. Of course, most mathematics teachers and parents recognize the intuitively obvious proposition that problem-solving and math skills are inseparable. Even in an age of calculators and computers, students must have "number sense." This means that students not only must be able to compute that $9 \times 9 = 81$ but they must also be able to understand that the number 81 is comprised of nine groups of nine and comprehend the notion that there are many other ways to achieve a product of 81. For example, consider these three levels of mathematical understanding, using the same example that begins with the question, "What is 9×9?"

The lowest level of understanding is expressed by the student who grabs the calculator and punches the buttons: $9 \times 9 =$ receives the answer 81. The next level of understanding is the student who recalled from memory that the product was 81 and did not need the calculator for assistance. But neither of these levels of understanding approaches the sophistication of the student who not only understands that $9 \times 9 = 81$, but also understands that since $3 \times 3 = 9$, then 81 is also the product of $3 \times 3 \times 3 \times 3$. For this student, the study of exponents in a future grade will be intuitive and easy. He will immediately grasp that $3^4 = 81$ rather than perceive exponents as a new and foreign mathematical concept that must be memorized without understanding. In other words, students need both the basics and thinking skills. The two are complementary, not competitive concepts.

Similarly, we expect students to have a deep understanding of causes and effects in history and science. But these deep understandings will elude students who do not have the ability to read and understand the paragraph before them. Moreover, the thinking skills involved in understanding the interplay of politics, geography, economics and conflict will elude students who did not study the factual details of those subjects. Thus, anyone who contends that an emphasis on standards excludes a commitment to basic skills has not carefully read the standards. I have met with angry parent groups whose concerns about standards were allayed when presented with the actual words of the standards. The academic standards make clear that students must not only master thinking, reasoning, and analysis, but also must understand how to read, write, and compute, as well as know the content associated with the foundational academic subjects.

understanding

Will Standards Mean the Elimination of Music, Art, and Physical Education?

There is a legitimate concern expressed by many parents that the overwhelming emphasis in state tests and standards on mathematics and language arts will exclude music, art, and physical education in some schools. In most successful schools I have studied, mathematics, social studies, science, music, art, and physical education are an integral part of the academic life of the school. For example, students in music class routinely use melody, rhythm, and song lyrics as a bridge to better understand history, learn new vocabulary, and master fractions. Students in art class use the visual images of art to expand their vocabulary and enhance their ability to compare and contrast different images. Moreover, students in effective art classes are able to master the art of scale and ratio, measurement, and the relationship between different geometric figures. There are wonderful physical education classes in which students acquire a better understanding of measurement. When the coach has given students the choice to run a millimeter or a kilometer, and the students make the wrong choice, the lesson on metric measurement tends to remain with them for a long time. Moreover, I have seen effective physical education teachers conduct vocabulary relays and math relays in which students must not only run fast but also must understand vocabulary and mathematical information in order to continue the race. This is the ideal intersection of the academic, the aesthetic, and the athletic.

Many middle schools and junior high schools have attempted to offer so much to so many different students that they have forgotten their fundamental mission: helping students to enter high school with confidence and success. It is clear from my interviews with high school teachers that the most important skills middle school students need are reading, writing, time management, and organization. Because classes in physical education, art, and music all can help to build these skills, they are not frills, but essential to the preparation of students for high school. The essential nature of these classes, of course, depends on teachers who understand that every class contains an academic component and that they are not a "teacher of music, art, and physical education," but rather a teacher of children.

the ideal intersection

Does My Child Really Have to Meet All of the Standards?

One of the weaknesses of standards as they have been articulated in most states is the failure of prioritization. In fact, not every standard is of equal value. Some standards recognize the need of basic skills, including reading, writing, and arithmetic. Moreover, the standards recognize the need of students to analyze and understand a relatively narrow set of facts. But neither every fact nor every skill has equal value for the student. Thus, it is not accurate to say that children have to meet every single standard elaborated by the state. One method of distinguishing the more important standards from those that are interesting but less valuable is the concept of "power standards." Chapter 5 provides more detailed elaboration on this concept.

What Happens If My Child Doesn't Meet the Standards?

When children do not meet academic content standards, the most immediate response should be the opportunity for additional learning. In other words, the immediate consequence for the failure to achieve a standard should be neither a low grade nor the repetition of an entire year of school. Rather, the initial consequence should be the opportunity for additional learning. This recognizes what all parents know to be true: Students learn at different rates. Many states have implemented high-stakes tests that are associated with academic content standards and some of these tests have dramatic consequences. For example, in some states, students must pass a reading proficiency test in order to enter the fourth grade. In other states, students must pass middle school proficiency tests in order to enter high school. A growing number of states—twenty-six at this writing—have established high school graduation examinations, which must be successfully completed by students in order to receive a high school diploma.

In the best school districts, the student performance on these examinations is rarely a surprise. In fact, students have multiple opportunities to prepare for important tests. Parents also have many opportunities to know well in advance of the test whether their children need additional help. Unfortunately, many school districts have a reactive response to high-stakes tests. Remediation and opportunities for additional learning only take place after a student has failed a test. Worst of all is the fallacy of remediation in high school for problems that have their roots in elementary and middle school.

If you are concerned about the performance of your child on a high-stakes test, then the use the letter format on page 92 to inquire of your school administration what specific testing policies will affect your child. Once you have this information, identify the particular knowledge and skills that your child will be required to have. Then you will be able to identify the gap between what your child knows at this time, and what your child will need to know and be able to do when the test is administered.

Parents frequently make the same mistake as schools, becoming involved in a child's academic challenges only after a student is experiencing difficulty in school. The most successful parental involvement occurs long before a child has experienced academic difficulty. Therefore, if you are concerned about the performance of your child in an upcoming test, the time to become involved is now, not after you receive your child's score.

My Child Just Doesn't Get It. What Do I Do?

Lots of frustrated parents share your concern. Most of us attempt to teach our children in the same way that we learned. In other words, if we learned by having someone read to us or speak to us, we assume that our children learn the same way. If we learned by having instructions written out for us, then we assume that our children will benefit from our own written instructions. Fortunately, children have a way of emulating some but not all of our characteristics. One of the things that they may not inherit is your learning style. As a result, please do not assume that your child "just doesn't get it" simply because the child is not learning the same way that you did.

You can discover your child's learning style by identifying the circumstances in which your child performs at a very high level. For example, perhaps your child plays a game exceptionally well. Perhaps your child enjoys a particular story, chapter, or book so much that she is able to recall it with astonishing detail. Perhaps your child enjoys writing to a relative or receiving mail. These will give you clues about the ways in which your child acquires information, processes that information, and applies information to the task at hand. Of course, just because a person prefers one learning style does not mean that the rest of the world will always accommodate that need. Therefore, children need to be able to process information from written text, oral instructions, and the context of the world around them. By finding your child's preferred method of learning, you can capitalize on that strength and also be more attentive to building skills in those learning methods that do not come so easily to your child.

When you become frustrated with your child's performance, one of the most important things that you can do is to stop the common practice of giving your child a single set of instructions involving the performance of multiple tasks. The most common example is, "Clean up your room!" For some children, this instruction is clear. For others, we must be more clear by breaking down the tasks: "Take the clothes off the floor and put them in the hamper." Then, after the successful completion of that task, "Empty the trash." Then, "Let your brother out of the closet," and so on, until the task of cleaning the room is completed. The breaking down of complex instructions into individual tasks is essential in the academic context as well. The only way you can isolate the difficulty your child is having is by providing clear instructions in a step-by-step manner. You may find that the problem is neither an inability to comprehend your instructions, nor an unwillingness to act on them. The difficulty, rather, may be that your child, like all of us, prefers some types of instructions to others. It is also quite likely that there is a difference in understanding when your child hears instructions compared to when the same instructions are printed on a page and your child must independently read and respond to them. The difference between oral and visual strengths is not the only learning style you should consider. Some children who do not respond well to oral or written instructions can perform the same tasks well if they see a physical model of the expected result, watch a demonstration, or engage in trial and error. The point is not that one of these learning styles is "right," but rather that every person learns in different ways, yet all of us occasionally are compelled to acquire information in a manner that does not correspond to our strengths. By understanding the need to listen, read, or observe demonstrations, a parent can support a child's strengths and offer encouragement and practice to deal with learning styles that are less familiar and, in the past, less successful.

Another common reason for children having difficulties in school is the disconnection between previous learning and current expectations. For example, students are bound to have difficulty with seventh-grade math requirements, such as finding the area of a circle by multiplying the square of the radius of the circle by pi, if they failed to master multiplication and exponents in earlier grades. Students are not going to be able to create a three-paragraph essay in eighth grade if they were unable to write coherent sentences in earlier grades. One of the principal benefits of the standards movement has been the requirement that teachers communicate with one another so that, in the best standards-based schools, there is a seamless transition from one grade to the next. An eighth-grade teacher has confidence about what students learned in the seventh grade because the seventh-grade curriculum was not based on the personal preferences of the teacher, but rather on a coherent curriculum that led directly to the instructional needs of the eighth-grade classroom. This process of building from one grade to the next should begin in elementary school. Students are not going to be able to create a satisfactory paragraph in fifth grade if they did not learn how to construct a proper sentence in earlier grades, and these same students will be frustrated in eighth grade when faced with the challenge of writing a persuasive or expository essay. The curriculum of each grade should be designed to equip students with the skills and knowledge required to master the curriculum of the next grade. It is fair to say, however, that this ideal, seamless transition from one grade to the next is the exception rather than the rule in most American schools. Moreover, many schools have high rates of student and teacher mobility so that it is impossible to assume that every child in every class had a common foundation of learning.

The final consideration with respect to children who are having difficulty in school should be evaluation for learning disabilities. When you have tried to analyze a child's learning style with few results, and when you have attempted to help your child fill in the gaps from previous grade levels, it may be that your child continues to have immense difficulties in school. In these cases, it is appropriate to request an evaluation of your child for a variety of learning disabilities. Some parents fear that if they request an evaluation of their child, a label with negative connotations such as "special education" may be applied to their child. It is essential to note that both federal laws and public perceptions have changed markedly in the past several years on this issue. If your child is among the eleven percent of students nationwide with an identified learning disability, it does not mean that your child is "stupid" or otherwise incapable of great performance. The fields of law, medicine, music, and governmental leadership include many men and women who have learning disabilities. Indeed, identification of and compensation for a learning disability are the keys to their success. It is also very likely that children who are evaluated will not have a learning disability, and that work by those children, along with parents and teachers, on academic and behavioral issues will help them reach their full potential.

What If My Child Has a Learning Disability?

More than eleven percent of students across the United States have some sort of learning disability. We have made great strides in this country in diagnosing, understanding, and even valuing the diversity of learning styles that different students bring to class, and this includes learning disabilities. The notion of "valuing" a learning disability is not merely a politically correct posture designed to make students and parents feel good about a bad situation. Marcus Buckingham and Donald Clifton of the Gallup Organization, one of the leading polling and management consulting firms in the world, provide examples of how even the profoundly challenging reading disability, dyslexia, can result in positive effects for students and adults who recognize the disability and carefully plot strategies for dealing with it. Students with learning disabilities have clear legal rights expressed in the

Individuals with Disabilities Education Act (IDEA). Moreover, the students frequently have rights that are protected by local district policy and state law.

Foremost among the rights of learning disabled students is the right to have the "least restrictive environment" for learning. This typically means that learning disabled students are sitting next to students in regular education classes with regular teachers. The students, therefore, must have accommodations and adaptations made for them, particularly when it is time for a test. The most frequent accommodations and adaptations include time, environment, reading, and writing. The adaptation of time is provided to students who process information slowly, but accurately, and thus taking more time on a test allows them to accurately express what they know. The adaptation of environment provides for a quiet and secluded test-taking environment for students whose learning disability limits their concentration. The adaptation of reading allows students who understand words, but cannot process words in printed form, to have tests read aloud to them. Finally, the adaptation of writing allows a student who can speak words, but cannot write them, to dictate test responses to an adult for the writing portion of the test. Of course, these are only some of the many adaptations that are available to students with disabilities.

It is absolutely vital that parents and teachers distinguish between appropriate accommodation and the reduction of rigor for a test. Many professions include members who are extraordinarily gifted and intelligent, and yet suffer from some learning disability. The gifts of these professionals would never have been recognized had their teachers and parents reduced rigor rather than sought the most appropriate adaptation for the needs of the students. There are instances in which parents and teachers harbor grave misconceptions about the distinction between appropriate accommodation and an inappropriate reduction in rigor. Such misunderstandings are usually revealed in the form of a statement such as, "She's in special education so I had to give her a B," or, "He has a learning disability, so even though he didn't take the test or complete the project, I had to give him a C." Such statements are at odds with both federal law and the best interests of the child. The focus of IDEA is appropriate consideration of individual needs. There is not a single sentence in the law or accompanying regulations that requires teachers to lie to parents about the nature of student performance. Indeed, the requirements for individual considerations in curriculum and assessments are not a prescription for "dumbing down" requirements, but rather a requirement for appropriate accommodations and adaptations. When those adaptations are offered to students, it is typical that the report card will indicate that the student "achieved standards with appropriate adaptations and accommodations." Moreover, when a student does not meet an academic standard, the appropriate and accurate report should reflect that "the student met these objectives in the educational plan and did not meet the other objectives in the educational plan." The path to improved performance by all students, including students with learning disabilities, is accuracy and honesty in assessment.

For more information on students with learning disabilities, please consult Chapter 9.

accuracy and honesty

What If I Disagree with the State and Local Standards?

Standards are political documents. They represent the efforts of a group of people who have endeavored to identify what students should know and be able to do. Nevertheless, as with any product of any committee, the documents are typically flawed. One can accept the obvious notion that some standards are too broad, some are too narrow, and most remain "works in progress," and nevertheless grasp that standards are superior to the poorly described curriculum or pedagogical anarchy that preceded them. It is entirely reasonable, and even likely, that thoughtful parents may disagree with some of the standards. Perhaps you disagree with the quantity of standards, with their specificity, with their vagueness, or even with their content. For example, I have heard a parent exclaim, "I don't care if my children can write, as long as they can read!" This was in direct response to the requirement of the state academic standards that children must be able to write coherent paragraphs. While this parent has a legitimate right to express such a point of view and, ultimately, to remove the children from the state school system, the parent should not have the right to require teachers to have a different set of standards for those children than for other children.

In many districts, parents have an extraordinary degree of influence on what the expectations are for their children. Unfortunately, these expectations are often used to reduce expectations and rigor and, as a result, dumb down the curriculum. In the example cited above, I confess to a prejudice. The research is clear and unambiguous: Writing is an effective way for students to think, reason, and learn. The fact that some parents may wish that their children did not have to write is not a sufficient justification for the absence of the requirement. I have worked in other schools where parents have asked the rhetorical question, "Why do these kids need algebra anyway? They will never use it." These parents, too, deserve a thoughtful hearing, but do not deserve to have their advice govern the curriculum standards for the school, district, or state that must serve all children.

There are other circumstances, however, in which the standards genuinely have deep flaws that contradict the philosophical, moral, or religious beliefs of parents. In these cases, parents have an opportunity to make their concerns known. Parents can exclude their students from tests and from subjects of study that they find objectionable on religious or moral grounds. Most schools ask parents specifically for permission to discuss issues involving human sexuality, birth control, religion, and other sensitive subjects. Schools routinely offer an alternative area of study and alternative literature to respond to parent wishes.

How Can I Deal with Stress and Anxiety about Tests?

Stress and anxiety are undeniably important parts of test performance. Most readers of this book can recall an instance in which they were well-prepared for an examination, or other challenge, and nevertheless performed below their ability. The reason for their poor performance was the stress and anxiety associated with a circumstance under which they had to perform. Although parents cannot completely eliminate childhood stress and anxiety, they can mitigate the negative impact by giving students healthy coping skills. These skills include the "second look" view of any situation in which children feel unprepared or uncomfortable. If the first look at a test question or other challenge reveals the student does not immediately know the answer, some students will simply assume that the challenge is impossible, emotionally shut down, succumb to the pressure at hand, and give up not only on the question before them but on the entire test. Other students, by contrast, have the ability to take a second look at a question or challenging circumstance. The second look of the student is comparable to the runner's second wind. This boost of energy occurs when students are able to use strategy, rather than mere recall, to address the question or challenge at hand.

Although parents need not conduct a test preparation academy from their home, they can give their students the ability to maintain and expand their repertoire of second look skills. Examples of second look skills include the following:

Two-pass technique—This technique suggests that students focus first on the questions to which they know the answer. Because every question typically has the same point value, students can generate the greatest yield on their investment of time when they focus first on those questions to which they immediately know the answer. After they have made the first pass going through all questions on a test, students can return to the beginning of the examination and devote additional energy to those questions that are ambiguous or more difficult. In most cases, students are well served to eliminate one or two obviously wrong answers, then guess the answer to these questions and quickly move along to the next challenge.

Outlining—Whenever students are faced with an essay question, there is a direct relationship between the amount of time spent outlining an answer and the time saved in creating the final answer. When students immediately launch into writing the final answer, they frequently produce an aimless and disorganized essay. When, on the other hand, students take the time to outline an answer first, they have the ability to produce a crisp and well-organized essay. Moreover, the very presence of the outline makes it clear to the teacher that the student understands the question and has taken the time to provide a detailed and well-organized response.

Process of elimination—In some cases, the right answer is not clear. Sometimes this is due to the difficulty of the test item. In many cases, however, this is due to the deliberate ambiguity of the test items. This is particularly true in the case of national standardized tests in which the test writers have determined that there must be a wide variation in the "difficulty value" of the test items. That is, some items are constructed in a manner so that many students will get them correct, and other items are constructed so that very few students will get the correct response. In the latter category, the cause for such a few number of students finding the correct answer is as likely the ambiguity as it is the difficulty of the question. In such cases, the students with the ability to persevere and take a second look at the question will find that, despite the difficulty or ambiguity of the question, they can at least eliminate one wrong answer and therefore have a higher probability of guessing the correct response. There is a great deal of mythology with respect to guessing on tests. In most cases, however, guessing strategies need not be mysterious at all. On many examinations, there is no "guessing correction factor" and therefore students should always guess if they do not know the right answer. On other tests, students are penalized for every wrong answer. In those cases, it only makes sense to guess if the student can eliminate one or two wrong answers. Consider these examples:

Mary is taking a test without any guessing correction factor. It is a multiple-choice test with four possible answers: A, B, C, and D. After reviewing her work, there are still eight questions that she just can't understand. Should Mary guess? Absolutely yes. If she just marks "A" for each of those eight questions, she has a one-in-four chance that "A" is correct, and thus she is likely to get two out of the eight questions correct. That is an extra two correct answers that she otherwise would have missed if she just left them blank.

In our second example, however, the rules are a little different. Bob is taking a similar test, with four possible answers. But for each question Bob misses, he will be penalized $\frac{1}{3}$ point. Bob also has the same chance of guessing correctly that Mary had, and indeed, he answered two out of eight questions correctly. But what about the other six questions? Because Bob lost $\frac{1}{3}$ point for each of those six, he was penalized two points ($\frac{1}{3} \times 6$), and thus he gained no advantage guessing.

What if Bob was able to eliminate two possible wrong answers? In other words, he is not guessing among choices A, B, C, and D, but only among choices A and B, because he determined that C and D were not possible right answers. Now Bob has a 50/50 chance—it's either A or B—of guessing correctly. With eight questions, he probably will get four correct. He will be penalized $\frac{1}{3}$ point on the other four, for a total of $1\frac{1}{3}$ points ($4 \times \frac{1}{3}$). Because Bob could eliminate two possible wrong answers, it was a good strategy for him to guess.

The suggestions offered here are essential elements of educational and psychological strategy. One of the most powerful forces operating in the life of the empowered child is emotional resilience. Children with the ability and willingness to persevere in the face of seemingly great odds have the gift of emotional resilience. This lifelong ability has importance that extends far beyond test taking and academic pursuits. We routinely see parents encourage the skill of perseverance and emotional resilience in athletic competition. "You can do it!" the proud parents exclaim. The same level of perseverance can be encouraged through parent support for the resubmission of student work after the first draft did not meet the standard, encouraging more than one attempt at an essay, and encouraging one additional try for success at the mathematics homework. This encouragement is the source of emotional resilience that will be as valuable in algebra class as it is on the soccer field. In the future, this sense of empowerment, perseverance, and resilience will serve your child well in college, in relationships, and in any professional endeavor.

What If My Child Is Not Ready for a Test?

It is relatively uncommon for children to say with confidence, "I'm ready for this test and I'm going to ace it!" More often than not, we have created a sense of fear and loathing for tests, including those tests for which students are reasonably well-prepared. Parents have an important role to play here. First, parents have an obligation to help students be prepared for tests. The first step is simple: Mark test dates on the family calendar. When it is clear that Thursday is a test day, then Wednesday is not the ideal evening for a movie or an appeal for a later than usual bedtime. Most teachers—particularly at the secondary level—confirm that the difference between the superior students and the vast majority of their students is more a matter of time management and organizational skills than intellect. While parents cannot take tests for their children, nor should they, parents can give students the gift of organization and that includes a calendar, appropriate focus on test preparation, and a consistent theme that performance on tests is improved with preparation and hard work. Parents must obliterate the notion that prevails among many children that, "either you've got it or you don't —studying doesn't make much difference." In fact, the harder they work, the better they will perform in school and most other areas of life.

Consider the typical exchange between parent and child: "Do you have any homework tonight?" When the response is in the negative, parents need to ask a few more questions. The absence of homework might be genuine. On the other hand, the absence of homework, particularly in middle school and in upper elementary school, might be due to the fact that there is a test the next day. Students of every age should maintain a calendar with important dates on it. This is one of the key lifelong time management skills that everyone must master. The skill and discipline of maintaining an accurate and up-to-date calendar and task list not only separates successful students from unsuccessful students, but also distinguishes people in the professional and business world from one another. When there is a test the next day, the result need not be endless anxiety, trepidation, and fear. Rather, there must be a systematic approach to test preparation.

The systematic approach to test preparation includes the following steps. First, students must outline exactly what the test entails. Sometimes it is clear, such as all the traditional spelling tests in elementary school. At other times, a chapter test in a book will provide a clear and accurate preview of the test that students must face in the classroom. At other times, however, the content of the test may not be so clear, and some questions must be asked. If this inquiry takes place at half past nine o'clock the evening before the test, there are few alternatives other than an investigation into the mysteries of the backpack and notebook. If, by contrast, this inquiry takes place several days before the test, there is an opportunity to give the student responsibility for asking the teacher for help and for seeking additional guidance from other sources.

Second, students should prepare a sample test. One of the most effective learning exercises is for students to create a test. For younger students, acting as a teacher is a fun and engaging way to learn. For older students, such an activity may lack pure enjoyment, but the intellectual advantage is nevertheless very significant. In addition, when students practice creating and taking a test, they have not only provided themselves with a cognitive edge over their peers, but they also have provided themselves with an emotional safety net. By facing the unknown in friendly circumstances—the family room or bedroom—the student has the opportunity to endure natural test jitters in an environment that is far less consequential than in the classroom the following day. Moreover, it is my experience that students generally ask themselves far more difficult questions than those posed by the teacher.

In a Technological Age, Why Should Kids Take Paper and Pencil Tests?

It is a common parlor game for people to fantasize about the future. For years we have contemplated a world in which pencils and paper would become obsolete. The "paperless office" has been a concept considered by business people for years. Alas, the reality of our daily lives flies in the face of our fantasies. In fact, both students and people in the world of work must be able to create visual images, words, sentences, and paragraphs using pencil and paper, white boards, chalkboards, and a host of other media. In addition, the use of pencil and paper to slowly and carefully express ideas offers students the ability to think through problems without necessarily resorting to the guesswork involved in a multiple-choice question.

It is true that twenty-first century students must achieve a degree of technological literacy. Nevertheless, we also expect students to achieve a high degree of thinking, reasoning, and analysis. Those skills are best reinforced when students must take pen or pencil in hand, express an idea, communicate their thinking, and subject their reasoning to the critical review of others. Although computers clearly will play a role in the classroom and the future of today's students, technology does not replace the need for students to communicate clearly, accurately, analytically, and yes, legibly, in written form.

appropriate help

How Can I Help My Child with Homework and Projects Without Doing the Work Myself?

The subtext of this question is quite revealing. Every parent has observed instances in which the work presented to the teacher is clearly the product of a parent rather than the student. Such projects reveal far more about parental ambition than they do about student ability. The problem is that parents do not like to see their children become frustrated, angry, and ultimately disengaged from school. So how much "help" is appropriate and when do we cross the line from appropriate coaching and assistance to the inappropriate substitution of our own efforts for those of our children?

Parents are best served when teachers provide clear expectations for student performance. Some teachers are also clear about the nature of acceptable help and the instructions will clearly say, "Ask a parent or friend for help on this part," or, "Do this part all alone—don't get help from anyone else." Unfortunately, this level of clarity and specificity is the exception rather than the rule. One method that is particularly helpful when students are doing projects is the use of a scoring guide (sometimes called a "rubric" in educational jargon). When there is a clear set of teacher expectations, parents are able to help students not by doing work for them, but by asking students this critical question: If you were the teacher and you were grading this assignment using the scoring guide or rubric that the teacher provided, what grade would you give?

The cognitive scientist Benjamin Bloom made a tremendous contribution to the field of education when he recognized that the abilities to synthesize and evaluate information were essential for the intellectual development of children. When parents ask students to evaluate their own work, they are challenging students to engage in the advanced skill of evaluation, something too frequently left only to the teacher. If the teacher has provided a clear scoring guide or rubric—particularly a scoring guide that is expressed in student accessible language—then students can place themselves in the role of the teacher-evaluator and ask themselves how they would evaluate their own performance.

Too frequently, however, students merely do their best work, or do the work in the minimum amount of time given the exigencies of an upcoming television program, and assume that the teacher will evaluate the work in his or her own mysterious wisdom. This common practice of reserving evaluation responsibilities exclusively for the teacher denies students the opportunity to evaluate and learn. Make no mistake: This is not an exercise in making children feel good about themselves or engaging in unwarranted self-congratulatory smiling faces affixed to non-proficient work. Rather, the practice of evaluation and reflection requires thoughtful criticism, evaluation, and in many cases, rewriting, correction of errors, and the improvement of the quality of work. When parents insist that students engage in evaluation, they are doing far more than helping students on an individual homework assignment. These parents are giving their children the lifelong skills of reflection and evaluation.

a sense of accomplishment

How Much Homework Is Reasonable?
How Much Is Too Much?

In the early elementary grades, students revel in sharing school work, stories, and projects with parents. It hardly seems like "homework," but rather is a chance to share a daily sense of accomplishment. Some practice and reinforcement on basic skills, as well as a review and revision of school work, might require fifteen to twenty minutes each school night. As students enter the fourth and fifth grades, teachers are mindful of the need to prepare students for the homework demands of middle school. Most upper elementary teachers require about 30 minutes of homework each evening. In the middle grades (usually sixth through eighth grade), students should expect about 90 minutes of homework each evening. It is important to note that these are averages. Before you conclude that your child has too much homework because of a project that requires four hours to complete, it might be useful to note whether the project was assigned three weeks ago. If that is the case, don't be surprised if, the night before the project is due, you hear the claim that "My teacher gave me five hours of homework!"

If the averages noted above are consistently exceeded, then it might be reasonable to have a conversation with the teacher about how the student can better use classroom time to finish work and how the homework burden can be made more reasonable.

In addition to the quantity of homework, parents should attend to the quality of homework assigned by teachers. Are students building skills, conducting independent research, reading for understanding, and building confidence? These are the characteristics of effective homework assignments. If, on the other hand, students are bewildered, unfocused, bored, or completing worksheets on skills they have already mastered, then the value of the homework assignment is subject to question. The best way to approach the teacher is not with a complaint about "too much homework" but rather with the request that homework be challenging and meaningful. "I understand your desire to instill discipline through daily work," you might say, "and I want to be supportive of those habits as well. Perhaps we could work together to find assignments that will be best suited to my child's needs."

The most important contribution that parents can make on the homework front is to make it a priority, with a consistent place and time for the completion of daily work. When no homework has been assigned, the place and time remain available for learning activities in this book as well as those that you and your child create. In this way, you have a regular commitment to learning at home that will sustain your child whether or not homework has been assigned by the teacher.

What If I Can't Help My Child with a Subject in School?

I have a confession to make. I studied and taught mathematics, and yet sometimes I find my own children's homework in that subject baffling. Even more embarrassing, I have given my children the wrong answers when I violated my own rules and helped them too much with their homework. If these mistakes can be committed by a former teacher and professor, how much more likely is every parent to make them? If you have ever felt intimidated by your children's homework, you certainly are not alone.

Even if you can provide the answer, this is rarely the most appropriate way for you to help children. When your children ask for your help, here are some steps that will produce better results than insisting they do everything themselves, or doing their homework for them.

First, ask the child to make an attempt. In some cases, this means breaking the problem down into steps. For example, if there is a multi-step story problem in mathematics, and the child does not know how to frame the answer to the problem, an appropriate step toward solving the problem might be creating a picture that accurately describes the problem. This is particularly effective coaching because many children understand visual images of a problem better than they do the words of the story problem. This also makes the point that the key to answering a problem successfully is the accurate understanding of the problem, not merely asking the parent for help.

Second, ask the child to solve a single part of the problem. If, for example, the problem involves a complex series of geography questions, and the child does not have all the answers, encourage the child to answer only one or two of the possible problems. Every time we break a large and complex problem down into its component parts, the problem becomes more approachable. This gives your child not only excellent task and time management skills, but also reduces the anxiety associated with the majority of complex and difficult problems.

Third, it is entirely legitimate for the child to write down these words: "I don't know the complete answer—I tried, but this is as far as I got." The child then makes a good faith attempt to respond to the challenge at hand. This demonstrates to the teacher that the child considered the problem, thought about the problem, and genuinely did not know the answer. This is far more important information for a teacher than when a child merely leaves a piece of paper blank or turns in nothing at all. In such cases, the teacher is unable to distinguish between work that has been ignored and work that was attempted, but completed unsuccessfully. Moreover, this builds a skill too rarely discussed in the context of homework and academic achievement: the skill and habit of intellectual honesty. Leaders in professions, businesses, and academic institutions can all attest to the rare circumstances under which the words "I don't know" have been uttered. Nevertheless, the courageous people who say those words are often well regarded by their peers. When leaders express this trait, it becomes clear that honesty, rather than bluffs, is the acceptable code of conduct.

explore your options

What about Extracurricular Activities?

The research involving extracurricular activities is unambiguous. When students are participating in extracurricular activities such as sports, music, leadership, service, drama, debate, and a host of other wonderful activities, their academic achievement improves. Although these activities do take some time, and occasionally they even take time away from homework and academics, the overall research is not even a close call. Attendance and grades improve when students are busily involved in extracurricular activities, and the most effective schools seek to encourage every student, not just the most talented athletes and the most gifted musicians, to participate in activities beyond the classroom. Parents are well advised to encourage their children to participate in extracurricular activities. Moreover, schools must challenge themselves to give recognition to the most inclusive extracurricular activities in addition to the most exclusive extracurricular activities.

As valuable as extracurricular activities are, involvement can be carried to an unhealthy extreme. I know of children whose days begin with 7:30 chess club, followed by a full day of school, followed immediately by science club from 3:30 to 4:30. Religious school follows from 4:45 to 6:00. Eating a sandwich in the car, the child barely makes the 6:15 piano lesson. Basketball practice starts at 7:00 p.m. sharp and the child arrives home, exhausted, about 8:30 p.m. The cycle will repeat itself tomorrow, with soccer practice in place of basketball practice, a violin lesson replacing the piano lesson, and student council replacing science club. A reasonable rule might be, "one sport at a time" or "no more than one private lesson per week."

What If My Child Is Assigned to a Bad School?

The first question that must be considered is what makes a "bad" school. More often than not, parents evaluate schools the same way that real estate agents do, with a review of test scores. It is more than ironic that the same parents who seek out schools with high test scores express shock when those schools demonstrate that they take tests seriously. Moreover, it strikes administrators and teachers as deeply distressing when parents choose a school based on its academic excellence, and the same parents immediately try to change the policies of the school, expressing discontent that it is "too serious" and requires too much work for their children.

It is essential to identify what choice parents have in your school district. There is a national trend toward giving parents greater choice with respect to the assignment of students to different schools, but this is by no means a universal characteristic. Frequently, students are assigned to a school and parents have no choice within the public school system. Chapter 6 provides step-by-step procedures for exploring your school choice options.

Conclusion

When you are confronted with uncertainty, there is no substitute for information. While opinions and rumor abound, solid evidence and reliable information are frequently scarce. Because you want to have information that is directly relevant to *your* needs and the education of *your* children, there is no substitute for direct personal inquiry. You may be more comfortable with letters than with personal meetings or telephone conversations. However difficult the initiation of communication may be with the teachers and administrators at your children's schools, or the leaders at the district office, this challenge is worth the effort if you are able to begin the process of open dialogue, respectful communication, and accurate information.

seek reliable information

Chapter 5

What Your Child Is Expected to Know and Do in School

The academic standards at the back of this book can seem intimidating to parents, students, and teachers. You may experience many common apprehensions as you ask these questions: How can one child possibly do all that? How can a teacher possibly cover all of that material? What were these people thinking when they wrote all of these expectations for my children? This chapter puts the list of standards into focus by identifying some of the most important expectations for your children.

Before we begin, consider the most important question: What would parents be doing to help their children if we had no standards at all? We would probably do our best to build skills in reading, writing, and mathematics. We would help our children to understand that school is important, that diligence is a worthy character trait, and that perseverance in the face of difficulty is the way that one learns to master difficult tasks. In other words, if you simply followed your instincts as a good parent, you would impart to your child many of the most important elements of academic standards. With standards to augment common sense and good parenting, you need not guess at the details. You will understand what every student is expected to know and be able to do to become a successful student.

The inevitable question arises: Does my child have to master every standard in order to be successful? The straight answer is no. The details of academic standards—particularly with respect to social studies and science—represent more content than many teachers and parents understand. That even successful students have not mastered 100 percent of this material should be no surprise. In addition, each of you will find important information—perhaps things you learned in school—that appears to be missing from this chapter and from the state academic standards. This presents every teacher and school leader with a paradox: There are simultaneously too many and too few standards. The standards that exist require more time than is available in the school year; the standards that exist omit some subject matter that many parents and teachers find interesting or even vital. This paradox simply establishes what most parents are forced to admit rather early in the lives of their children: Perfection is not an option. The use of standards in school is no exception to this maxim. Therefore, use the standards as a guide, not a straitjacket. If you follow your instincts and help your child build academic skills in reading, writing, and mathematics, and if you consistently model and reinforce the development of sound character traits, your child will be successful in school.

Reading

Chances are that you began reading to your children while they were still babies By your early efforts, you were building a love of books, an understanding of the power of stories, and the belief that words on a page have meaning. In addition to reading, you probably provided plastic books on which your baby chewed, drooled, and even appeared to "read" as the vivid images captured the attention of the infant. As babies become toddlers and new words seemed to spring from their lips every day, reading together becomes a magical experience. Even before they know letters, very young children associate words with images and thus can fill in words in the picture books that parents are reading. When I ask parents about their favorite times of learning together with their children, these early days of eager discovery, quick mastery, joint experience, incredible wonder, and lots of laughter are the times recalled most fondly.

By the ages of four and five, the association between print and words is clear to most children, and they appear to "read" because they have memorized certain symbolic patterns. These so-called "sight words" help give children confidence, and therein lies one of the early misunderstandings about what it means to become a successful reader. While we naturally celebrate the ability of children to memorize symbols and their meaning, we also must understand that reading is more than the memorization of symbolic patterns. In order to become successful lifelong readers, we must build on the initial skill of memorization and add the following critical elements: decoding, comprehension, summarization, conclusions, and predictions.

As children enter adolescence, they naturally express a desire for more independence. Bedtime stories and long hugs give way to a peck on the cheek and a brief "good night!" Nevertheless, the fundamental need of middle school students is comparable to that of students in elementary school: Kids need to be competent, successful, and appreciated by the important adults in their lives. There is much in the lives of adolescents that seems out of control. Their bodies change, relationships are unstable, and emotions are out of control. One of the few things that offers stability to the adolescent is the mastery of academic skills, including reading. Parents who nurture and reinforce these skills provide reassurance, consistency, and stability to the teenager for whom these attributes are in very short supply.

successful reading

Literacy: Still the Most Essential Skill

Many parents and teachers of middle school students make the faulty assumption that reading proficiency is a certainty for fifth and sixth grade students. After all, they reason, children should have learned how to read and write in the first grade. Although it has been a few years since parents have heard their middle school children read a bedtime story, their ability to read directions, signs, and labels surely must indicate that literacy isn't a problem for these students. Such an assumption is fundamentally flawed for three reasons. First, many parents and teachers misunderstand what "good reading" really is. Many adults listen to a first grade child read aloud and exclaim, "My, what a good reader you are!" When the same child is identified a few years later as reading below grade level, the parents and teachers respond, "The test must be flawed. She is an excellent reader! In fact, she was able to read stories aloud without making a single mistake." Unfortunately, the oral pronunciation of words is not all of what "reading" really means. At the middle school level, students must be able to read long passages of 200 to 800 words silently; then they must be able to accurately recall and summarize the ideas, events, and people that were described in the passage. Good reading is much more than reading aloud.

The second reason that the presumption of "good reading" is potentially flawed is that students in elementary school tend to focus on fiction, while the reading requirements in middle school tend to be nonfiction. In one analysis of third grade reading I conducted last year, the ratio of fiction to nonfiction reading was 90 to 1. In middle school, however, students must be able to read nonfiction passages, including text on subjects such as social studies and science, in which students may not have a personal interest.

The third reason that parents must double-check their assumption that their child is a "good reader" is that the higher students progress in elementary school, the less detailed is the assessment of reading skill by teachers and school officials. Kindergarten and first grade teachers tend to keep detailed records of student progress in letter recognition and vocabulary development. These educators frequently maintain records that show which letters and words the child understands and where they will place particular emphasis in the weeks ahead. Teachers in the upper elementary grades discard such detailed record-keeping as their curriculum demands grow. Thus, a very bright and capable student can receive excellent grades, speak with confidence and assurance in class, impress most of the adults with whom he is in contact, and yet enter the sixth grade without the ability to read, comprehend, or write at a sixth grade level. In the upper elementary and early middle school grades, the discipline of reading gradually becomes a study of literature. Students and teachers discuss stories, characters, plots, and settings. Most of these discussions take place in groups, and there is little accountability for an individual student to read and understand the text. Indeed, the clever student can participate actively in a literature discussion, asking good questions and reflecting on the comments of classmates, without ever having read the text that is being discussed. Parents must therefore be willing to suspend their understandable confidence in their own children and ask the pointed question, "Can they really read and understand the pages of middle school textbooks?"

Whether or not reading is a problem for your child, there are two simple things that every family can do to improve the reading comprehension skills of every student. If your child is a superior reader, these ideas will elevate her skills to a higher level. If your child needs help in reading, you can quickly identify the areas where help is needed and build skills on a daily basis. Neither of these ideas will take more than 20 minutes of your time. First, have your child read aloud. The necessity to read aloud with clarity and confidence is important well beyond elementary school. Middle school students rarely get practice in the skill of oral reading, yet the development and maintenance of this skill is essential for their classroom success in middle school, high school, and beyond. Reading aloud can be a wonderful family activity and the selection of reading material can range from plays, in which each family member takes a part, to texts selected in turn by each member of the family In my family, we lingered around the dinner table for a few minutes every night and each person at the table, including children and adults, would read a paragraph. Sometimes it was an article about outer space, while other evenings it was a story. Often it was a brief article from an encyclopedia, usually hauled out to settle an argument. During certain seasons of the year, religious texts were read that were consistent with our family tradition. Whatever you select, these brief minutes will allow your children to develop confident reading skills in a safe and loving environment. If they make a mistake, the result will be your gentle encouragement rather than the snickering of classmates. If there is a serious problem in reading ability, you will learn about it firsthand and not be fooled by the awarding of a B in English class.

The second way families can improve the reading comprehension skills of middle school students is the "instant book report." Traditional book reports provide superficial summaries and evaluations of books and, at the middle school level, are written once every two or three months. The instant book report takes 20 minutes, with ten minutes of reading followed by ten minutes of writing. The child can select any text, although the parent may wish to alternate the genre between fiction and nonfiction. After ten minutes of silent reading, the child closes the book, takes out a piece of paper, and writes a brief summary of the text. If this is an activity that you do regularly, you also may wish to ask your child to compare the text of today's reading to the text that she read a few days ago. While the child is writing, the parent can read the text so that the actual reading passage can be compared to the child's summary.

These two reading strategies, reading aloud and reading silently before producing a written summary, are simple but powerful ways for parents of middle school students to get at the heart of what "good reading" really means. Because the number of students assigned to each teacher in middle school is significantly greater than was the case in elementary school, few middle school teachers have the time for this sort of individual attention to students and detailed analysis of reading ability. It is up to you, the parent, to provide this, and it only takes 20 minutes of your time.

Books: Just so Twentieth Century

This book, as with most of those published in the twenty-first century thus far, is written on a computer. Much of the research that I conduct comes from Internet searches and electronically published journals. If computers and electronic communication are to be the future of the written word, why should parents invest money and time in old-fashioned books? You might as easily ask why you should attend a live symphony orchestra concert when there are so many fine compact discs available. Why should you write a thank-you note with pen in hand rather than send an e-mail? The answer to these questions is that there are intangibles to the heft of a book and the resonance of the symphony hall, and to holding a letter that someone else took the time to write that are absent when technology, no matter how elegant or sophisticated, replaces physical contact.

There is, of course, an important role that technology will play in the future of our children. There are some wonderful computer programs that are successfully used to help children develop skills. As I write these words, my seven-year-old is explaining the nature of pulleys and levers to his five-year-old friend using illustrations from a clever science program. As with many education matters, this is not an "either/or" proposition. We can nurture a love and respect for books while encouraging an understanding of appropriate uses of technology. Our priorities, however, must be clear. My observation is that there are many more students who can troll the Internet than who can write a sentence with appropriate grammar, spelling, and punctuation.

the most effective strategy

Writing

Although most educators and parents properly place an exceptional emphasis on reading, we dare not neglect the importance of writing. It is also essential to recall that language development does not proceed in a neat linear fashion in which we first perfect speaking skills, then polish reading skills, and only then proceed to writing. In fact, as students improve their writing, they also improve their ability to read, particularly with regard to the advanced skills of comprehension, summarization, and prediction. Student proficiency in writing also is associated with improved student achievement in mathematics, social studies, and science. In fact, of all the strategies that teachers and parents can use to boost student achievement, improved formal writing is the single most effective strategy that provides benefits in every other area of the curriculum.

Some parents may question whether writing is really that important when state academic tests and college admissions tests are typically multiple-choice exams. The answer is not that there is some magic in a number two pencil, but rather that writing—particularly formal nonfiction writing—requires students to think, reason, analyze, and communicate. Those skills will help students deal with multiple-choice tests and every other challenge that they face in school. Indeed, the best teachers I have observed do not see writing as a trade-off with multiple-choice tests, but rather combine these two testing methods. They routinely require students not only to choose the correct response, but also require written explanations of why one response was chosen and another possible answer was rejected. Such an approach transforms multiple-choice tests from a guessing game into a challenging and engaging intellectual task.

Some parents and teachers regard writing with pen or pencil as an ancient craft, soon to be displaced by computers. I respectfully dissent. If we think of writing not merely as a means of communication, but also as a means to enhance thinking, reasoning, analysis, and communication, then writing will not "go out of style" until thinking goes out of style. Moreover, children and adults who are able to convey in handwritten form their deep emotions and sentiments such as sympathy, appreciation, and encouragement, will find that they have a far more profound impact on those with whom they communicate than if they are brought up to rely solely on a word processor. Technology will replace neither emotions nor the need to communicate them. Thus writing, including the ability to write legibly and without the aid of a computerized spell-checker, remains an essential characteristic of the educated child.

Rewriting: The Key to Improved Writing

Think of the things your child does well. Perhaps she plays soccer. Maybe he plays the violin or piano. She might be a great swimmer. Every child has something in which enjoyment and skill coincide. Now consider how that skill was developed. It never—not once—occurred with a single effort. Many soccer balls were kicked far from the net before that first glorious goal. A fair amount of screeching preceded the successful completion of "Minuet in G" on the violin. The first attempt at the G-major scale probably omitted the F-sharp. Skills are never developed in one-shot endeavors. Children know intuitively that practice makes perfect and that the remedy for failure is additional practice. Why then, is so much written schoolwork submitted on a one-shot basis? The habit of writing a rough draft, submission to a parent or teacher for correction, and rewriting, is not merely a habit for writing; it is a habit of mind that displays perseverance and character.

developing skills

The Basics: Spelling, Grammar, Punctuation, and Legibility

Some of the best support for the proposition that the basics of English communication are important in every academic and vocational setting has come from several unexpected sources. The president of an urban electricians' union, for example, addressed an audience of technical school students and parents and provided a passionate defense for the literacy requirements. "Successful members of this union must be able to read and write instructions. Mistakes in writing can mean putting yourself and others at safety risk. We require people to be good writers." Many high schools have conducted focus groups of former students who were invited to share their responses to the question, "What do you wish you would have had in school?" With remarkable consistency, students in universities noted that they were required to write not only in English class, but in history, music, economics, and every other discipline. They needed more formal writing, they admitted. Individuals in technical schools and the world of work similarly expressed their concern that they were required to write on a regular basis and that they needed additional training to do so. Whether the former student was a dispatcher in a truck stop or an undergraduate in the Ivy League, the consistent theme was a request for more writing. Of course, none of these chastened high school graduates requested more writing during the course of elementary, middle, or high school classes. The role of teachers and parents in this and many other areas is not to give children what they want, but what they need. Writing is, in brief, a skill that they need, but rarely request.

It is important that parents and teachers are specific about what "writing" really means, for too often students have been left with the impression that aimless reflections in journals fulfill the requirement for written expression. Whatever merit journal writing may have, the self-absorbed and frequently scatological reflections of teenagers do not develop the formal writing skills that students need. They need to write paragraphs with topic sentences and essays with a clear beginning, middle, and end. They need models of good writing and clear criteria for what constitutes acceptable and exemplary composition. In any other area of skill development, specificity is essential. Children would laugh at the notion that they should be creative with regard to where the soccer ball should go. Thankfully, they do not find the need to be creative with regard to the tones to which the violin is tuned. Yet, there are remarkably creative and gifted soccer players and musicians. The strict application of structure, in other words, does not remove creativity, but rather creates a clear framework within which creative expression can occur.

The overwhelming majority of writing by students in elementary and middle schools is in the form of a creative narrative. While this genre of writing is important, it is not sufficient. Specifically, students must be able to write for several purposes. First, students must write to inform. That is, they must describe an object, sequence of events, person, or situation with clarity and accuracy. Second, students must write to analyze. Typically, analytical writing involves the comparison of two different events, people, or activities. When students write analytically, they carefully explain similarities and differences between the objects of their analysis. Third, students must write to persuade. Effective persuasive writing is not an expression of personal preference, but rather an argument supported by evidence, examples, and illustrations. Although the labels of these types of writing may vary from one class to another, students must understand differences between creative writing and description, analysis, and persuasion. Middle school students can be asked to compare different books and describe the characters, settings, and plots of novels. It is particularly important for students in middle school social studies and science classes to be able to express a conclusion and support it with evidence. My interviews with secondary school and college faculty members reveal that the single greatest deficiency among their students is writing, and in particular, nonfiction writing in the form of description, analysis, and persuasion. College students who persist in the illusion that a successful argument begins with the words "I feel" have, at some early point in their academic career, been denied the opportunity to learn the craft of writing.

Mathematics

The controversies involving mathematics education have mirrored the phonics vs. whole language debate. Typically, the terminology of the math wars includes "problem-solving" and "number operations," with advocates of the "new, new math" preferring the former over the latter and traditionalists taking the reverse point of view. While few thoughtful people doubt that problem-solving is a useful skill in mathematics, it is baffling to me that anyone would think that skill in solving mathematical problems can be developed without an understanding of calculation. Conversely, no mastery of the times tables replaces the necessity to read a story problem and write a clear explanation for a solution. The debate between these extremes implies a dichotomy that is illogical. Students must have both the ability to read and write about mathematics, as well as a sound grounding in the fundamentals of arithmetic.

One common source of friction is the use of calculators. Indeed, calculators are commonly used in math classes, based on the "obvious" proposition that students would be foolish not to make use of the best technology at hand. Evidence reported in the *Wall Street Journal* (December 15, 2000, p. A1) indicates that students who make frequent use of calculators in class perform at much lower levels on state tests than students who use calculators only two or three times a month. This is no surprise to the parent or math teacher who has witnessed a child instinctively reach for a calculator when asked to multiply three times three. Worse yet, if the student hits a wrong key and the screen says that the answer is 25, she may have been conditioned to place more confidence in the calculator than in her own understanding that three groups of three cannot conceivably yield a product of 25. This is not merely an issue of discipline and the "basics." Some of the most sophisticated mathematics at the secondary school and collegiate levels require students to be able to estimate. Their ability in "mental math," and their confidence in making a judgment about what a likely answer might be, is an important input into some statistical and financial equations. In sum, calculators do not replace the need for the disciplined thinking in mathematics any more than word processors replace the need for thoughtful analysis in an English class.

building sound skills

If You Are Intimidated by Math

It is possible, even likely, that your own experiences in mathematics were not favorable in school. Moreover, the format, content, and sheer size of mathematics text-books can be intimidating. Nevertheless, there are many things you can do to help your children develop sound mathematical skills. In addition to the many activities suggested at the back of this book, there are four common household themes that will build the math skills of your children. These include games, money, time, and measurement. Children love games, and keeping score is normally part of this family activity Parents may be tempted to take on the scorekeeping duties in the name of accuracy or speed. This is a missed opportunity. My experience is that if one child is keeping score, every other child at the table will be doing the same thing, keeping an eagle eye out for errors. When the parent keeps score, children may passively accept the calculations. Money offers an exceptional opportunity to build mental math skills. If children are paid an allowance or compensated for chores, parents should make a point of providing money in different denominations and combinations. Middle school is a wonderful opportunity for budding entrepreneurs to mow lawns, baby-sit, sell popcorn and soft drinks, or engage in other creative ways to make money and, of course, keep careful track of the income and expenses of the enterprise. A regular review of the business records creates opportunities to practice the arithmetic involved in subtracting expenses from income to yield profit, and to introduce questions that involve common middle school challenges such as percents, decimals, fractions, and ratios. The power of these authentic situations is that they give genuine value and meaning to the field of mathematical problem-solving. These situations are no longer the academic questions of a textbook, but real-world situations that have relevance to your child's activities. How well does Pepsi sell compared to Dr. Pepper? How did sales change from week to week during the summer? If I charged a flat fee for the lawn job, how much did I make per hour?

Time is a theme that governs many households, yet the predominance of digital clocks prevents many children from learning to tell time or to solve problems regarding the intervals between different time periods. Daily reinforcement of these skills can occur with questions such as, "What time is it now, and how many minutes before school starts?" Finally, the theme of measurement offers abundant opportunities for the building of math skills in the kitchen, the yard, home construction jobs, or marking off athletic fields. Because measurement refers to space and volume, these lessons cannot be learned by reading a chapter in a math book about measurement. Students learn about measurement by measuring, by observing the impact of measurement mistakes, by making corrections, and by learning the carpenter's rule to "measure twice, cut once."

Science a spirit of inquiry

As intimidating as mathematics may be, the science curriculum can be even more baffling to many parents. The traditional curriculum of weather, dinosaurs, and volcanoes has been replaced by an early emphasis on the physical, chemical, and biological sciences. Both state standards and school texts can present remarkably sophisticated challenges for students. Despite these challenges, there are several things that parents can do that will improve the scientific thinking of their children.

Parents can encourage a spirit of inquiry, helping children to understand that science is not just about providing answers, but also about asking questions. Real scientists are not just smart people who have all the answers. Even very famous scientists, such as Galileo, have been spectacularly wrong about many of their theories. Science advances through the process of generating a theory, developing alternative hypotheses, and then systematically testing those hypotheses. For science to advance, we must disprove hypotheses. This means that for every gain in scientific knowledge, some very smart scientist was proven wrong. This does not diminish the credibility or importance of scientific work. Indeed, the researcher's aphorism is, "We learn more from error than from uncertainty." This is a good rule in the lives of students as well. When they don't know the answer, testing an idea—even if such a test proves their previous conceptions to be untrue—is better than proceeding in ignorance.

Scientific observation can occur in the home every day when children pose the hypothetical question, "What will happen if I do this?" If we announce the answer, we deny our children the opportunity to generate a hypothesis and then test it through systematic observation. Children are full of "why" questions that are directly susceptible to the generation of hypotheses and systematic testing.

- **Why do some years have 365 days and other years have 366 days?**

- **Why is it colder in January and hotter in July in the Northern Hemisphere, but the other way around in the Southern Hemisphere?**

- **If I drop a penny and a baseball from the top of a ladder, which one will hit the ground first?**

The list is endless. The key is not for parents to attempt to become walking encyclopedias, but to build a spirit of inquiry and testing in which children are not afraid to generate thoughtful guesses and then test those guesses. Real scientists, and thoughtful students, are not afraid to routinely write the words, "My hypothesis was not supported by the evidence." This approach to learning values evidence over alchemy and thus is not only a sound intellectual trait, but an opportunity to build sound character as well.

Social Studies

The amount of content in social studies curricula can be overwhelming. Spanning the subjects of history, geography, civics, and economics, social studies texts can add many pounds to your child's backpack and nevertheless omit many important subjects. Despite the bewildering array of complex ideas in the subjects involved in social studies, parents can reinforce some fundamental understandings that every child should have.

The first and most important principle to understand is that advancement in social studies is directly related to student proficiency in reading and writing. Make no mistake: If your child needs help in reading and writing, then you and the teachers must devote time to these areas as a priority. Of course, it is possible to use reading texts that include history and government. There is, however, no substitute for absolute proficiency in literacy as an antecedent to the study of social studies. I have never heard a secondary school teacher say, "I wish that more students knew the capital of South Dakota," but I have heard hundreds of them say, "I wish that more students could read my textbook."

Government and Civics

At the end of the Cold War, President Gorbachev of the former Soviet Union famously said to General (now Secretary of State) Colin Powell, "General, you will have to find yourself another enemy." While Americans who grew up in the 1940s and 1950s rejoiced at the diminution of world tensions, and the reduction in the likelihood that our own children would face the prospect of nuclear war, the demise of the Soviet Union also changed conversations in schools and homes. For the last decade, we rarely talked about the difference between democracy and authoritarian forms of government with the same urgency that we did when our own form of government seemed to be threatened. These are distinctions that remain important and are among the fundamental concepts that students must know. If you can take your children to see any democratically elected body in action, it is worth the trip. If you live near the state capital, watch the legislature in session. Better yet, arrange to have your child serve as a page in one of the legislative chambers for a day. If distance from the capital prevents such an excursion, then take your children to a meeting of the school board, county commission, or city council. The concept of representative democracy is fundamental and every child should understand that one of the distinguishing parts of our heritage of freedom is the ability to vote, selecting men and women who do the public's bidding. Of course, parents who wish to encourage good civic behavior by their children must vote, and you may wish to consider taking your children with you to observe this most fundamental civic right and obligation. There can be little doubt in the aftermath of the presidential election of 2000 that every vote has an important influence on the future of the nation.

History

History has been the subject of the most hotly debated state standards. Part of this controversy stems from the idiosyncratic manner in which history has been taught in schools, with the principal source of differentiation being the personal preference of the teacher. Some teachers devote weeks to the building of scale models of the Coliseum as a substitute for the study of ancient Rome, while others devote the month of November to an historically inaccurate drama inevitably focusing on Pocahontas and John Smith. Other classrooms devote weeks to Custer's Last Battle, while others linger for months on the Civil War. Few, however, stop to ask what the study of history is all about and many leave students with the conviction that it is simply "a bunch of facts" that are regurgitated on demand. If the teacher deliberately avoided the fact-based approach to history, then students would have the impression that history is a series of disjointed dramas and personal stories. The presence of social studies standards offers the beginning of some coherence to the study of this discipline.

Let us first put to rest the "facts vs. themes" controversy. Students need to learn historical facts. It is preposterous to assume that students can apply higher order thinking skills to history, geography, and economics without understanding that the Civil War preceded Vietnam, that the Balkans are not the Baltics, and that there is rarely a singular cause for an historical or economic effect. While not every date is of equal importance, a sense of sequence in the broad sweep of history is essential if students are to have an appropriate context for their understanding of historical events, political decisions, and cultural artifacts of the time. The words of the song, "Battle Hymn of the Republic" have a profoundly different meaning for students who have studied the words as part of their understanding of 19th century history.

Parents can reinforce this understanding of historical context by talking about family history. Family trees and time lines can lend context that many children do not understand. If your children have parents, grandparents, or great-grandparents who fought in a war, then encourage serious family discussion about those events. For today's students, Vietnam is simply one more piece of history, as removed from their reality as the World Wars of the last century, or the many conflicts of centuries long past. If you can add profound family context to these events, the lessons learned by your children will have value far beyond a few paragraphs in a textbook. Every community has historical landmarks and most have museums. Although the events commemorated in those monuments may not be the focus of your school's textbooks, there is nothing to match the visual impression of personal observation. If your family has the resources to take a vacation, then plan to spend a week or more in the nation's capital. Let your children see the Constitution, the Declaration of Independence, and the words of Lincoln beneath his majestic statue.

adding context

Foreign Language, Music, and Art

Although this book focuses on the core academic areas of language arts, mathematics, social studies, and science, parents are wise to reinforce their children's pursuit of studies in foreign language, music, and art. At the very least, study of a foreign language will help to build English vocabulary, and at best will improve your child's understanding of other cultures. Much of the world's classic literature first appeared in languages other than English, and by opening the door to the study of other languages, you will provide a lifelong gift with which your children can explore other cultures and lands. Even a slight familiarity with another language allows your children to recognize the value of courtesy when they are guests in other nations.

The study of music is one of the most important disciplines for children. It is not necessary for your child to become a concert pianist or to play first chair in the saxophone section of the school band. The study of music, however, will improve your child's understanding of mathematics with the study of rhythm and notation. The study of songs will build your child's vocabulary and reading skills. The occasional performance will build confidence and presence.

The study of art allows your child a creative outlet that can be successfully combined with many other disciplines. Because vivid images are one of the best ways for children to acquire understanding and knowledge, the study of art should include not only the creation of original pieces of art, but trips to the museum and the observation of the art work of the world's great artists. The connection between art and written expression is particularly important. A wonderful way to build your child's skills in analytical writing is the comparison of two pieces of art. Moreover, students can illustrate their creative and nonfiction work with vivid illustrations that reflect their words.

respect, teamwork, and integrity

Behavior

No discussion of learning at home is complete without addressing the issue of behavior. Veteran teachers frequently complain of the extent to which behavioral education has been transferred from parents to schools, and teachers readily acknowledge that schools are ill-equipped to begin teaching respect, teamwork, and integrity in a classroom for six hours a day if those values were not taught before a child's schooling began and reinforced before and after the school day.

Although every family has its own code of behavior, these differences need not obscure some fundamental obligations that people, including school children, have in a civil society. Parents may differ about the need to call adults "sir" and "ma'am," but every parent has an obligation to instill in children a respect for the authority of teachers and school leaders. No amount of parental guilt due to absence and no amount of parental recollections of unsatisfactory relationships with their own parents justifies the wholesale abandonment of behavioral training. Even more shocking than the abandonment of parental attempts to instill codes of civil behavior in children is the frequent support of student behavior that is disruptive, rude, and dangerous, as if the school had an obligation to conform to the behavioral code of the children, rather than the reverse.

In addition to encouraging a fundamental respect for adult authority, parents can build sound behavior in their children by insisting upon good organization in everything from the toy box to the dresser, closet, and backpacks. The adage, "A place for everything and everything in its place" may not conform to the adults who routinely display messy desks and ridicule their more organized colleagues. Nevertheless, secondary school educators routinely speak of students who fail not because of poor intellectual skills, but due to lack of the most fundamental organizational skills. The teachers assumed that children would learn these skills at home, while parents assumed the children would pick up these traits at school. Meanwhile, school lockers resemble toxic waste dumps, completed homework assignments are lost in a backpack full of trash, and bright students flounder because they lack simple organizational skills and habits.

The most important consideration with regard to building strong organizational skills is to establish the fact that good student organization is a skill, not an inherited genetic trait. Writing assignments in a notebook, making daily lists of things that must be done, and putting away books and toys are not matters encoded in DNA; they are skills and habits that are taught, learned, practiced, and developed over time.

What to Do When You Can't Do it All: Power Standards

Having reached the end of this chapter and not yet confronted the list of standards at the end of this book, the skeptical reader might be tempted to exclaim, "Twenty minutes a day? He's got to be kidding! I could devote hours every day to the reading, writing, mathematics, science, music, and art, and never even get to the behavior and organizational stuff. Attempting to make a difference in 20 minutes is sheer fantasy."

Your skepticism is understandable. Moreover, this perception of standards and school curricula as overwhelming burdens is shared by many teachers and school leaders who know that even the most diligent teacher may not produce students who know and understand every single standard. Nevertheless, the plain fact remains that your time does matter and that 20 minutes a day makes a world of difference. Without question, the homes in which independent reading routinely takes place probably have other characteristics, including access to books, caring adults, quiet space, and time. Nevertheless, the evidence is clear. Student achievement can dramatically improve without transforming school and home into a joyless test prep center. Rather, the ideas in this book, implemented incrementally and balanced between academic and behavioral objectives, serve to have a clear and dramatic impact on student success.

Given the overwhelming number of standards and the many activities in this book, a fair question to ask is, "Where do we start?" The concept of "power standards" provides one mechanism for parents, teachers, and students to choose wisely among many available alternatives. The notion of power standards suggests that the choice is not necessarily based on popularity, but on impact. Power standards must pass three thresholds. First, they must have endurance. In other words, some information memorized for a particular test is liberated from our neurons within nanoseconds after the completion of a test. While the knowledge that Pb is the chemical symbol for lead may be of use when the *Jeopardy* category is Chemical Symbols, it is not a piece of knowledge that has endurance. While the scientific method endures, memorization of chemical symbols and, for that matter, the dimensions of the stegosaurus do not.

The second criterion for power standards is leverage. This chapter has already highlighted a skill that provides students with leverage, that is, it has impact on many different subjects. When students write more frequently, particularly when that writing includes formal submissions with rewriting based on teacher feedback, student achievement improves not only in writing, but in mathematics, social studies, and science.

Another example of leverage is the skill involved in creating tables, charts, and graphs, and the understanding necessary to draw inferences from the graphic representation of data. This requirement not only appears in the mathematics standards, but also in academic standards for science, social studies, and language arts. Time invested in the development of a skill with leverage will pay dividends in many different academic areas.

The third threshold that power standards must cross is that they be necessary for success at the next level of instruction. Whenever I have challenged teachers to narrow the focus of their curriculum and omit a chapter, activity, or unit, they frequently respond that "everything I do is important" and besides, "The children will need this information for the next grade." When I ask the same teachers to provide advice for a new teacher who has the responsibility for students in the next lower grade, the story changes. While the sixth-grade teacher may insist that "everything I do is important," the seventh grade teacher is quite willing to provide a very brief list of requirements for sixth grades. The sixth grade teacher is similarly willing to provide clarity and focus for a suggested fifth grade curriculum. In contrast to the lists of standards and test objectives that include scores of items and extend to several pages, the lists of requirements for the next lower grade that I routinely receive from teachers rarely exceeds a dozen items and seldom exceeds a single page. Part of this phenomenon may be the very human characteristic that it is easier to give advice than to take it. The inescapable conclusion, however, is that teachers and parents know that hasty and superficial coverage of massive amounts of curriculum is not as effective as thorough student knowledge of the most important elements of the curriculum.

While reasonable people may differ with regard to the ideal curriculum, no parent wishes students to be in a classroom where reading is not valued. Few parents would find competent the teacher who provides writing requirements only on rare occasions. In other words, while reasonable people may disagree about the universe of standards, most parents and teachers can apply the three criteria—endurance, leverage, and readiness for the next grade—and quickly arrive at a consensus on the most important pieces of information that are the non-negotiable. These are the areas of knowledge and skill that students must absolutely, positively have in order to be successful. This might mean that the scale model of the Coliseum gives way to improved reading instruction, that the eighteenth annual dramatization of Pocahontas yields to the need to master fractions, and the recollections of summer vacations are supplanted with a better understanding of the Constitution. In brief, power standards help teachers and parents make choices in the real world of limited time.

What's Worth Fighting For

Although it may appear that the burdens of standards are staggering, there are only a few areas on which parents must absolutely insist both with regard to student work at home and the curriculum in school. Those areas worth the assertion of parental authority include thinking, reasoning, and communication. If you find that students are only being asked to complete drill sheets rather than engage in deep and thoughtful analysis, it is essential that such practices are challenged with the evidence that the path toward greater student achievement lies not in mindless test preparation, but in extensive analysis, reasoning, and writing. If you find that students are taking exclusively multiple-choice tests and rarely if ever are required to write, then it is essential that such practices are challenged with the evidence that more frequent student writing not only builds thinking and reasoning skills, but also improves student performance on multiple-choice tests.

Although parents may not win every issue of contention over curriculum and testing, these discussions with teachers and school officials will make clear that the obligation of the parent is not merely to support homework and reinforce the skills required by the school. Sometimes the most important obligation of the parent is to provide complementary skills in those areas that the school is short-changing. If writing is underemphasized, then it is important that parents pay particular attention to writing requirements as part of your 20-Minute Learning Connection. If math calculation is underemphasized in the name of improved problem-solving techniques, then parents must make up the shortfall with an emphasis on the development of sound basic skills in addition, subtraction, multiplication, and division. If the discussion of literature takes precedence over the development of reading comprehension skills, then parents must give children the opportunity for independent reading—both aloud and silently—at home. Most importantly, parents must ensure that students can understand the text before them and write a brief summary that is accurate and complete.

When parents are proactive as advocates for their children, then they not only help future generations of children, but also immediately and decisively intervene in the educational lives of their own children.

be a proactive advocate

Chapter 6

Before School Begins: Planning for School Success

The 20-Minute Learning Connection begins long before children enter school. Part of the success of parent planning is a commitment to being proactive rather than reactive when dealing with school issues. This chapter addresses the strategies parents can use to maximize their influence on their children's educational opportunities.

Much of the recent discussion about parent choice in schools has been focused on the politically volatile issue of school vouchers. Although only a very few school systems in the nation offer publicly funded vouchers that parents may choose to use for a private school education for their children, there is frequently a great deal of choice that parents can and should exercise with regard to the educational opportunities for their children.

Choosing Schools

In some school districts, a parent's request for school "choice" is welcomed as an indication of positive involvement. Even some large urban school systems pride themselves on the claim that more than ninety percent of parents and children receive their first choice of school. In other school systems, however, choice of school is something exercised only by the administration, with boundary lines, program assignment, and bus schedules, all matters that are announced to parents, rather than decisions that invite participation and comparison among alternatives.

If you wish to get the straight story about parent rights and choice in your district, it is important that you ask the right questions. Figure 6.1 provides an easy guide to the specific questions you should ask school administrators in your district about your rights as a parent. Don't settle for a form letter or impromptu policy statement by a harried administrator. Ask the questions and write down the answers.

FIGURE 6.1
What Are My Choices?

School Administration Telephone Number:_____

Name of Administrator:_____

Introduction:

"Hello. My name is _____ and my child is a student in this district. I would like to ask some questions about the choices of schools available to my child. Are you the right person to talk with about this matter?"

If "no": "Thanks very much. Who should I speak with about this?"

 Name:_____

 Phone Number: _____

If "Yes": "That's great. Do you have a moment so that I can learn more about this?"

"Does the district have a voucher program that provides funding for private schools?"

❏ No

❏ Yes

❏ Details:_____

"Does the district have any charter schools?"

❑ No

❑ Yes

❑ Details:_____

"Is my child required to attend the school nearest to me, or may I select any of the public schools available?"

❑ Your child must attend local school. That is:_____

❑ Your child may choose any school.

❑ Your child may go to another school, but must deal with certain restrictions.

❑ Your child may go to another school, but families living close to each school have first priority, and people outside of the boundaries of that school are only permitted to enroll if there is space available.

❑ Additional details:_____

If no choice at all: "I understand that you are saying I have no choice of schools at all. Is that correct? So that I understand this clearly, are you saying that there are no situations in the school district at all in which students are attending a school other than their official assigned school? Could you please tell me about these exceptions to your normal policy?

If choice is available: "That's great. Is there a written policy that governs the choices that I have as a parent? Would you please send me a printed copy of that policy?"

"Just one more question. Where can I find information about the different schools? Is there an accountability report or other document that will provide detailed information about the enrollment, teaching staff, and academic programs of each school in the district?"

"Thank you very much."

Although most public school systems are far from a genuine market system in which consumers can make informed choices from among a variety of alternatives, there is frequently much more choice available than parents recognize. Although only a tiny minority of school systems offers publicly funded vouchers and only a few school systems offer charter schools that may appeal to some parents, virtually every school system with more than one school will provide some level of parent choice if the matter is pressed. The purpose for the inquiry is not necessarily to engage in political advocacy for vouchers, charters, or other forms of school choice. Rather, the purpose for your question is simply to ensure that you have the best possible information with which you can make a reasoned judgment.

choose wisely

Making the Best Choice

Once you have determined that you have some level of school choice, it is important that you choose wisely. The label of the school tells you very little about the quality of the curriculum and teachers. For example, some charter schools are among the very best in the nation; some charter schools have been abject failures. The label "charter" does little to assure a parent of educational quality. Rather, you must make specific inquiries about the curriculum, teaching, and leadership of the school. Sometimes these inquiries may be uncomfortable, as many schools have a history of operating free from parental scrutiny. Many other schools welcome parent questions and provide easy-to-understand accountability information for parents or any other member of the community. Regardless of the ease with which you acquire this data, the following questions will serve as a useful guide for your conversations about schools, curricula, teachers, and leadership.

Your inquiries must be specific. First, you'll want to know what the academic expectations of the school are. The assurance that "we are standards-based" or "we follow the state standards" is not sufficient. You deserve a direct answer to this question: "What is my child expected to know and be able to do at the beginning of the school year and at the end of the school year?" You should receive a specific list of the knowledge and skills with which your child should enter and leave each grade level. Anything less than a straightforward response to this inquiry is evidence that the school is "standards-based" in name only, and that curriculum anarchy prevails. The extent to which individual teachers can choose to make extraordinary departures from the curriculum is stunning to many parents. Some teachers offer little or no science, while others emphasize science to the exclusion of essential literacy programs. Some teachers invest extraordinary amounts of time in student performances, often with the enthusiastic encouragement and support of parents, omitting large amounts of academic requirements. A great number of teachers emphasize arts and crafts more than academic requirements. Kati Haycock, president of the Education Trust, recently observed that in classroom after classroom she witnessed more coloring assignments than reading, writing, and mathematics assignments. You must ask, "What is my child expected to know and be able to do?" The principal and individual teachers must be able to answer this question clearly and without hesitation. If the response is unclear to you, academic expectations will be the subject of mystery and ambiguity for your child.

Another important part of your consideration of curriculum is testing and assessment. Curriculum without testing is wishful thinking. All the elegant lesson plans, detailed curriculum documents, and heavy textbooks in the world have little impact if there is not a systematic method of determining the extent to which students are learning what is expected. Do not settle for unspecific assurances such as, "We do regular testing." Ask to see the results for the past two years of the state and district tests that are related to the academic standards and curriculum requirements of the school. Determine for yourself whether students in this school are learning what school leaders believe that students are learning.

Second, you want to know about the teaching qualifications of the staff. Teachers typically receive certifications for specific subjects, particular groups of grade levels, or both. While certification is no guarantee of quality, the evidence is over-whelming that students taught by noncertified teachers perform at significantly lower levels than students under the tutelage of certified teachers. Many school systems have emphasized reductions in class size. Unfortunately, they have filled some classrooms with well-intentioned, but untrained, people. You must insist that your child be taught by a certified teacher. In addition, the educational background and experience of the staff should be examined. Advanced degrees and extensive experience is no guarantee of quality, but you may wish to consider carefully whether your child should be in the classroom of a teacher with little or no experience.

Third, you want to learn about the leadership of the school. In some schools, the principal operates autonomously, with little or no oversight. In other schools, a collabo-rative decision-making body includes teachers, parents, and administrators. Sometimes these committees operate differently in practice than the theory with which they were originated. The best way for you to address this is to ask when the next meeting of the decision-making committee will be and plan to attend the meeting. Does the group make substantive contributions to the decision-making process? Do some groups dominate the discussion? Do parents have a real voice on matters such as curriculum, instruction, and policy? Finally, ask this specific question: "Can you give me an example of how parents have influenced the curriculum and instruction policies of the school?"

There is no doubt about this fact: You have a right to make these inquiries. Information about curriculum and teacher qualifications is not secret. If you receive anything less than completely forthcoming information, then you should make a written inquiry to your district superintendent. Figure 6.2 provides an example of how you can make these inquiries in a courteous and businesslike manner.

FIGURE 6.2

Inquiry Letter to School Superintendent

(name), Superintendent of Schools
(district name)
(address, city, state, zip)
Re: Information concerning _____ school
Dear (Dr./Ms./Mr.) _____:

On (date) I met with the principal of _____ school. The purpose of my meeting was to learn more about the curriculum, teaching, and leadership of the school my children may attend next year. I still have some questions about these matters and I would appreciate your assistance in responding to them.

With respect to the curriculum, I am particularly interested in the specific academic expectations of my children and how those expectations are assessed. If there are specific curriculum standards that every child is expected to meet, I would like to see them. In addition, I would like to know if there are district or state tests that address the extent to which the school has met those academic expectations in the past. I would also appreciate seeing the results from those assessments for the past two years. Please let me know if there are differences among the curriculum based on choices made by each teacher or if the curriculum is the same for each teacher. If there are differences, please elaborate on those differences.

With respect to the faculty, I would like to know about the subject matter and grade-level certification of the staff, their educational backgrounds, and teaching experience. If some faculty members have particular interests or areas of expertise, please share that information as well.

Finally, I am very interested to learn about the leadership of the school and particularly about the manner in which parents are able to participate in school decision-making. If there is a governing or advisory body in which parents participate, I would like to learn more about the operations of this group and when its next meeting will be held.

Thank you very much for your assistance.

Sincerely,

(your name)

be courteous but persistent

Choosing Teachers

Parent choice of teachers is a delicate subject. Reasonable people may disagree on the matter. Those advocating parent choice see it as a way of encouraging parent involvement and ensuring that parents have a vested interest in supporting the teacher and encouraging their child to succeed. Certainly most parents believe that they know their children better than anyone and are therefore best equipped to determine which teachers and educational programs are best suited for their children. Those opposing parent choice of teachers see this practice as an inequitable device in which activist parents get better teachers for their children than parents who do not have the time, ability, or interest to attempt to influence school administrators. Moreover, some administrators fear that parent choice is more of a popularity contest fueled by rumor than a choice based on professional abilities. In addition, some administrators worry that teachers might make unwise educational decisions in an attempt to be popular with parents. Finally, there is the concern that since teaching ability and popularity never will be equally distributed among various teachers in a grade level, some classes might be overburdened with too many students in a quest to meet the demands of parents.

Whatever the policy of your local school, it is important that parents take the time to understand the extent of their ability to influence the assignment of students to the classroom. Even if there is an official policy against parent choice, parents are entitled to ask questions about the differences among teachers with regard to certification, education, experience, and educational practices. While some of this information may be obtained through public documents, other matters, such as the educational practices of individual teachers, will only be revealed through interviews and observation.

When you make your initial inquiries about teachers, you will likely be told, "All of our teaching staff are excellent. Besides, we all have state standards, so you'll find that pretty much every class is the same. That's why we handle teacher assignment." You should be courteous but persistent in pursuing your inquiries. After you have learned the basics—certification, education, experience—you will need to dig deeper. Talk with your child's prospective teacher, preferably in the classroom. Plan to spend more time listening than talking. This is not the time for you to articulate your educational philosophy, but rather the time for you to determine what the philosophy and practices of the teacher will be. This is a difficult but important consideration: Your time is better spent finding a school and teacher that conform to your philosophy than attempting to convince a school and teacher that they should change their philosophies to agree with you.

Here are some things to notice as you enter the classroom:

☐ **Student work:** Is student work prominently posted around the room? If so, is there clear and specific feedback on what work is acceptable and what work needs improvement? Does every paper, including poor work, have a "smiley face," or does the teacher provide encouraging but clear guidance on how to improve? Are there samples of exemplary work that represent the educational target for students?

☐ **Class rules:** Are there high standards of behavior that are clear and unambiguous? Does the appearance of the classroom indicate that students take good care of their personal property and school property?

☐ **Teacher's desk:** Does the teacher set an example of organization and neatness?

☐ **Availability:** Were you welcomed into the classroom at any time or was your entry into the classroom restricted to specific pre-announced times? Were other parents actively volunteering, participating, and improving the learning environment?

Following is a list of things you should discuss with the teacher. It is absolutely important to take the time to listen to the responses without interruption. You want to solicit clear and unambiguous answers. You might need to draw the teacher out with some encouraging phrases such as, "Please tell me a little more about that."

❑ **What should a child know and be able to do at the beginning of the school year? In other words, what preparation should a successful student have before coming to your class?**

❑ **What should a student know and be able to do at the end of this school year? Please be as specific as possible.**

❑ **How do you assess student progress? May I please see an example of one of the tests you routinely use to assess student progress? What is the consequence when a student does poorly on a test? Can you please provide an example of a time when you changed the curriculum based on your analysis of the assessment results of the class? If my child does badly on a test, how soon will I be informed? Are there reports of student progress other than the report card?**

❑ **Please tell me about your favorite things to teach. Are there certain areas for which you provide extra emphasis based on your personal interest and knowledge?**

❑ **Are there some areas that you are not as comfortable teaching? Are there certain areas that you tend to emphasize less as a result?**

❑ **As a parent, how can I be most supportive of my child's education? Are there particular things that the parents of students in your class should do?**

❑ **Please explain your homework policy. How much homework should students normally have? What is the consequence when a student fails to turn in homework?**

❑ **What is your policy with regard to parent volunteers in the classroom?**

- [ ] What is the practice of the school and your class with regard to extracurricular activities? If these activities occur during the regular school day, do students make up for lost instructional time? If so, please explain.

- [ ] May I please see a copy of the report card form? Please explain how grades or other marks on the report card are determined. Is there a written grading policy? May I please have a copy of it?

- [ ] What happens when students learn and complete their work at different levels of speed and proficiency? What assistance is provided to students who are slower or less proficient? What enrichment is provided to students who are quicker or more proficient? If enrichment work is provided, could you please show me an example of such a task?

While these questions are certainly not exhaustive, they provide the basis for a continuing conversation and mutual understanding between parent and teacher. Even if there is absolutely no parent choice with regard to teacher and class assignment, this conversation will allow you and your child to begin the year with greater clarity and less ambiguity. Such a conversation also makes clear to the teacher that you are genuinely interested in the education of your children and that you are willing to be helpful and supportive of the teacher.

When You Need to Change Teachers

Many teachers are wonderful. They are dedicated professionals who work extra hours, take a personal interest in every child, and who are remembered by generations of students who were lucky enough to be in their classroom. Students in these classes may not come home every day having had fun, but they always come home having been challenged to do their best. Many teachers are solid practitioners, perhaps a little cynical because of their treatment at the hands of administrators and school boards. These teachers have had a few run-ins with parents, and those experiences left the teacher wondering whether the parents really wanted to support education or just wanted a babysitting service for their child. These teachers can provide a solid education for your children, but they are not the exceptional educators who will inspire a child to excellence. A few teachers are truly incompetent. Their classrooms are out of control, perhaps dangerous. Sometimes they scream; sometimes they are silent in the face of belligerent behavior that appears to be tacitly approved by their silence. They play favorites and the incomprehensibility of their evaluation system makes it impossible to tell how grades are awarded. Some of these terrible teachers embrace every new fad, sometimes to the exclusion of educational basics; others have learned nothing since they left college, perhaps decades ago. They rarely ask students to write, and the teacher's own writing is full of errors in grammar and spelling. Their personal understanding of the subjects that they teach rarely extends beyond the textbook, so that if there were errors in the science or social studies text, they would be unlikely to notice.

In the course of thirteen years of education, from kindergarten through the completion of high school, your children will probably have more than fifty different teachers, assuming one or more teacher for each elementary grade and six or seven teachers for each middle school and high school grade. Of these fifty teachers, some will be wonderful, some will be solid practitioners, and perhaps a very few will be incompetent. If that is the case, you have an obligation to intervene. In some cases, such as with an unclear grading policy, the situation may improve with a simple request. In most cases of a true incompetent, however, no amount of cajoling or complaining will change the fact that the person in the classroom is not equipped to do the job. Whatever the inconvenience, you will be less aggravated and your child will be better educated if you insist on a change. You may be able to change to a different teacher within your school or it may be necessary to change schools. In extreme cases, where the district and school administration are extremely uncooperative, it may be necessary to change to a different public school system or to find a charter or private school that will meet your child's needs. The impact of this disruption is negligible when compared to the impact of a lost year of learning.

If you request a change of teacher, you must have your facts straight. Present to the principal a written request, identifying the specific objections you have. If there were particular behaviors by the teacher to which you object, identify with as much specificity as possible the circumstances, the exact behavior (not the attitudes or motivation, just the behavior) that you observed, and precisely when it occurred. You should expect to have the principal listen to you politely, and then refuse your request for a change. In general, school administrators deplore change and are supportive of teachers in most instances of teacher-parent disagreement. Remain calm, make your case with clarity and specificity, and ask for a written notice of the principal's decision. If the decision is against your wishes, ask also for the written notice to include information on the next level of decision authority. There is no such thing as a decision that cannot be appealed, and you must pursue the matter with the district administration if necessary.

One final issue should be considered before you proceed to change teachers, schools, or systems. You must ensure that the alternative is genuinely better. That means that you have taken the time to have the same conversation with the prospective teachers in the other classrooms or alternative schools that you had with your child's current teacher. You cannot assume that simply because a school has a good reputation, is a charter school, is a private school, is exclusive, or is expensive that the individual classroom to which your child is assigned will be one of quality and challenge. There is no substitute for asking the questions listed above, starting with the simple, "What is my child expected to know and be able to do at the end of this year?"

Parents' Checklist for the Week Before School Begins

☐ Gradually begin to move your child's bedtime back (getting up at 6 a.m. can be quite a shock after "summer hours").

☐ Do any last minute shopping for school supplies. Try not to leave it all until the week before school starts, as the shelves may be stripped. Instead, try to start shopping for school supplies two or three weeks before school starts.

    ☐ Plan ahead. Know what you need to buy before you're in the store.

    ☐ Try office supply stores and warehouse stores. You'll find better prices.

    ☐ Try to involve your child in the shopping and decision-making. After all, these are the notebooks and pencils she'll be using.

☐ Let your child choose something special to wear or bring on the first day of school. A new backpack or his favorite shirt may help make things less overwhelming.

❑ If possible, visit school before it opens, and locate the places your child is likely to visit often. Once school begins, don't be surprised if your middle school student does not want you around to be helpful.

  ❑ Restrooms

  ❑ Counseling office

  ❑ Main office

  ❑ Nurse's office

  ❑ Gym

  ❑ Cafeteria

  ❑ Where to buy lunch tickets

  ❑ Locker

  ❑ Where to catch the bus

❑ Get a copy of the bell/class schedule and look it over along with a map of the school.

❑ If your child will be bringing a sack lunch to school, consult her on the menu.

❑ If your child will be walking to school or to the bus stop, make sure he is familiar with the route and with "safe places" along the way (friends' houses, stores you frequent, etc.).

❑ Be open, alert, and sympathetic to any and all questions about school, as well as to moods and behaviors that may indicate fear and anxiety on the child's part.

Parents' Checklist for the First Week of School

❑ Once again, be alert. Ask a lot of questions and make eye contact and affirming comments when your child answers. Make sure he knows you want to be involved and that you are listening to him.

❑ Some direct questions to ask:

  ❑ Where is your locker? Is it conveniently located? How often can you go to it? Do you have to carry all your books all day long?

  ❑ Where is lunch? Do you have someone to sit with? Do you know how to get through the lunch lines? Do you know where to buy lunch tickets?

  ❑ Are you having trouble with any kids?

  ❑ Are you thinking of trying out for any sports or plays, or joining any clubs? How can I help?

❑ If you happen to have one of those kids who doesn't answer direct questions, here are some indirect ones to try:

  ❑ What was your favorite part of the day?

  ❑ Was there a high part? What was it?

  ❑ Was there a low part? What was it?

❑ Pay close attention to any handouts your child brings home. The important guidelines and forms tend to be sent home in the first few weeks. If your child is not forthcoming with handouts, a "backpack search" may be in order.

❑ With your child, go over any homework, artwork, tests, or other papers she brings home. Talk openly about what was difficult and what was easy, her likes and dislikes about the assignment or project.

❑ Never be afraid to call the teacher! If something doesn't seem right or is simply unclear, a phone call at the beginning of the school year can often ward off bigger problems later.

❑ Realize that your child may be tired, overwhelmed, and even cranky the first week of school. Try to help him relax.

❑ Leaving notes of encouragement in a backpack or lunch box is a pleasant surprise that even older kids enjoy. Help them remember that you support them even if you can't be there.

The Emergency Supply Cabinet

We all remember running home from school one day saying, "Mom! I have a project due tomorrow! I have to make a replica of the Coliseum… do we have three pounds of clay and a yard of brown felt?" If it hasn't happened to you yet as a parent, it will. You can't get through even one child's school career without a school supply emergency of some sort. Here are a few things to keep on hand so that you'll be better prepared for such an occasion:

school supplies

❑ Glue and/or glue stick

❑ Construction paper

❑ Extra computer paper

❑ Extra toner or ink cartridge for the printer

❑ Blue and black ink pens

❑ Lined paper

❑ Poster board

❑ Colored pencils

❑ Markers

❑ Tape

❑ Scissors

❑ Ruler and/or yardstick

❑ Stapler and staples

❑ Paper clips

❑ Stickers

❑ Glitter

- ❑ **Dictionary**
- ❑ **Thesaurus**
- ❑ **Atlas**
- ❑ **Globe**
- ❑ **Encyclopedia**

Chapter 7

But What Do I Do Tomorrow?

The 20-Minute Learning Connection is not a quick fix. Rather, it is a commitment that will become a habit for you and for your child, leading to success in school as well as learning, discipline, intellectual development, discovery, and most importantly, the connections between parents and children that are far more important than any test or homework assignment. The path to this commitment, as with all great achievements, begins by recognizing what could go wrong and anticipating these developments. One of the first things that might go wrong is that your child might not share your enthusiasm for spending these 20 minutes together every day. This chapter suggests some practical ways for dealing with the typical differences between what children want (freedom, television, and Nintendo) and what they need: guidance, discipline, and the development of skills and knowledge that will last them a lifetime. We will consider some typical responses of children who will resist your attempts to engage them in new and challenging enterprises.

"I Can't Do This!"

Perhaps the most frequent complaints of school children and, for that matter, adults, is the allegation that because they cannot do something, it must be impossible. I am reasonably certain that the young Michael Jordan did not sink his first basket, nor did Tiger Woods ace his first golf shot. Van Cliburn probably muffed a scale or two long before achieving stardom as a concert pianist. In the abstract, we know that hard work and many mistakes, along with an occasional dose of frustration, are part of learning. When the abstract becomes our reality, however, it is much easier to succumb to the logic that the past is prologue, and that what I was unable to do yesterday I cannot do today, nor will I ever be able to do it.

Children do not invent such a negative image of their ability to learn. They are taught this pernicious lesson through the example of many adults, including teachers and parents. Every parent knows that there is a wide gulf between pride in the accomplishment of a difficult task and the anxiety that preceded the first step toward such an achievement. Whether the challenge is the first step of the baby, the first word of the toddler, the first chapter of a book, the first soccer kick, or the first sonata, there is an inevitable sequence that includes challenge, doubt, failure, perseverance, and ultimate success. The chasm from challenge to success is a wide one, but it is not filled merely with obstacles and heartache. This path also includes encouragement, small victories, glimpses of future success, and growing confidence that the goal is worth the effort. When we hear the fear-filled complaint from children, "I can't do this!" our response must be more than superficial encouragement. Rather, we must provide an immediate shift in focus away from the insurmountable goal and toward an immediately achievable objective. In other words, our focus must continually be on what children can do now and our encouragement must be focused on the immediate next step. This establishes a clear incremental process: challenge, self-doubt, encouragement, small steps, and then, the next challenge.

"I Don't Have Any Homework!
Why Should I Have to Do This?" learning

The 20-Minute Learning Connection offers parents an excellent opportunity to make learning part of life rather than mere drudgery confined to the school day. This habit can be developed as a routine, no more onerous than making one's bed or washing the dishes, and no less pleasurable than a short walk around the neighborhood or enjoying a hot cup of tea. Even though there are many other things to be done, parents and children still manage to engage in the ordinary duties and pleasures of everyday life. Learning ought to be one of those simultaneous duties and pleasures.

In order to develop the habit of learning, parents must counter the prevailing notion that the only context in which structured learning should take place is when homework is assigned by the teacher. Indeed, some parents may be skeptical about asking their children to engage in any additional activities because of what they have heard about excessive homework that today's children must endure. The myth of the sixth-grade student with five hours of homework every night should be challenged for what it is: either the result of the most grievous educational malpractice or, far more likely, the result of the fevered imagination of those who are persuaded by rumor rather than evidence. In fact, the far more common problem in many schools is the complete absence of homework, even at the secondary level. Teachers increasingly find that it takes too much time to grade, that students refuse to complete it, and that parents and even administrators fail to support the requirements that teachers place on students. When I hear complaints about excessive homework, including in my own home, I am generally inclined to examine the facts. The "five hours of homework" was, in fact, thirty minutes of homework, plus four and a half hours of phone calls, computer games, television, and other diversions. Even when there is an extensive homework assignment that might have required many hours of work, further investigation reveals that the teacher provided the requirement weeks in advance of the due date, and it was poor planning on the part of the student that caused all of the work to be required in a single sitting. The plain fact is that for the vast majority of middle school students and secondary students, the problem is not too much homework, but the habitual absence of homework that has convinced students that they ought to be liberated from anything resembling learning beyond the confines of the school day.

The skills and knowledge contained in this guide will, in fact, build confidence, speed, and efficiency in the completion of homework. Moreover, these activities offer the opportunity for parents and children to enjoy learning together, whereas the typical homework assignment is something that the teacher expects students to complete independently.

figure it out together

"It Doesn't Make Any Difference What I Do! I Just Don't Get It!"

I wish that I could offer a response to the frustration of a child that would mix the wisdom and certainty that Dr. Spock (the pediatrician and best-selling author, not the alien on *Star Trek*) offered to parents of the 1950s. Readers would recognize and challenge the superficiality of easy answers to challenging problems. In fact, children can become plagued by self-doubt, and their absolute knowledge that "I just don't get it" quickly becomes the ingrained belief that "I just *can't* get it." Here are some ideas to consider when dealing with a child who expresses feelings of inadequacy, self-doubt, and hopelessness.

First, recognize the value of these feelings. When children accurately say, "I don't get it," they are expressing the first step toward understanding. After all, it is far more difficult to convince someone to accept instruction when they think that they have the right answer and are unwilling to admit that they don't know everything. Thus, the parent's response to uncertainty and self-doubt should be clear and unequivocal affirmation. "You're right," the parent can acknowledge. "You don't know it. And you know what? You have to be *really* smart to know that you don't know something! Let's see if we can figure it out together…"

Second, determine what the child knows. For example, if the child is bewildered by the words of an authentic historical document, such as the Declaration of Independence, start with what your child knows. "So you're saying that the words of the Declaration of Independence are pretty strange, right? Well, let's start with what you already know. Why were the colonists angry at the British?" You might hear some answer about taxes or other colonial grievances that have been discussed in class. Then continue, "The Declaration of Independence includes a lot of reasons that the colonists were upset. Let's go through each one of them and put it into your own words."

Third, break the task into incremental steps. Too many textbooks, academic standards, and test requirements involve many different tasks masquerading as a single step. If the student does not recognize that there are many separate tasks, then frustration is inevitable.

For example, consider this typical item from an early middle school math test:

"Herb is a gardener who loves tomatoes. In fact, that is all he plants in his backyard garden. In his side yard he has a 12-square-foot garden with zucchinis and azaleas. In the front yard, he has a pond in the middle of his 32-square-foot flower garden. However, the backyard garden is all tomatoes. His backyard garden is 7 feet wide and 24 inches long. There are 4 tomato plants in each square foot. If each tomato plant has an average of 3 ripe tomatoes, how many tomatoes will Herb harvest?"

Some students might tackle this problem with gusto. In fact, they might do it so quickly that they will include information about the side yard and front yard gardens or forget to convert 24 inches into two feet. Other students will find the sheer quantity of information so overwhelming that they will become bogged down in some of the irrelevant details. An effective method of helping students tackle a multistep problem is the clear identification of each step. A good rule of thumb is this: If you are not sure whether you need to add an extra step, then add it. It is much less risky to have a step that you do not need than to skip a step that you did need.

Here is one approach to breaking this problem down into incremental steps.

First, circle the question—what am I supposed to know? In this case, the question is, "How many tomatoes will Herb harvest?" Whatever I do, I know that the final answer is not about feet or inches, it is about the number of tomatoes that Herb will harvest.

Second, make all the units the same. The garden is "7 feet wide and 24 inches long." To make these the same units, I need to know that there are 12 inches in one foot, and that 24 inches is the same as 2 feet. Third, draw a picture. Why? Because pictures are easier to understand than words. On some tests, students are required to draw a diagram for math problems. However, even when such a drawing is not required, it is a great idea to convert words into pictures because it makes the problem easier to understand. My picture might look like this:

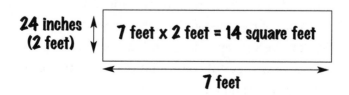

24 inches (2 feet) ↕ **7 feet x 2 feet = 14 square feet**

7 feet

Fourth, write the problem in words. It might look something like this: "The number of tomatoes that Herb will harvest is equal to the number of tomatoes on one plant (3) times the number of tomato plants in one square foot of his garden (4) times the number of square feet in his garden (14)." Some tests require that students explain their answer in writing. However, even if it is a multiple-choice test and no one but the student will see the diagram and sentences, it is an excellent idea to write out the sentences that explain the answer. Fifth, put numbers with the words of the sentence. "The number of tomatoes that Herb will harvest is equal to 3 tomatoes per plant times 4 tomato plants per square foot times 14 square feet, or 168 tomatoes." Sixth, go back to the question in step one. Ask yourself, "Have I answered the question?"

This may seem to be a laborious process for a relatively simple math question. On the contrary, the easiest way to tackle this or any other math problem is to break it down into simple steps. Some of these steps will be the same on every single math problem, from fifth grade math through graduate school statistics. For example, the first step is always, "Circle the question—what am I supposed to know?" The last step is always, "Go back to the question in step one—have I answered the question?" This process is essential for a student to move beyond calculation into real mathematical problem solving. There are many students who know the times tables and math facts, but who cannot solve the problem of Herb's tomatoes. They do not read the problem carefully, they include irrelevant data, or they provide elaborate answers in square feet when the question is asking about the number of tomatoes that Herb will harvest.

This problem illustrates an important component of the 20-Minute Learning Connection. In this illustration, the parent was not imperiously demanding, "Don't you get it? It's 168 tomatoes!" Rather, the parent was breaking down a complex problem into steps and the child proceeded systematically through the problem.

"Everything Is Okay. Just Leave Me Alone!"

Self-reliance is a wonderful thing. A few school children still read Emerson's essay on the subject and are enjoined to revel in the independence of spirit enjoyed by that rare individual who is dependent on no other person. As a student and as a parent, I have experienced both sides of the tension that result when a parent wishes to be helpful and the child prefers to assert independence. It is at this point that the normal stress of homework can explode into a tearful confrontation. Thus, the parental response to "Just leave me alone" must be careful and measured.

Start with a positive statement. "You must be very confident to want to do this yourself without any help. I am proud of you. Please show it to me when you are done." This is not a request; it is a requirement. If the Emersonian spirit is alive and well, your self-reliant student will submit flawless work that will elicit unrestrained praise. When that daydream is interrupted, however, it is far more likely that "Just leave me alone" was a way of saying, "I don't know how to do this, but I really don't want you to think that I'm stupid. If you would just stay away, then I won't know it, but at least you won't know that I don't know it."

This is a delicate point in a conversation with any child. Whether your child is in second grade (my youngest) or twelfth grade (my oldest), the need for independence is strong. There is a world of difference between the parent who in exasperation demands, "Let me show you how to do it right," and the parent who says gently but firmly, "I'm really proud of your independence. Please show it to me when you are done." Your time is limited. Invest it wisely. If the child's confidence is appropriate, then parental support for that confidence should follow. If the child needs help but will not admit it, then no humiliation is required. The certain knowledge that a loving and supportive parent will look at the final work product will lead to a request for help. For the strong-willed, independent child, the response to a request for help is far better than imposed assistance.

a positive beginning

Daily Checklist for School Success

Whether you have one child or six, checklists are helpful ways to transform the chaos of the morning into a positive beginning to the school day. While every family has its own rituals and requirements for the start of the day, here are some items you may want to include in a visible checklist for daily review by children and parents:

❑ **Assignment notebook complete.**

If not, call a friend, call the "homework hotline" if your school has one, or call the teacher at home. If it is not written down in the assignment notebook, it will not happen.

❑ Backpack empty and repacked.

Archaeologists of the future will find some student backpacks and be unable, in at least a few cases, to differentiate them from time capsules. The accumulation of literature, culture, and food represent the accumulation of epochs of civilization. Let your child find a better way to be famous than in the diorama of a natural history museum of future centuries. Empty the backpack completely every night and repack it, with a place for everything and everything in its place.

❑ Projects, tests, and other important dates on the family calendar.

There are few more discouraging moments than finding "important" notes squashed in the residue of the bottom of a backpack that involve dates that have already passed. There should be a single large family calendar that has everything from the volunteer activities and business trips of parents to the school activities, project due dates, and tests of children. Without such a combined calendar, conflicts are inevitable.

❑ Homework checked.

This does not mean homework done by the parent, nor does it imply homework completed at all. It means that the parent knows what has and has not been done. The child knows that accountability begins at home and that the requirements of the parents are at least as stringent as those imposed at school.

❑ Long-term projects reviewed.

The myth of "five hours of homework" is frequently revealed as the month-long project that has been concealed and postponed until the night before it is due. The requirement of fifteen minutes a night for twenty nights thus became five hours in a single night, with the teacher portrayed as the architect of student misery. While it is important that parents ask about projects due "tomorrow," it is equally important that future projects and tests become the subject of daily conversation.

The "Refrigerator Curriculum"

Ray Simon and Janine Riggs are leaders in one of the most remarkable stories of educational progress in the nation. Their "Smart Start" initiative in Arkansas focused on literacy and math and created nationally recognized progress among students of every economic and ethnic group in the state. Their methods were hardly revolutionary. They set high standards and clear expectations for every child. They also had the wisdom to know that parents were essential contributors to student success. One of their most successful innovations was the "Refrigerator Curriculum," so named because it was designed to be affixed next to student work proudly displayed on the refrigerator door. This document expressed on a single page the essential knowledge and skills that students needed for each grade level. Unless you have a large refrigerator, you will not have enough space to display every state standard. Nevertheless, you can identify the most important skills that your child must acquire, and reminders of those essentials should roughly correspond to the frequency with which you open the refrigerator door.

If your child's school does not offer a refrigerator curriculum, then consider creating one. The plain fact is that every standard and academic requirement is not of equal value. Determine those that are most important and reinforce them frequently. Ask your child's teachers and school administrators this simple question: "If I can't do everything that you'd like me to do at the end of the day, what are the most important things for my child to know and be able to do in order to be successful in the next grade?" When the question is phrased in this way, the response should be brief. It will not include a laundry list full of scores of standards. Rather, the list will include some academic requirements, a focus on literacy, and an emphasis on appropriate behavior, time management, and organizational skills. These are worthy of a place on your refrigerator door.

Conclusion

Advice about how to raise the perfectly behaved and flawlessly educated child can be overwhelming, unreasonable, and silly. There is simply too much to do and not enough time to do it all. One of the central themes of this book is that even on the typical day when perfection is elusive and you cannot "do it all," there are nevertheless important and constructive things you can do in order to make a positive difference for your child. As this chapter suggests, not every conversation is easy, nor is every offer of parental support welcomed by a child. Nevertheless, in 20 minutes you can update the calendar, check the backpack, help break a complicated problem down into small steps, provide some encouragement, and maybe even share a laugh. In other words, even on the busiest day, you can make a difference.

make a positive
difference

Chapter 8

Standards and Tests in Illinois

Putting It All Together: Standards, Tests, and Accountability

"Standards, Tests, and Accountability"—the very words have the rhythm of "Lions, Tigers, and Bears" from Dorothy's scary walk along the Yellow Brick Road. That which is unknown and mysterious is, to both students and adults, the source of fear and anxiety. This chapter will demystify the Illinois Standards Achievement Test, known as the ISAT. While the ISAT is not easy, the more students know what to expect, the less fearful they will be. It is important to note that this chapter is not a definitive guide to the content and format of the Illinois middle school tests.

You should expect to see periodic changes in testing policy on everything from the standards addressed to the grades tested. What this chapter does offer is sound advice for helping your student succeed on any state test. Even if the format and content change, your student will learn sound test taking principles and the importance of reading comprehension and written analysis as the keys to test success in every subject. For the latest information about the content and format of the ISAT, visit the Illinois State Board of Education's website at www.isbe.state.il.us. Interactive multiple-choice tests offering immediate feedback for students are available at tp1.clearlearning.com/ISBE. These online tests provide a no-risk opportunity for students to get used to test questions in a low-stress environment. In addition, parents can observe the thought processes, emotional reactions, and strategies that children use during the test.

Is Test Preparation Unethical?

There is an important difference between mindless test drills and the teaching of a curriculum that is thoughtfully linked to the assessments that students must take. Although the phrase "teaching to the test" is often used critically by those who oppose any sort of testing, consider the alternative. If teachers did not link their curriculum to state assessments, then students would be set up for failure, with every test a mystery and every question a surprise. Inevitably, anger, frustration, fear, and anxiety would stem from the failure of schools to link their instruction to the requirements placed on students during tests.

Parents are rightfully concerned when they hear rumors that a thoughtful and rigorous academic environment has been transformed into a boot camp for test preparation I personally have investigated many such claims, including the complaint that "all students do all day is prepare for the state tests." Each time I hear such a statement, I make a point of asking for more detail. "Tell me," I inquire, "about the schedule of the most test-obsessed teacher in the entire school. How much time every day is spent on test preparation? For how many weeks does such a regimen last?" The most recent inquiry resulted in the admission that the "test-obsessed" teacher devoted one hour a day for three weeks to test preparation. That is fifteen hours out of 1,080 instructional hours (180 school days times 6 hours a day), or about 1.4 percent of the time in school.

That is not, by anyone's standards, an inappropriate obsession with test preparation. My typical recommendation to educators is that they devote about twenty minutes a week to the "life skill" of test taking. We teach students many life skills, including pedestrian and bicycle safety, avoidance of alcohol, tobacco, and drugs, and a variety of skills that extend beyond the academic curriculum of school. Test taking is also a skill that students use throughout their lives. Twenty minutes a week—about twelve hours a year—is hardly transforming American schools from an academic paradise into a test preparation boot camp.

Finally, let us consider the ethical issue itself. Even at twenty minutes a week, does test preparation cross an ethical boundary? Certainly, it would be unethical if a teacher were to procure questions from the state test, copy them, and encourage students to memorize the answers. Such behavior can result in felony convictions and jail time for teachers and administrators in some states. No thoughtful person recommends such behavior. It is, however, entirely fair and reasonable for teachers and school administrators to say, "This test will require reading and, more specifically, require students to write a summary of the stories and nonfiction passages that they read. This is not only a test requirement, but the requirement for any well-educated student. We would do this even if there were no state test. Therefore, every day when students read a passage in their textbook or read a story, we will require students to write a brief summary of what they have read."

This is good educational practice, not unethical "teaching to the test." The same is true of requirements for students to write, know their geography, or understand mathematics. It is good education, not any sort of ethical breach. In fact, the real ethical challenge is presented by teachers who refuse to give students the information they need to be successful on tests and in the next grade. Some teachers refuse to acknowledge the value of aligning their curriculum with the skills and knowledge students need to succeed on tests. These teachers are committing an ethical violation as serious as the driver education teacher who sends students to take a driving test without an understanding of stop signs or the operation of the brake pedal.

The Illinois State Board of Education is very clear on the professional ethics of test preparation. The board published a document called *Professional Testing Practices for Educators* that states the following:

Test preparation activities must have two goals: (1) Ensure that all students have the opportunity to learn in accordance with the Illinois Learning Standards so that they are knowledgeable about the content covered by the tests and (2) give all students occasion to become familiar with the types of items used on the test (writing prompts, multiple-choice questions, and extended-response questions) so that they are tested for their knowledge, not their test-taking skills . . . Practices essential for proper test preparation [include the following:]

■ Administrators, curriculum directors, and teachers shall rely on the Illinois Learning Standards as a primary resource for curriculum development and instruction, thus providing students the opportunity to learn the content covered by the tests.

■ Administrators and teachers shall ensure that students are familiar with the testing formats. Teachers must teach relevant test-taking skills, especially at lower grades, including how to approach multiple-choice items, write essays, and answer extended-response items.

What Students Need to Know for the Tests

The most important clarification with regard to standards and testing is this: Students do not have to be proficient on every single standard in order to be successful on the Illinois tests. Although the Illinois Learning Standards provide excellent guidelines for teachers and parents, it is impossible for any test to address every standard for each grade level. Therefore, the Illinois tests cover only a small part of the school curriculum, with a particular emphasis on reading, writing, mathematics, social science, and science. So if someone were to ask, "What does a student need to know and be able to do in order to be successful on the Illinois tests?" the answer would be, "The student must read, write, understand elementary mathematics, and be familiar with the basics of the middle school science and social science curriculum. While some content knowledge – the facts of history, geography, and science – are helpful, the most important areas for students are reading and writing."

There are five tests of concern to middle school students in Illinois. These tests include:

Grade 7 Science and Physical Development/Health: Two testing sessions, with each session including thirty-five multiple-choice science questions and five multiple-choice physical development/health questions.

Grade 7 Social Science and Fine Arts: Two testing sessions, including one session with forty multiple-choice social science questions and one session with thirty multiple-choice social science questions and ten multiple-choice fine arts questions.

Grade 8 Reading: Three testing sessions, including one session with eighteen multiple-choice questions and one essay question, one session with twenty-eight multiple-choice questions, and one session with nineteen multiple-choice questions and one essay question.

Grade 8 Writing: Two testing sessions, including one session with a single assigned prompt (a question or topic assigned by the test writers) and another session in which students choose one of two different prompts.

Grade 8 Mathematics: Three testing sessions, including two sessions with thirty-five multiple-choice questions and one session with "extended response" questions – math questions that require students to write out their explanations using sentences, diagrams, charts, graphs, or other appropriate explanations of their work.

Illinois does one of the best jobs in the nation of linking its tests to its published academic standards. In addition, any student, parent, or teacher can go to the Illinois State Board of Education website and find practice test questions that will give students a good preview of what to expect on the test. While the exact questions on the test will be different from those on the practice exam, students and parents who review the practice items will have a much better idea of whether the curriculum in school matches the expectations of the tests.

The writing test for eighth-grade students is very demanding, and students should begin their focus on writing well before the eighth-grade year. While many students in upper elementary school and early middle school have traditionally focused on creative writing, students must be able to write a proficient essay that is persuasive and informative. The "rubric" or guide to evaluators who score student writing is a public document and available to every teacher and parent. The best teachers use this rubric in their classroom on a regular basis so that the expectations for student writing are the same in the classroom as they are on the test. Some of the state's expectations for eighth-grade student writing include the following:

- Clearly sets purpose of paper through use of effective thematic introduction, a specific preview, or may attempt more sophisticated strategy with some success; could be developed inductively

- Clearly maintains logic throughout

- Effective closing which unifies the writing

- All major points developed by specific detail

- Most key points are developed evenly – to the same degree of specificity

- Extensive development of Support through multiple strategies (e.g., explanation, evidence, and example)

- Word choice enhances specificity

- Structure is clear and appropriate to purpose

- All points appropriately paragraphed

- Coherence and cohesion demonstrated by effective and varied transitions or other devices (e.g.,transitions, parallel structure, pronouns, repetition, etc.)

- All points are logically presented and interrelated

- Varied sentence structure and word choice produce cohesion

- Mastery of sentence construction

- Few run-ons or fragments in proportion to amount written

- Mastery of subject/ verb agreement

- Correct use of pronouns

- Mastery of common grade-appropriate punctuation/capitalization

- Few minor and very few major errors in proportion to amount written

- Fully developed for grade leve

- Clear and purposeful Focus; in-depth balanced Support; lines of reasoning identified and developed coherently and cohesively throughout

These criteria represent the expectations of the state for the highest score on the writing test. Most students will fall short of that mark. The essential consideration for parents, teachers, and students is this: If we fail to understand the expectations for the highest score in student writing, then it is unlikely that classroom assignments or work at home will strive for this level of writing mastery.

The "Basics" Are Still Important in Middle School

Middle school students and teachers frequently face a dilemma. Teachers want to cover a curriculum that is more complex than the basics that dominated elementary school, but they frequently find that students did not master reading, writing, and mathematics during the elementary grades. Because the state academic content requirements are very specific and demanding, some teachers and parents are tempted to forge ahead to the requirements of the eighth-grade test, whether or not students have mastered basic skills. This is a critical error. Let us briefly review the basic skills necessary for success on the middle school tests.

The reading and writing items on the ISAT require students to read long passages (two to four pages) of grade-level text and understand the main idea, the author's point of view, the meaning of common vocabulary words, as well as the meaning of unusual words that will be unfamiliar to the student but that can be defined using the context of the reading passage. Students must also spell correctly, use proper grammar, and write paragraphs and essays that have a clear beginning, middle, and end.

The mathematics questions on the ISAT require students to read questions (this is very important: the "math" test is, in fact, very much a test of reading ability as well), understand what the question is asking, solve simple number operations (addition, subtraction, multiplication, and division), and find the "next step" in solving mathematical problems. Make no mistake: math facts are important. Just as was the case when you were in school, children must know addition and subtraction facts from second grade on, and multiplication and division from third grade on. If your child is in a later grade and was told that, in the age of calculators and computers, math facts are not really important, then it is not too late to break out the flash cards and correct this omission in his or her education. If your child has a teacher who believes that learning the "times tables" and other drudgery is unimportant, then you need to seriously consider changing teachers. There are many areas in education about which reasonable people may differ, but this is not one of them. While the logical and analytical skills involved in mathematical problem-solving are important, they are not a replacement for understanding and knowing—and yes, that means memorizing—the facts of addition, subtraction, multiplication, and division. Although students may use calculators on the Illinois Grade 8 Math test, the majority of problems require reasoning, thinking, analysis, and "mental math" such as testing the reasonability of an answer.

Writing: The Best Way to Build Thinking Skills

One of the best ways that parents can help student gain essential knowledge, not only for the Reading and Writing tests, but for success throughout the school years ahead of them, is to require students to read for at least twenty minutes, write a summary of what they have read, and then edit and correct their summary. While reading is important, the creation of a written summary, along with the editing and revision of that summary, provides one of the best ways to build the skills of thinking, comprehension, analysis, synthesis, understanding, and communication. Students may not think that they have time to create a brief outline of what they are going to write. In fact, students will find that the creation of a brief outline will save time and improve organization.

Student writing is required on almost every element of the Illinois examinations. Whether the subject is reading, writing, or mathematics, students must write clearly and coherently. Of all the skills acquired in elementary and middle school, the one with the greatest weight on the state test is, by pleasant coincidence, the skill with the greatest impact on student success in secondary school and college: nonfiction writing. If parents and teachers feel overwhelmed with too much academic content and wonder where they should focus their energies, the development of writing, editing, and rewriting skills would be at the top of my list.

It is important that parents understand that the term "writing" can be applied to many different activities, and some are more helpful to students than others. While journal and story writing may be entertaining, these activities are not as useful as writing that requires students to hone summarization, analytical, descriptive, and explanatory skills.

Writing Activities to Build Thinking Skills

■ **Summarization:** Listen to a parent read a chapter in a novel, a short story, or an article from a newspaper or magazine. While you are listening, make a few notes about the general ideas and the details. Write a brief summary of what you have just heard.

■ **Comparison and Analysis:** Listen to a parent read two related but different stories. Make a list of what is similar and what is different between the two stories; then write three paragraphs. The first paragraph should contain a brief introduction, followed by a statement of how the two stories are similar. The second paragraph should contain statements describing how the two stories are different. The third paragraph should draw conclusions about the stories and make an evaluation about which one the student prefers.

■ **Description:** Look at an object, animal, or activity for five minutes. Write down what you notice, using as many senses as you can. Then write a paragraph describing the object, animal, or activity in as much detail as possible.

■ **Explanation:** Look at a process—perhaps a math problem or a science procedure. Explain in writing how to solve the math problem or how the scientific procedure works.

Some readers may wonder about such an emphasis on writing. Aren't the majority of questions on the test in a multiple-choice format? Student skill in writing, however, not only improves performance on the written questions on the tests, but writing skills are related to higher performance on the multiple-choice questions as well. The research is unambiguous in demonstrating that a greater emphasis on nonfiction writing builds the thinking, analysis, and reading skills of students. These skills, in turn, are associated with improvements on multiple-choice test scores. Finally, writing is a complex skill that improves only with consistent effort and reinforcement. Because writing takes on even greater importance in secondary school and college, middle school educators and parents are well advised to place an exceptional emphasis on writing.

Test Format and Test Preparation

The majority of test questions are multiple-choice in format. This means that students can choose an answer from among the four or five possible responses provided by the test. The multiple-choice format has an important implication for students, teachers, and parents:

It is not only important to know the right answers to test questions, but also to find the wrong answers and eliminate them.

Although this may seem obvious to parents who have experience in taking multiple-choice tests, the implications for students are profound. This means that test taking need not be a game of mere memorization in which students conclude, "Either I know it or I don't, and if I don't, then I might as well give up." Rather, this focus on knowing both the right and the wrong answer gives students multiple opportunities to be successful on the test. It also gives students an incentive to persevere on a problem even if the right answer is not obvious to them. Most importantly, this insight gives teachers and parents the ability to move far beyond traditional practice tests and enhance the thinking and reasoning skills of students.

Consider this sample question:

Tamika and her family are making a round trip by car between New York and San Francisco. The distance between the cities is 2,921 miles. Her brother says that they should take the station wagon, but Tamika is concerned about the cost of gasoline and suggests the family take a smaller car instead. The station wagon consumes about one gallon of gas for each 18 miles traveled, while the smaller car consumes about one gallon of gas for each 25 miles traveled. If gas prices are $1.92 per gallon, how much money will the use of the smaller car save?

A) Cannot be determined from the information given

B) 7 miles per gallon

C) $174.48

D) $1,744.80

This could be a very time-consuming problem if each individual step is calculated. Let's use two different methods to solve this problem. First, let's solve the problem the slow way: Always start with the question: "How much money will the use of the smaller car save?" That tells us right away that the answer must be an amount of money – not miles, miles per gallon, or any of the other sorts of numbers provided in the problem. First, we need to know the total miles traveled. The total round trip distance is twice the one-way distance, or 2 x 2,921, or 5,842 miles. Next we need to figure out the amount of gas each of the two cars would consume. With the station wagon traveling 18 miles on one gallon of gas, we can divide 5,842 total miles by 18 miles per gallon, with a result of 324.56 gallons consumed. With the smaller car traveling 25 miles on one gallon of gas, we can divide 5,842 total miles by 25 miles per gallon, with a result of 233.68 gallons of gas consumed. The difference in gasoline consumed is 233.68 subtracted from 324.56, or a difference of 90.88 gallons saved. With gasoline costing $1.92 per gallon, we then multiply $1.92 times 90.88, and determine that the smaller car would have saved a total of $174.48. That was a lot of work! There must be a faster and easier way to deal with this sort of multi-step problem.

Consider a different approach. Again, start with the question: "How much money do we save?" Let's estimate the round trip distance to be about 6,000 miles – 3,000 miles each way. The smaller car gets 25 miles to the gallon, so for each 1,000 miles it travels, it uses 50 gallons of gas. Over a 6,000-mile trip, the smaller car will use about 300 gallons of gas. Gas costs about $2 per gallon, so the cost of gas for the smaller car is about $600. The larger car get 18 miles to the gallon, or about a third less than the station wagon. Let's estimate that we'll save about 1/3 of $600, or $200. Before spending any time on more calculations, let's see if the $200 estimate allows us to quickly answer this question and move on. In reviewing the choices, it's clear: the test writer is trying to catch students who read the question wrong with the choice of B: we're not looking for miles saved, but for money saved. Choice D will catch students who misplaced a decimal–something that is very easy to do when you are performing a lot of manual calculations. That leaves C as the clear choice–$200 is close enough to $174.48 so select that answer, save several minutes on the test, and move on to the next question.

The problem-solving section of math and science tests is challenging for many students, so it is a good idea to practice both ways–the slow way and the fast way – so that students build confidence both in calculation and in estimation. On the test, however, estimation can save a lot of time and avoid mistakes that frequently occur in a series of many different calculations. It is also important to know that, from an educational point of view, this sort of practice is not the "mindless test prep" that critics of standards and testing so frequently assail. In fact, this approach to the practice problem improves students' reasoning, reading, estimation, and problem solving—all skills that are essential even if state tests were eliminated tomorrow. Moreover, the habit of moving from the search for the right answer to the elimination of wrong answers builds a student's power of logic and reasoning, helping to improve success on tests for many years to come.

When parents and teachers analyze multiple-choice problems in this way, they are moving far beyond the low-level test preparation that critics of standards and testing have so frequently criticized toward the thinking skills that students need. It is fair to ask this question: If all tests were eliminated tomorrow, would my student still need to think, read, write, and compute? If you answered in the affirmative, then these exercises are not merely a matter of preparation for tests, but preparation for life.

Student Writing

The Illinois exams include questions requiring short and long written responses. The long responses require students to develop skill in organization and planning to gain the maximum score. Students typically will have plenty of time to create an outline, write a rough draft, and then produce a final copy. Students who immediately start writing in response to the question frequently submit work that is poorly organized. One of the most important skills that you can instill in your student is the habit of rewriting. Students never should presume that their first written product is their last. Most editors would argue that this is a good rule for authors of any age. By focusing on the habit of rewriting, parents provide both an intellectual and an emotional advantage for their students. Successful writers must not only write, but also rewrite and after thought, reflection, and feedback, rewrite yet again. This intellectual attribute is directly related to the emotional trait of persistence. Students will not have the ability to rewrite unless they have the emotional strength to persist in the face of difficulty and challenge. One of the most important gifts any parent can give to a student is the habit of persistence, resilience, and rising once again to a challenge. In simple terms, rewriting is an emotional and intellectual gift to students, and it is as important as the initial gifts of reading and writing that were bestowed by parents in the earliest days of literary exploration.

Does *Every* Student Have to Take the Test?

Illinois laws and administrative regulations place a heavy emphasis on the inclusion of all students in testing and the vast majority of students must take the tests prescribed by the state. The clear intent of both the law and the policies of the Illinois State Board of Education is to have maximum participation. Students with disabilities must take the assessment with appropriate accommodations and adaptations unless their Individualized Education Plan (IEP) specifies in writing that the student must be excluded from testing. Even in those cases, the IEP must provide for other means of assessing student progress.

What If Parents Object to the Tests?

Because of the clear emphasis on 100 percent participation in the state testing program, some parents may be legitimately concerned that their students are being subjected to inappropriate testing. Because of the complexity of federal laws guaranteeing the rights of individual students to appropriate testing and the Illinois statutes that intend to have 100 percent participation, parents must serve as advocates for their students in those cases where testing may not be appropriate. In general, every student, including the profoundly disabled and those unable to speak English, will be assessed. The vast majority of those students will be assessed using the standard English Language test forms, although teachers are required to provide reasonable accommodations to students with specifically diagnosed learning disabilities. Only in the most rare cases can students be excluded from state testing, and even in those cases, it is the responsibility of the school to administer an appropriate alternative assessment.

What About the Other Tests in School?

Although the state-mandated standardized tests receive the lion's share of the publicity about testing in school, there are other tests that students routinely take that can have very significant consequences for a student's future educational opportunities. Some of these tests include so-called I.Q. (Intelligence Quotient) Tests and Aptitude Tests. These tests frequently are used to determine the eligibility of a student for "gifted and talented" programs or for participation in special education programs. Educational assessment experts have strong differences of opinion on what these tests mean. One leading national testing company explains "aptitude" as follows:

> A combination of characteristics, whether native or acquired, that is indicative of an individual's ability to learn or to develop proficiency in some particular area if appropriate education or training is provided. Aptitude tests include those of general academic (scholastic) ability; those of special abilities such as verbal, numerical, mechanical, or musical; tests assessing 'readiness' for learning; and tests that measure both ability and previous learning, and are used to predict future performance – usually in a specific field, such as foreign language, shorthand, or nursing. (Harcourt Educational Measurement website, www.hemweb.com/library/glossary)

Some scholars question the very existence of aptitude as a consistent quality in young students, arguing that interest, environment, and early education are all variables that change rapidly in the life of a young student. Moreover, the announcement of such a quality as aptitude can become a self-fulfilling prophecy. There are large numbers of students who have been told that they lack an aptitude in math and science based on a test at an early age. This test result discouraged these students and their parents from the pursuit of the more advanced—and potentially more interesting—science and math courses. Not surprisingly, the "predictions" appeared to be accurate, as these students did not perform well in high school and college on science and math tests. Consider the case of a student who is told, "You're going to be fat, so there is no reason for you to even consider diet, exercise, or a healthy lifestyle." When that student becomes an obese and unhealthy adolescent and adult, do we blame the student or would we question the wisdom of the prediction that, not surprisingly, came to fruition?

There is a cautionary tale from comic genius Matt Groening, the creator of the television series, *The Simpsons*. In one episode, Bart, the ne'er do well son of Homer and Marge, is accidentally identified as "gifted" when his test paper is switched with that of another student. As Bart exhibits the same behavior that had been routinely ridiculed and berated by teachers and school administrators, he is now applauded for his wise insights and extraordinary "gifts." The test had miraculous powers of prediction, though not in the way that its creators had intended. In this cartoon, as in real life, tests do a much better job of predicting the actions of the adults to read and believe the results than they do of predicting the success and failure of the students who take the tests.

Just as the term "aptitude" has been subject to debate among researchers, so also the term "intelligence" has been the subject of considerable controversy. Although the notion of measurable intelligence was regarded as a scientific fact in the early twentieth century, researchers in the last two decades have cast considerable doubt on the notion of general intelligence. These complex controversies have filled volumes. For the purposes of this book, suffice it to say that a few things are fairly clear. First, the younger a student is, the more variable the scores on intelligence tests tend to be. Therefore, it is wise for parents to avoid reading too much into the results. Tuesday's gifted student may, with a little more fatigue and distractions, become Wednesday's student in need of special intervention. The same student, in turn, becomes Thursday's student who is destined for a career in music because of the chance playing of an engaging song on the radio and the ability of that student to replicate a music and rhythm pattern on the way to the office of the school psychologist.

These observations do not indict all tests administered to all students, but only indicate the obvious: the smaller the number of measurements, the greater the opportunity for error. No adult would submit to a life-changing decision based on a single test. If the physician prescribed surgery after a single blood pressure reading, we would demand more tests. We should be no less insistent on additional measurement when someone makes life-changing decisions that affect our children.

creating balance

Questions for Teachers and School Leaders

The tests in Illinois have consequences, both intended and otherwise, for students and parents. The most draconian consequence is the possibility of forcing a student to repeat a grade in school due to failure to pass a test. While there are many areas of educational research that yield ambiguous results, the issue of student retention is not one of them. In a tiny fraction of cases, such as those where a student started school at an inappropriately early age or where overly aggressive parents insisted on skipping the first or second grade, the requirement for a student to repeat a grade may be appropriate. In the vast majority of cases, however, the repetition of a grade is a classic example of the faulty logic demonstrated by repeating the same activity and expecting different results. It simply doesn't work. If the student has a reading deficiency, then the appropriate intervention is intensive and immediate reading instruction, not another year in which reading constitutes only sixty minutes a day of the curriculum. Because retention has such negative consequences for the students retained and, ultimately, for all students in the classroom, it is important that parents ensure that their children take the tests seriously, are well prepared, and perform well on them. Because the consequences of inadequate preparation are so serious, it is appropriate and fair for parents to ask these questions:

- How is the curriculum in my student's class related to the ISAT?

- What opportunities will my student have to become familiar with the requirements of the ISAT?

- If my student is not making adequate progress toward preparation for the ISAT, when and how will this be communicated to parents?

- What intervention plan does the school have for students who are having difficulty so that students receive this intervention long before the ISAT is administered?

- Do the teachers and administrators in the school believe that these tests are important?

While most parents have observed the obnoxious behavior of the Little League Dads, and their academic counterparts who are incessantly berating teachers and students about their performance, these questions are neither inappropriate nor intrusive. The unfortunate fact is that parents cannot assume that teachers know or care about tests. There is a backlash against testing in some areas of Illinois, and many teachers and school administrators continue to regard the classroom curriculum to be the exclusive domain of the teacher. Thanksgiving plays, Halloween parties, and scores of hours devoted to dioramas, crafts, and coloring all have hallowed traditions and have been supported by generations of teachers, students and, indeed, parents. But none of these is more important than learning to read.

While the primacy of reading, writing, and mathematics may be obvious to some readers, a backlash to the standards movement has resulted in a growing number of places where an emphasis on academic excellence is regarded as politically incorrect. Even well meaning parents have jumped on the bandwagon, opposing standards and testing, and decrying the increased emphasis on academics in the classroom. One wonders if the same parents would protest against the physicians who delivered the bad news that kids could benefit from cutting back on the corn chips, soda, and Twinkies. If those, too, were fixtures in classrooms for generations, a reduction in them might cause frowns and protests from students. Presumably, if the matter at hand were the health of our students, we would endure the whining about a reduction in junk food. There is no doubt about this point: Success in school, including proficiency in reading, writing, and mathematics, is a health issue. Students who are forced to repeat a grade are at substantially greater risk for dropping out of school later in life, and students who drop out of school exhibit a broad range of high-risk behaviors that threaten their very lives.

Test Preparation Without Test Anxiety: The Delicate Balance

The challenge for parents and teachers is the manner in which we convey this complex message to students. We want them to understand that the tests are important and we want them to be willing to work hard to learn in school. We also want them to have fun, enjoy school, love learning and most importantly, deal with the inevitable stress and anxiety that occur in school without becoming paralyzed by negative emotions. While the perfect balance may be elusive, we certainly know what does not work. Telling children that "It's no big deal" or "You're wonderful and you really don't need that stuff" may be comforting in the short term, but it lays a foundation of academic quicksand for students. False reassurances now lead to failure, stress, and anxiety later. By contrast, gentle but firm challenges now are necessary for the reduction of anxiety in the months to come. Many of these gentle but firm challenges occur in school under the guiding hand of a devoted, caring, and knowledgeable teacher. The vast majority of such challenges, however, must come from home where daily routines, including the 20-Minute Learning Connection, will give students confidence, skills, perseverance, and ultimately, success.

Chapter 9

Children with Special Needs

Your Rights As a Parent

I choose my words carefully here: The rights of people with disabilities are civil rights. The last century will be marked in history not only for technological advances, world wars, and economic booms and busts, but for the battle fought and won on behalf of the disadvantaged. If you are the parent of a child with special needs, whether the child is blind, hearing-impaired, cognitively disabled, or suffers from any other disability, then school officials are not doing you a favor when they provide accommodations for your child any more than your local officials do you a favor when they allow you to vote. Meeting the needs of persons with disabilities is a civic responsibility. Having those needs met is a right, not a privilege.

If you are already confident in the accuracy of the diagnosis of your child's needs, then you may wish to proceed directly to the end of this chapter and find more detailed information on organizations that are specifically oriented to the needs of your child. If, however, you do not know if your child has a learning disability or other special need, then this chapter may offer some ideas for you to consider as you enter this very complex and challenging area of education.

In the context of standards and testing, the discussions surrounding special needs students frequently have been polarized. At one extreme are those who stereotype every special needs student as cognitively unable to meet academic standards, and thus every effort is made to exclude these students from testing. At the other extreme are those who recognize no impairment that would interfere with testing and insist on including every child in testing. In reality, the essence of the legislation at all levels regarding children with special needs is designed to protect the *individual* needs of the child. This chapter, therefore, cannot provide guidance about all children except in the most general sense. Every sentence that follows must be interpreted through the parental lens that is best able to focus on the individual needs of your child. Whether your child is included or excluded from special education, whether your child meets academic standards with or without accommodations, and whether your child participates in regular state examinations or alternative examinations that are more appropriate, is not a matter of blind bureaucratic policy, but rather an individual decision made based on the individual needs of your child.

What Are Special Needs Anyway, and How Do I Know If My Child Has Them?

Some special needs are obvious. Children with profound physical, neurological, or developmental challenges clearly need additional assistance in order to deal with the challenges of daily life, including the challenges of a school environment. Other children may be unsuccessful in school, and yet there is no clear developmental or physical disability. How then can you tell if your child needs the additional assistance that is legally guaranteed? Parents must separate the normal challenges of daily life from the challenges faced by students with developmental impairments. As the complexity of pediatric neurology grows, the field is understandably intimidating for any parent. One thing is clear: Your child will never have any advocate that is more knowledgeable and caring about the individual needs of that child than a parent. Your lack of a professional credential must not limit you from playing an active role as the primary advocate for your child. In this respect, it is important for you to advocate accuracy. You are not an advocate either on behalf of participation in special education programs nor exclusion from them, but rather you are an advocate on behalf of accurate, complete, and meaningful diagnoses of your child's needs.

independent evaluation

The Limits of "Field Diagnosis"

The field of special education includes professionals who are gifted educators and diagnosticians. When your child is entrusted to this select group of educators, psychologists, and medical professionals, their wealth of experience and personal attention to each child, as well as their expert administration of a wide battery of tests and other diagnostic assessments, will provide a high probability that the diagnosis of your child's learning disability—or the absence of any disability at all—is accurate. Unfortunately, schools across the nation are governed by resource constraints, where one school psychologist may be assigned to serve the needs of more than a thousand students. Specialists in the diagnosis of learning disabilities are overwhelmed with the immediate needs of students whose needs are obvious and profound. In some cases, this leaves the diagnosis in the hands of amateurs who have neither the experience nor technical skills to make an accurate diagnosis. Here are the most important words in this chapter:

Before you allow your child to be categorized as "special education" or "learning disabled," it is imperative that you have an independent evaluation of your child done by an independent psychologist (doctor of psychology who specializes in learning disabilities and their diagnosis—not a practitioner, regardless of degree, who gives diagnostic tests on a part-time basis).

Why is independent diagnosis so important? The literature is full of tests and questions that appear to create a link to potential learning disabilities. Among these "diagnostic questions" I have found, a parent might be alarmed to find the following:

☐ **Does the child have difficulty in understanding new concepts?**

☐ **Is the child restless in class?**

☐ **Does the child fidget in his seat?**

☐ **Does the child seem less mature than his classmates?**

By these standards, every one of my children would have sent alarm bells ringing on any given day, even though all of them have managed to perform at very high levels in school. Indeed, by these standards, I know of few children who would not send parents scurrying to a specialist in search of a diagnosis to these obvious "problems" which, in another age, we called normal childhood behavior. This does not diminish the very real presence of learning disabilities and the need for their diagnosis and treatment. Yet, when I hear of regular schools with no greater population of disabled children than the average, and more than thirty percent of the children have been labeled as "special education," then I must wonder if the problem is really with the children or in pervasive presumptions of disabilities and the need for accompanying accommodations when, in fact, the children are quite normal.

an important clue

Context: Where Does Your Child Excel?

One important clue to your child's needs is the context in which your child has difficulty and that in which your child excels. For example, a child who does not write well in class, but who at home is able to compose wonderful stories with exciting plots and characters does not have a writing disability, but rather has a disinterest in the type of writing that is presently being required in class. The child who refuses to read aloud in class may not have the suspected reading disability, particularly if the same child is able to read with enthusiasm when alone with Grandma. Some parents have been told that the requirement for multi-step mathematical problem-solving is developmentally inappropriate for their child, and yet the same child is able to engage successfully in playground games that require multi-step conditional problem-solving and to keep the score with meticulous accuracy.

Thus, the first step in your reflection on your child's learning needs is to ask the question, "Where does my child excel?" I have heard some parents and teachers insist that there is no response for such a question and that every activity involves failures. When I persist, I will sometimes get a shrug of the shoulders and the rueful observation that, "Well, at least he can excel at Nintendo!"

Curious, I persist. "Tell me more about this success in Nintendo."

"It's awful," the parent complains. "He'll sit there for two hours, hardly blinking an eye, and proudly announce that he has made the 'next level,' whatever that means. He even compares scores with seven other kids at school who seem to devote every recess period to talking about how to get better at the dumb game, and he rattles off their scores every night as if he were announcing the league standings for the NFL."

"Please let me make sure that I understand this," I respond. "This is a child who at school appears to have memory problems and a complete inability to focus and concentrate. Homework seems futile because the child cannot remember simple facts from the previous day. Just sitting and talking about schoolwork often provokes an angry and tearful confrontation and, eventually, you both give up and the child retreats to the Nintendo game, and that way at least you both get some peace and quiet. Is this a fair summary?"

"Every blessed night," the parent sighs.

"Okay, I want to make sure I understand this," I continue. "The child has memory problems, but gives a daily recitation of seven different changing Nintendo scores. The child has attention problems, yet remains engaged in a complex game with multiple levels for hours at a time. The child does not like to discuss even for a moment his areas of failure, but will revel at length in stories of his success. Let's think about where this child can excel. The child excels first when other students are similarly enthusiastic about the activity. The child also excels when there is immediate feedback— in fact, every few moments in a Nintendo game, the child knows if there is success or failure, and every session reveals whether a 'next level' has been achieved. And, it is fair to say that this child, like most humans, enjoys talking with those he loves and respects— his parents—about his successes much more than he enjoys dwelling on his failures. And when he talks with his friends, he talks about how to get better, not about how terrible his failures make him feel."

"So what?" the parents counter. "Playing Nintendo won't get him into college. In fact, it won't get him into the seventh grade, and that's what we're worried about right now."

"That's true, and as someone who (I trust my children will never make it to this chapter) has hidden the family Nintendo machine for several months now, I share your frustration with what seems like a mindless game that robs time from homework and other more appropriate pursuits. But let me share what I have learned from Nintendo and my good friend, Dr. Jeff Howard. Dr. Howard is the founder of the Efficacy Institute. He's a Harvard-trained psychologist who has devoted a good deal of his life to helping students on whom many other people have given up. Jeff doesn't like Nintendo games any more than I do, but he made me pay attention to what they offer that kids need. He asked me one day, 'How long would those kids be playing Nintendo if their scores were put in a package and given to them at the end of the week?' After I thought about it, I knew that the answer would be, 'Not very long.' Then Dr. Howard persisted, 'They stay focused on Nintendo because the feedback is immediate and relevant. They know when they succeed and, even if they fail, they have an immediate chance for redemption. When was the last time a homework assignment did that? In fact, it gets shoved into the parent packet and the child sees it at the end of the week, if ever, and the feedback inevitably focuses on their failure to do something that was required many days (an eternity for a sixth grader) earlier. Trust me—the kid can focus, memorize, and excel, but only if there is feedback that is timely and relevant, and only if the conversations about the activity focus on success rather than failure.'"

"So," the exasperated parent demands, "You and Dr. Howard want kids to play Nintendo?"

"Not at all," I offer reassuringly. "We just want students to apply the Nintendo Effect to the classroom and to family discussions of schoolwork. What would happen if we applied these rules to learning at school? First, feedback doesn't happen at the end of the week amidst a sea of red ink in the parent packet, but it happens right away. That means that you ask the teacher for immediate feedback, so that whenever there is an error, your child has the opportunity to correct it immediately. Teachers almost always have some free time built into the day, and this could be devoted to allowing your child to leave the school day with success rather than with ambiguity or failure. At the very least, your child could take the work home and deal with it Monday night rather than over the weekend—typically Sunday night after an exhausting weekend. Second, your child might be encouraged to talk with friends and parents about strategies to get better, and even an incremental gain—each time he reaches the 'next level'—is the cause of some celebratory phone calls. That might be a new chapter, a new reading level, or a new performance level in writing. Each gain may be, like Nintendo, only a few points, but it is at least as worthy of celebration as is game success."

The point of this extended dialogue is not to suggest that Nintendo will solve the development challenges of children. Rather, the central question must always be, "Where does my child excel?" Whether or not your child has a learning disability, the context, conversation, and process of those areas where your child excels will provide clues for application to other areas where your child needs help. This is one of many areas in which the lessons of special education can be broadly applied to every other area of education for learners of any age.

Adaptations, Accommodations, and Truth

Children with special needs are entitled to the "least restrictive environment" for learning. They are also entitled to adaptations and accommodations that allow them to participate in regular classrooms to the maximum extent possible. The greatest entitlement, however, for students with special needs and their parents is the truth, including the truth about what the student has and has not yet accomplished. Too frequently, the discussions surrounding adaptations have as the underlying theme that an adaptation is equivalent to a loss of rigor. This is summed up in statements such as, "She was in special education, so I had to give her a B," or, "Sure, he passed the test, but only because he received special accommodations, so it really doesn't mean very much." There is a more appropriate way to discuss student achievement, and that is with an unwavering focus on truth.

If a child were blind, few people would presume that the Braille version of the test had less rigor than the printed version used by children with no visual impairments. In fact, some might argue that success on these tests by students who are blind requires more memory and better analytical skills than are required by other students. After all, the student reading Braille has to solve the Pythagorean theorem on a middle school math test, whether the problem about right triangles is posed in print or the problem is presented in the form of raised symbols. Now let's consider a child who has a different disability that is less obvious. The child has no guide dog, cane, or other external indicator of a disability, but nevertheless this student has an impairment that prevents the processing of printed text. The accommodation in such a case might include the presence of an adult to read the test. For another child with an attention deficit, the accommodation might include testing in a different room. For another child, there might be a scribe who writes the answers as dictated by the child. But all of these children must solve the problem with the Pythagorean theorem. In other words, the presence of an accommodation does not necessarily indicate a reduction of rigor. If these students can solve that equation, then it would be prejudicial in the extreme to conclude that they didn't "really" know that the square of the hypotenuse is equal to the sum of the square of the two sides.

Let's consider the case of a student who, perhaps due to a cognitive delay, does not correctly solve the problem. Rather than conclude that, "This child cannot do the Pythagorean theorem," or more broadly, that the child has a mathematics disability, we should focus our attention on truth and accuracy. We know what the child has not done yet, so what *can* this student do? Special educators are masterful at breaking standards and other academic requirements down into incremental tasks. In this example, the special educator might say that the real problem is text processing, not an inability to manipulate numbers. When the problem is presented as a story problem, the child "can't" do the Pythagorean theorem, but when the problem is presented with symbols and numbers, the child quickly calculates that $c^2 = a^2 + b^2$ or otherwise solves the problem without relying on text. Perhaps the student does not understand exponents, but does understand multiplication, or in this example, $c \times c = (a \times a) + (b \times b)$. Or perhaps the child does not yet grasp multiplication, but does understand the nature of addition as the total represented by groups of other numbers or objects. And so the task of incremental analysis continues. It is not done until we have more than the obvious information, such as the test item that the child missed. Our task as educators and parents remains incomplete until we have identified what the child can do, and the small incremental steps that are ahead of us, separating the present moment from the ultimate solution of the problem. A well-drafted Individualized Education Plan (IEP) will contain a series of such small increments, including a clear identification of what the student has already accomplished and the next steps to be accomplished.

The Individualized Education Plan (IEP)

The IEP is an important document that governs everything from classroom expectations to curriculum to assessment. This plan, as the name implies, must be focused on the individual needs of each student. While accommodations may be similar for several different students, the plan itself must be distinct, unique, and individual. The IEP is an evolving document, and the needs of your child may change. As a student gains skills, improves development, modifies behavior, or otherwise changes over the course of time, the IEP should also change.

The IEP is the result of the careful collaboration of a group of teachers, frequently labeled the IEP Team. This includes the classroom teacher, special education specialists, other specialists (such as speech pathologists), and school administrators. Parents should be personally involved in the IEP Team and should plan to attend meetings of the team. Your observations about the successes and challenges in the daily life of your child will provide valuable information that is more detailed and timely than may be obtained from classroom records.

Reporting Student Achievement of Standards— Beyond the Report Card

A frequent source of miscommunication between educators and parents has to do with the student report card. Many parents have contributed to this confusion by insisting that teachers must use a regular report card because parents perceive that this document is part of the "inclusion" to which their child is entitled. Although it is true that "regular" students routinely receive a traditional report card, this is among the many practices applied to regular education students that are of questionable value. For students who need very specific feedback on what they can do and have not yet done, the traditional report card provides inadequate information. Rather than focus on the report card, parents should focus on the imperatives of accuracy and fairness. What they really need to know is what standards their child has met and what specific incremental steps remain to be achieved in those areas where the student has not yet met a standard. When teachers and parents pretend that a standard has been met, or otherwise indicate achievement on a report card that is at variance with the facts, then the child does not benefit. In fact, when the adults in the system focus on factors other than objective indicators of real achievement, the child is left wondering what the meaning of success and failure really is. One of the best ways to resolve this dilemma is to make better use of the IEP and other documents that teachers and IEP members have collected. In fact, one of the best ways to individualize curriculum and instruction for a student with special needs is to start with an individualized report card that includes narrative descriptions, the IEP itself, evidence of student achievement in a portfolio, and narrative descriptions of what the child has achieved. This is far superior to the traditional set of letters and numbers that represent judgments which are typically inconsistent and poorly related to the individual needs of your child.

assistance and support

For Further Information

There are a number of national organizations devoted to helping parents of children with special needs advocate for their children. Because the needs of your child are likely to be complex and significantly different from the needs of other children, it might be helpful to find a group of parents across the nation who face similar challenges. You may feel that your circumstances are unique in your school, and thus you and your child can be made to feel very isolated. In fact, there are many parents who share the same challenges and successes, frustrations and triumphs. Here is a partial list of such organizations that you may wish to contact:

Children and Adults with Attention Deficit/Hyperactivity Disorder
(800) 233-4050
www.chadd.org

Council for Exceptional Children
(888) CEC-SPED
www.cec.sped.org

Learning Disabilities Association

(412) 341-1515

www.ldaamerica.org

National Center for Learning Disabilities

(888) 575-7373

www.ncld.org

National Information Center for Children and Youth with Disabilities

(800) 695-0285

www.nichcy.org

International Dyslexia Association (formerly, the Orton Dyslexia Society)

(800) 222-3123

www.interdys.org

Access America

www.disAbility.gov

Federation for Children with Special Needs

(617) 236-7210

www.fcsn.org

Alexander Graham Bell Association for the Deaf and Hard of Hearing

(202) 337-5220

www.agbell.org

American Foundation for the Blind

(800) 232-5463

www.afb.org

Autism Society of America

(800) 3AUTISM

www.autism-society.org

Brain Injury Association

(800) 444-6443

www.biausa.org

Tourette Syndrome Association, Inc.

(718) 224-2999

www.tsa-usa.org

Contact Numbers and Websites for the Illinois State Board of Education and National Resources

If you are interested in staying abreast of the latest educational policy as well as finding various ways to support and supplement your child's education, the numbers and sites below should prove helpful.

Illinois State Board of Education

http://www.isbe.state.il.us/

National Resources

U.S. Department of Education's Main Site

www.ed.gov

(800) USA-LEARN

Individuals with Disabilities Education Act (IDEA)

www.ed.gov/offices/OSERS/IDEA

National Assessment of Educational Progress (NAEP)

nces.ed.gov/nationsreportcard/site/home.asp

(202) 502-7458

National Center for Educational Statistics (NCES)

nces.ed.gov

(202) 502-7420

No Child Left Behind (President Bush's Statement on Education)

www.ed.gov/inits/nclb/index/html

Safe and Drug-free Schools

www.ed.gov/offices/OESE/SDFS

(800) 624-0100

144

20-Minute Learning Connection   **Contact Numbers and Websites for the California Department of Education and National Resources**

ILLINOIS

LEARNING

STANDARDS

with Home Learning Activities

Illinois Learning Standards* with Home Learning Activities

• English Language Arts • Mathematics • Science • Social Science

Annotated with Home Learning Activities by Abby Remer

The activities in this section are designed to help your child master the knowledge and skills required by the state of Illinois for students in middle and junior high school. Although there are many ways to approach the standards and activities, here are some suggestions:

- Read through the standards for all subjects. This will help you understand how the "power standards" (see Chapter 5) apply to the Illinois Learning Standards. Although not every standard is of equal value, reading the complete set of standards will give you a general overview of the knowledge and skills the state expects your child's school to cover.

- Choose activities that will appeal to your child. If your child especially enjoys writing, drawing, music, drama, or athletics, the icons will help you identify activities in those categories.

- Look for activities that will build skills in an area where your child needs help in school. Ask your child's teacher to identify the standards your child needs to work on, and select corresponding activities for your 20-Minute Learning Connection.

- If you are concerned that the arts or physical education have been reduced at your child's school, this guide offers many opportunities to reinforce their importance at home. Icons for fine arts, performing arts, and physical education will help you identify activities in these categories.

Materials needed for each activity are identified by the following icons:

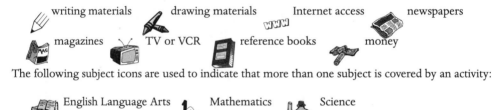

The following subject icons are used to indicate that more than one subject is covered by an activity:

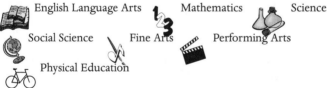

*The Illinois Learning Standards are reprinted in this guide with the permission of the Illinois State Board of Education. The Home Learning Activities in this guide, and their alignment to the Learning Standards, are the creation of the author and not the Illinois State Board of Education. Up-to-date information about the Illinois Learning Standards is available at http://www.isbe.state.il.us/ils/.

ILLINOIS

English Language Arts

Middle/Junior High School

State Goal 1: Read with understanding and fluency.

1.A.3a   Apply knowledge of word origins and derivations to comprehend words used in specific content areas (e.g., scientific, political, literary, mathematical).

Scientific origin game

 NOTE CARDS, TIMER *Have your child select an article on a scientific topic of interest. Read the article together and have your child highlight (or underline) any scientific terms. When you are done, have your child transfer the terms to individual note cards.*

Next, ask your child use a dictionary to find the origin of each word, writing its origin and definition on the back of the respective note card. Every night for three evenings, shuffle the "deck" with the terms facing up. Time your child as he goes through each term, defining it correctly in his own words, identifying its origin, and using it in a sentence. Each time your child gives the correct information, take the respective card out of the pile. Place any missed answer cards back into the deck. The game is over when your child has eliminated all the cards. Write down the time, and then compare this day's results to the next two games played on successive nights to see if you child can beat his own score!

1.A.3b Analyze the meaning of words and phrases in their context.

Switch-aroo

Have your child read aloud from a favorite book or magazine. When he comes across an unfamiliar word, look together at the surrounding word clues. Repeat the sentence aloud, saying "blank" in place of the unknown word, and then continue on. Ask your child what other word(s) might be substituted for the unknown word in the sentence so that it still makes sense. For instance, "José's mother is proud of him because he is <u>responsible</u>. *He always completes his chores on Saturday before he goes to the park." Ask your child to look for clues in the sentence that suggest a meaning for the unknown word. For example, José's mother is proud, so being responsible must be a good thing. Also, José does his work before he goes off to have fun. Then, ask your child to think of words that can be switched for the word* responsible *in the sentence; for instance, other words that might be used to describe José in this passage are* dutiful, reliable, dependable, *and* trustworthy. *Based on the surrounding word clues and the switched words, your child can conclude that a person who is described as responsible is "someone who does what he is supposed to do." Help your child understand whether the word(s) or definition he selected is close to the meaning of the original unknown word, asking him to use the dictionary as a resource. Ask your child to use the newly understood word in another sentence to enhance comprehension.*

www 📖 *Have your child study, interpret, and present a moving speech, such as Martin Luther King Jr.'s 1963 "I Have a Dream" speech at http://web66.coled.umn.edu/new/MLK/MLK.html or at http://www.7cs.com/king.html, or perhaps President Lincoln's 1863 "Gettysburg Address" at http://lcweb.loc.gov/exhibits/gadd/. How will your child's understanding of the speech impact the way he presents it to others? Afterward, discuss how it felt to speak passionate words spoken by a real person in history.* 🌐 🎬

1.B.3a   Preview reading materials, make predictions and relate reading to information from other sources.

Sneak preview

FICTION BOOK WITH DUST JACKET OR BACK COVER SUMMARY Have your child select a book from the library or at home that has information about the story on the jacket flap or on the back cover. Then, after reading it carefully at least three times, have your child predict the outcome of the book. After reading the story and comparing her predictions to the actual tale, have your child write her own version of the jacket/back-cover preview that will help grab the reader's attention without giving too much away!

1.B.3b   Identify text structure and create a visual representation (e.g., graphic organizer, outline, drawing) to use while reading.

1.B.3c   Continuously check and clarify for understanding (e.g., in addition to previous skills, draw comparisons to other readings).

1.B.3d   Read age-appropriate material with fluency and accuracy.

Past amusement

Tell your child that you are going to step back in time and entertain yourselves for the evening with a good book, never once using any electronic entertainment device for diversion, as people did for centuries before the technological age. Encourage your child to select material related to the same topic as a favorite show, online activity, or video game she might be missing.

1.C.3a Use information to form, explain and support questions and predictions.

What's next?

CHILDREN'S BOOKS Hone your child's ability to predict using existing information. While reading aloud (fiction or from the newspaper), stop at intervals and ask your child to predict what comes next. Ask which events or "clues" in the story led to her predictions. You can sharpen predicting abilities as well by repeating the activity with television shows (asking at commercial breaks what your child thinks will happen next) or stopping movies on the VCR at certain points for reflection. Also encourage your child to act out "what comes next," using a clear and articulate voice.

1.C.3b Interpret and analyze entire narrative text using story elements, point of view and theme.

Dear author

Ask your child if all readers share the same opinions about books, or if readers have personal preferences. Have your child read several (if possible, contrasting) reviews of a book he has read recently. (Online bookselling sites often feature a variety of reviews for individual titles.) Ask your child to compare and contrast the reviews. Does each reviewer support his or her position with details from the book? Do some of the reviewers express personal preferences that are consistent or inconsistent with your child's reading tastes? Then, have your child write a letter to the book's author sharing his interpretation. Your child's letter should demonstrate a careful reading and analysis of the work, and should be organized around a clearly stated main idea, supported with details from the story. After drafting, editing, and revising the correspondence (checking for correct spelling, punctuation, and grammar), mail the letter to the author in care of the book's publisher.

1.C.3c Compare, contrast and evaluate ideas and information from various sources and genres.

Titanic fact and fiction

Together, view the movie Titanic, *having your child take notes about the causes of the ship's demise and other historical information, such as the ship's technology. Then, ask your child to research information about the event in the library or explore the topic online using an Internet search engine. Afterward, have your child use his research to describe what in the movie version was fact and what was fiction. (For example, the movie version invents a romance in order to keep audiences involved.) Finally, check for comprehension by asking your child which sources he would rely on if making a documentary film about the Titanic, supporting the answer with clear reasons.*

1.C.3d   Summarize and make generalizations from content and relate them to the purpose of the material.

Northern/Southern perspectives

Have your child read Abraham Lincoln's Emancipation Proclamation (1863), which can be found by using a major Internet search engine or library resources. Help your child summarize the document's meaning and impact in her own words. Afterward, have your child imagine being a local newspaper reporter for a Southern journal who has just read the Proclamation. How will the reporter (your child) respond to Lincoln's words? Have your child think about the purpose of the Emancipation Proclamation, and how a reporter from the South might interpret the document. Then have your child take on the role of a Northern journalist. Your child's two revised and edited newspaper articles should include correct grammar, spelling, punctuation, and strong organizational structure, as well as convey a keen understanding of how Lincoln's ideas would have been received differently in the North and South.

1.C.3e   Compare how authors and illustrators use text and art across materials to express their ideas (e.g., foreshadowing, flashbacks, color, strong verbs, language that inspires).

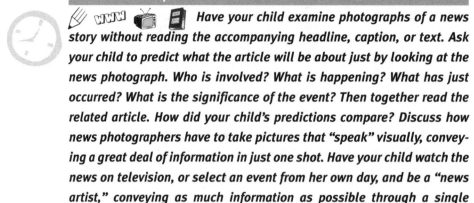

Have your child examine photographs of a news story without reading the accompanying headline, caption, or text. Ask your child to predict what the article will be about just by looking at the news photograph. Who is involved? What is happening? What has just occurred? What is the significance of the event? Then together read the related article. How did your child's predictions compare? Discuss how news photographers have to take pictures that "speak" visually, conveying a great deal of information in just one shot. Have your child watch the news on television, or select an event from her own day, and be a "news artist," conveying as much information as possible through a single image. Finally, examine your child's work and describe the information the image conveys. Then ask your child to explain the events and ideas she was trying to communicate in her image.

1.C.3f   Interpret tables that display textual information and data in visual formats.

STATE GOAL 2: Read and understand literature representative of various societies, eras and ideas.

2.A.3a   Identify and analyze a variety of literary techniques (e.g., figurative language, allusion, dialogue, description, word choice, dialect) within classical and contemporary works representing a variety of genres.

PORTRAITS Explain to your child that <u>dialect</u> is a regional pattern of speech. Authors use dialect to give readers information about where characters are from and how their speech sounds. Have your child read a book that includes character(s) who speak in dialect. (If you need help, ask your librarian to recommend a book.) Ask your child to find sections that include examples of dialect and read them aloud. What does the dialect convey about that character? What is it that the author is trying to communicate? Now, have your child be a "dialect detective." When watching television, ask your child to identify any character who speaks

with a dialect and describe how this helps build a sense of the person. Help your child detect various types of dialects and compare them and the information they convey. Finally, examine painted or photographed portraits and have your child invent a dialect for the person that helps convey something about his or her character based on the visual clues your child sees in the image.

2.A.3b Describe how the development of theme, character, plot and setting contribute to the overall impact of a piece of literature.

2.A.3c Identify characteristics and authors of various literary forms (e.g., short stories, novels, drama, fables, biographies, documentaries, poetry, science fiction).

Genre game show

LITERARY SELECTIONS OF NONFICTION, FICTION, DRAMA, AND POETRY Recruit another player for a game in which two contestants (one of which is your child) will compete to see who can correctly identify the genre for the greatest number of writing examples. Together, review the characteristics of the various genres. (Which genre is most likely to use quotation marks? rhymes? similes? dialogue?) In your role as game show host, select three to five different examples of each genre, without letting the contestants see your selections. Have the two contestants sit on separate chairs facing you. For each round, read a short selection from one of the examples and ask one contestant if it is A. nonfiction, B. fiction, C. drama, or D. poetry. The player gets a point if his or her answer is correct; if the answer is incorrect, the other contestant gets a chance to answer the same question and earns a point for a correct answer. If both players answer incorrectly, add the sample back into your selection for a later round. Have your child keep score. Alternate players for each round until all of your writng samples have been identified correctly. The first player to score ten points wins!

2.A.3d Identify ways that an author uses language structure, word choice and style to convey the author's viewpoint.

Analyze this!

POEM Have your child select a favorite poem or share one that you particularly like. Ask your child to imagine being an English professor teaching a class (household members) about the poem. Ask him to prepare the lecture by analyzing the poem, paying particular attention to how tone or meaning is conveyed through word choice, figurative language, sentence structure, line length, punctuation, rhythm, repetition, and rhyme. Your young professor should take "students" through the process of understanding the piece more deeply from his own findings. You, as one of the students, should pose questions or make observations about punctuation, rhythm, repetition, or rhyme to make the class more interesting and interactive.

2.B.3a   Respond to literary material from personal, creative and critical points of view.

Kid's view

WWW Tell your child that she can see her own opinions online. Have your child visit www.amazon.com, www.bn.com, or another book-selling site that encourages visitors to post reviews. Search for a book that she has read. On the page displaying the book, select the option of writing your own review. Have your child compose her own review, as described in the Standard, and then post in on the website.

Sports organizational review

Have your child read a sports article about a game that she played in or watched. Ask your child to reflect upon her personal experience of the game to offer insight into how and why the journalist chose to organize the account of the game in a particular manner. Additionally, have your child "review the review," by grading the effectiveness of the article's content, purpose, and organization. Afterward, have your child use her personal experience of the game to devise a different organizational structure for the article, and then draft and revise this new version.

Democratic book club

Have your child organize and run a book club for household members and friends. Before the first meeting, your child should create a list of recommended readings, with a brief, well-organized summary (without giving away the ending), and the reasons for the recommendation next to each title. Have your child organize his list of recommended readings by theme (stories set in the present, past, or future, for example), and then reproduce the list and give it to all book club members. At the first book club meeting, have your child orally elaborate on his summaries and the reasons for his recommendations, and then conduct a democratic vote to determine the order in which the books will be read and discussed at future book club meetings.

2.B.3b Compare and contrast common literary themes across various societies and eras.

Ancient constellation myths

WWW *Ask your child, "How can we prove that constellations have been around for centuries?" Together, read about the same star patterns we see today in the ancient constellation-related myths from different cultures (Greek and Roman, Native American—including Navajo and Iroquois—Chinese, and Indian) using library resources or any major Internet search engine. (Examples of Greek and Roman mythology of the constellations can be found online at http://www.emufarm.org/~cmbell/myth/myth.html.) Have your child chart the similarities and differences across cultures about the stars, their meaning, and the stories behind them.*

2.B.3c Analyze how characters in literature deal with conflict, solve problems and relate to real-life situations.

STATE GOAL 3: Write to communicate for a variety of purposes.

3.A.3 Write compositions that contain complete sentences and effective paragraphs using English conventions.

Now what?

✎ *MISCELLANEOUS HOUSEHOLD ITEMS Explain to your child that you are going to give her a "set up" for a story, which she will then develop into a written narrative. For props, find two unrelated household objects, such as an eggbeater, toothbrush, or Halloween mask. For the "set up," hold the items in your hands and then walk into the room, stop short, and ask, "Now what?" It's up to your child to take it from there, using the elements in the Standard to write a gripping tale, edited for correct spelling, grammar, punctuation, and tone.*

3.B.3a Produce documents that convey a clear understanding and interpretation of ideas and information and display focus, organization, elaboration and coherence.

3.B.3b Edit and revise for word choice, organization, consistent point of view and transitions among paragraphs using contemporary technology and formats suitable for submission and/or publication.

Chief editor game

✎ *WRITING SAMPLES Ask your child to imagine that she is the editor-in-chief of a magazine, and that she has been asked to consider three articles for publication. Use three samples of your child's writing (created for the activities in this book or for classroom assignments) as submissions. Ask your young editor-in-chief to consider each submission in relation to the Standard. Are sentences constructed properly? Is the punctuation correct? Are words spelled and used correctly? Ask your child to revise the three writing samples according to the guidelines in the Standard, as if she was editing the work for publication. As a first step in the revision process, have her re-read each piece and circle errors (misspelled words, incorrect grammar and punctuation, misplaced modifiers) on the original document. For the next step, ask her to review each writing sample sentence by sentence. Can any of the sentences be made*

more effective by simplifying them, or by combining them with another sentence to make one compound or complex sentence? Have your child write her editorial suggestions for stronger sentences on each original piece. Then, ask your child to play the role of the writer receiving these editorial suggestions, and have her rewrite each piece so it is fully polished for publication. Encourage your child to use this editorial process when preparing homework assignments.

Fine tuning

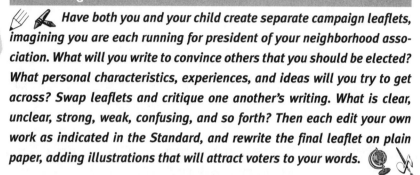

Have both you and your child create separate campaign leaflets, imagining you are each running for president of your neighborhood association. What will you write to convince others that you should be elected? What personal characteristics, experiences, and ideas will you try to get across? Swap leaflets and critique one another's writing. What is clear, unclear, strong, weak, confusing, and so forth? Then each edit your own work as indicated in the Standard, and rewrite the final leaflet on plain paper, adding illustrations that will attract voters to your words.

3.C.3a Compose narrative, informative, and persuasive writings (e.g., in addition to previous writings, literature reviews, instructions, news articles, correspondence) for a specified audience.

Put it in writing!

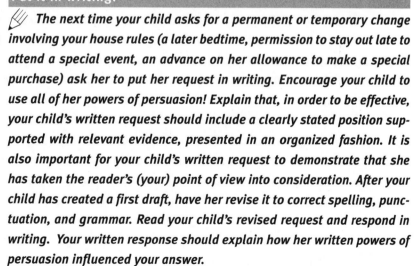

The next time your child asks for a permanent or temporary change involving your house rules (a later bedtime, permission to stay out late to attend a special event, an advance on her allowance to make a special purchase) ask her to put her request in writing. Encourage your child to use all of her powers of persuasion! Explain that, in order to be effective, your child's written request should include a clearly stated position supported with relevant evidence, presented in an organized fashion. It is also important for your child's written request to demonstrate that she has taken the reader's (your) point of view into consideration. After your child has created a first draft, have her revise it to correct spelling, punctuation, and grammar. Read your child's revised request and respond in writing. Your written response should explain how her written powers of persuasion influenced your answer.

Sports editor

 Ask your child to read an article or watch a television show about a favorite sport, team, or player (or attend a sporting event). Then ask her to choose one of the writing styles mentioned in the Standard and write an article about the event as the local newspaper sports editor. For example, she might choose to write a persuasive piece about why a particular player should be named Most Valuable Player, or an informative piece about the reasons a particular sport has become so popular. Before handing in the draft, have your young sports editor (your child) revise its organization for clarity.

3.C.3b Using available technology, produce compositions and multimedia works for specified audiences.

STATE GOAL 4: Listen and speak effectively in a variety of situations.

4.A.3a Demonstrate ways (e.g., ask probing questions, provide feedback to a speaker, summarize and paraphrase complex spoken messages) that listening attentively can improve comprehension.

Hiring help

 Tell your child to imagine that she runs a zoo, and you are coming to interview for a job. Have your child interview you as the prospective employee, asking about your talents, interests, and experience as it relates to working in the zoo. Before the interview, discuss with your child some of the different types of jobs available at zoos, including the individuals who feed and care for the animals, the ticket takers at the gates, the veterinarians who care for the animals' health, the architects who design the habitats for the animals, and so on. Then discuss some of the characteristics of good zoo employees: individuals who love animals, individuals who are knowledgeable about each of the animals' preferred diets and habitats, individuals who are observant (to notice when animals are sick or need things), individuals who are strong (for moving feed bags and equipment), and so forth. Explain to your child that, during the interview, she should

paraphrase your answers to each question to make sure she understands your response. At the end of the interview, ask your child which job she might place you in and why. Ask your child to cite the specific interview responses that led to her decision.

4.A.3b   Compare a speaker's verbal and nonverbal messages.

Actions speak louder than words

Together with your child, watch a videotape without the sound for a few minutes. (For this activity, you need to select a video with human actors—no nature shows or cartoons.) Ask your child to keenly observe how the actors convey ideas through body language. Discuss what you can infer from certain movements, facial gestures, or lack of them in the segment. Rewind and watch the tape with the sound on to see if your child's ideas about the meaning behind the actors' gestures are accurate. Periodically repeat this activity throughout the tape. Determine whether knowing more of the story and the characters as time goes on helps in this game. Later, mime out a short conversation between the two of you, using only body language and no speech, checking afterward to determine if you both truly understood what the other was trying to "say."

4.A.3c   Restate and carry out multistep oral instructions.

Application, please

APPLICATION FORMS FOR A VARIETY OF SERVICES First, have your child read an application and then restate the instructions in his own words. Then, have your child fill out the application (for a public library card, bank savings account, sports club, league membership) or help you fill one out for yourself. Use these applications without really submitting them, just for use with practicing the Standard. Review the importance of following all directions carefully in order to expedite the application process.

Cooking 101

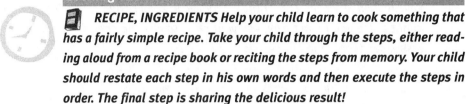

RECIPE, INGREDIENTS *Help your child learn to cook something that has a fairly simple recipe. Take your child through the steps, either reading aloud from a recipe book or reciting the steps from memory. Your child should restate each step in his own words and then execute the steps in order. The final step is sharing the delicious result!*

4.A.3d Demonstrate the ability to identify and manage barriers to listening (e.g., noise, speaker credibility, environmental distractions).

Distraction game

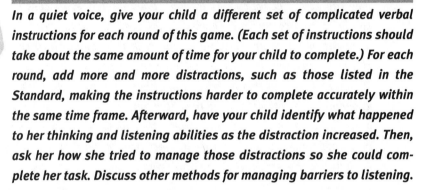

In a quiet voice, give your child a different set of complicated verbal instructions for each round of this game. (Each set of instructions should take about the same amount of time for your child to complete.) For each round, add more and more distractions, such as those listed in the Standard, making the instructions harder to complete accurately within the same time frame. Afterward, have your child identify what happened to her thinking and listening abilities as the distraction increased. Then, ask her how she tried to manage those distractions so she could complete her task. Discuss other methods for managing barriers to listening.

4.B.3a Deliver planned oral presentations, using language and vocabulary appropriate to the purpose, message and audience; provide details and supporting information that clarify main ideas; and use visual aids and contemporary technology as support.

You are there

Ask your child to close her eyes for a moment and think of a favorite place. Then without saying the name of the location, have your child describe as much as possible about it and her experience there. Can you guess the location from the description? Reverse roles and then discuss which aspects of the descriptions were most helpful in imagining the place. Afterward, both of you should draw your location and discuss how visual representations capture things that words might not, and vice versa. (For example, art might convey the exact color of the ocean or lake at a location, but not the sounds of the waves.)

4.B.3b Design and produce reports and multi-media compositions that represent group projects.

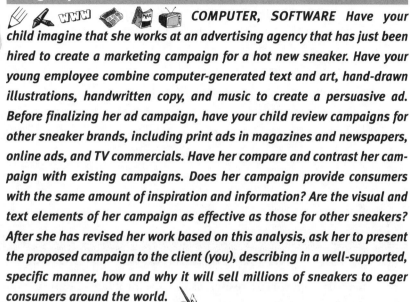

Ad agency

COMPUTER, SOFTWARE Have your child imagine that she works at an advertising agency that has just been hired to create a marketing campaign for a hot new sneaker. Have your young employee combine computer-generated text and art, hand-drawn illustrations, handwritten copy, and music to create a persuasive ad. Before finalizing her ad campaign, have your child review campaigns for other sneaker brands, including print ads in magazines and newspapers, online ads, and TV commercials. Have her compare and contrast her campaign with existing campaigns. Does her campaign provide consumers with the same amount of inspiration and information? Are the visual and text elements of her campaign as effective as those for other sneakers? After she has revised her work based on this analysis, ask her to present the proposed campaign to the client (you), describing in a well-supported, specific manner, how and why it will sell millions of sneakers to eager consumers around the world.

4.B.3c Develop strategies to manage or overcome communication anxiety and apprehension (e.g., sentence outlining, note cards).

With the greatest of ease

Help your child develop strategies for overcoming any anxiety when communicating to groups, with adults, or in formal situations. Select one of the activities in this book that requires a presentation and use it as a "practice run." Strategies to ease anxiety include rehearsing in front of a receptive audience, placing outlines or key words on note cards, stamping one's feet to bring oneself back into the room if feeling dizzy or light-headed, rehearsing the presentation enough times that it becomes second nature, thinking of everyone in the audience doing something embarrassing (thus making them very human), and inviting a friend to the real presentation for moral support. Have your child ask others what methods they use to dissipate anxiety, trying them all on for size to see which ones "fit."

4.B.3d Use verbal and nonverbal communication strategies to maintain communications and to resolve conflict.

Alternative result

Together, watch a videotape of a movie or television show that is new to both of you and that has conflict as a main theme. Stop it two-thirds of the way through and have your child articulate the main problem. Each of you will now be "screen writers," devising and writing a fascinating and unexpected resolution to the movie or show. Afterward, watch the end of the film to see how your screenplays differ from the original. Then, vote on which of the three was the best and why, making sure to discuss additional strategies for resolving conflict.

STATE GOAL 5: Use the language arts to acquire, assess and communicate information.

5.A.3a Identify appropriate resources to solve problems or answer questions through research.

Young consumer report

ACCESS TO CARD CATALOG, READER'S GUIDE TO PERIODICAL LITERATURE, A COMPUTER CATALOG Have your child research the very best sneakers (or backpack or sports equipment) on the market using the elements listed in the materials list above. Next, ask your young analyst to write a "consumer report" (with appropriate graphs and charts), supporting his findings with specific references and citations.

5.A.3b Design a project related to contemporary issues (e.g., real-world math, career development, community service) using multiple sources.

Extinct is forever!

ANIMAL AND ENVIRONMENTAL RIGHTS ORGANIZATIONAL LITERATURE Have your child pretend he is a speechwriter for an animal rights organization. Ask him to write and deliver a persuasive, well-

argued speech at a "press conference" meant to gain support for the group's cause. Your young speechwriter must research the topic before drafting a moving oration. He should use library materials, animal and environmental rights organizational literature, and or the Internet for information. (Helpful background on endangered species can be found at http://www.animalsindanger.com/and http://library.thinkquest.org/ 25014/english.index.shtml.) After researching the topic, have your child list and then organize the points he will make. How can your child order the facts and opinions to make the most persuasive speech possible? (For instance, perhaps facts with the most emotional impact should be saved for last.) Have your child deliver the speech in a clear, articulate, and impassioned manner to the press (household members and friends).

5.B.3a   Choose and analyze information sources for individual, academic and functional purposes.

Fad diets

With your child, watch television advertisements or listen to radio ads for diet products and weight-loss foods (or any "miracle" cure). Discuss which claims seem likely and which do not (such as losing ten pounds in two days). How does the fact that the advertiser's claims are broadcast publicly affect what you might believe about them? Would you be more or less likely to believe the claims if they were printed in a scientific or medical journal? How about if they were confirmed by a "real person" (as opposed to a paid actor) on TV? What if you heard the claims from a friend? Based on your conclusions, discuss the methods advertisers use to persuade customers to buy other categories of products (toys, clothes, sneakers, etc.).

5.B.3b   Identify, evaluate and cite primary sources.

First-hand history I

PRIMARY SOURCE MATERIALS SUCH AS FAMILY MEMORABILIA, LETTERS, GOVERNMENT RECORDS, PHOTOGRAPHS, NEWSPAPER CLIPPINGS, CERTIFICATES Have your child study the history of a relative (perhaps a grandparent or aunt or uncle) up close by examining <u>primary</u>

sources (those created during the time period being studied), including photographs, letters, and personal memorabilia. Together, search your home to assemble a variety of primary sources and piece together a "history" of the person's life. Together, identify the information each item reveals about the individual and discuss its significance in relation to the person's history and the era in which he or she lived. Move to the next step.

5.C.3a Plan, compose, edit and revise documents that synthesize new meaning gleaned from multiple sources.

First-hand history II

After evaluating each item, have your child write a journal entry reflecting a day in the life of the selected individual. Make sure she incorporates elements from the different primary sources she studied to enhance the diary entry and to provide a realistic description of a place and time in history.

5.C.3b Prepare and orally present original work (e.g., poems, monologues, reports, plays, stories) supported by research.

A bug's tale

Have your child select a bug to research—a ladybug, grasshopper, beetle, ant, butterfly, praying mantis, ant, or any other insect that catches his fancy. Help your child research the insect, using online resources and library reference materials. As your child conducts his research, show him how to use an index, a table of contents, an alphabetical listing, and online search engines such as Yahoo and Alta Vista. If possible, obtain a live specimen and use what you have learned from the research to create a safe, comfortable habitat for the insect so your child can observe its behavior. Based on his research, ask your child to write a "day-in-the-life" poem from the bug's point of view, and then set the poem to music. Your child can use an existing melody or invent an entirely new one, but his song should include several facts about the insect obtained from his research and observation.

For this activity, you and your child will write a poem together, including assonance, alliteration, and similes. To prepare, look up the definitions for the terms in a dictionary or find the definitions online by typing each term into any major Internet search engine. Next, together think of as many silly examples of <u>assonance</u>, (the repetition of vowel sounds, i.e., feet dare to meet), <u>alliteration</u> (the repetition of initial consonant sounds in neighboring words, i.e., jumping jars, pickled pixies), and <u>similes</u> (the comparison of two unlike things using "like" or "as," i.e., "Her eyes were shining like stars in the midnight sky.") as you can. (If you need help getting started, you'll find many entertaining examples in Lewis Carroll's poem, "The Walrus and the Carpenter" in Through the Looking Glass.) Then create a poem together, using your favorite examples from your practice session. Add assonance, alliteration, and similes to your everyday conversation for fun, and point out examples when you read together.

CHILDREN'S BOOKS Explain to your child that a <u>synonym</u> is a word with a similar meaning (delicious, tasty), an <u>antonym</u> is a word with an opposite meaning (fast, slow), a <u>homophone</u> is one of two or more words that sound the same but have different meanings (to, two, too), and a <u>homograph</u> is one of two words that are spelled the same, but have different meanings (wind: a breeze, wind: to twist or wrap around). Find some sentences in a favorite storybook and ask your child to name synonyms or antonyms for the adjectives and adverbs you point out. Then ask your child to create his own sentences and then substitute synonyms or antonyms for descriptive words to create new sentences. Give your child bonus points if he is able to incorporate homophones or homographs into the sentences!

5.C.3c   Take notes, conduct interviews, organize and report information in oral, visual and electronic formats.

Roots historian

Help your child generate questions to ask older relatives about why and how the family first came to the United States. Even if the original relatives who arrived are not available, your child can pose them to you or another knowledgeable adult. When interviewing, your child should take careful notes and then use them to develop an outline for an oral presentation that she will give at the next family gathering. Also, have your child create an illustrated "roots" poster, depicting the relatives who first came, where they began, how they traveled, and what it was like when they first arrived. Your child should use this poster as a visual aid during her presentation. Have her make smaller versions of her poster to give to family members as gifts.

If I had a pet giraffe

Have your child select a very unlikely animal for a household pet, such as a giraffe, crocodile, porpoise, or aardvark. Have him answer the question, "What would I have to do if I had a pet _____?" Have your child investigate online or at the library what he would have to do, learn, get, and change in your home to accommodate this new pet. After gathering all the information, have your child organize it into a persuasive essay that describes why getting such an animal would be a good idea. Then, have your child argue the opposite, stating in an opposing essay why it might not be such a wise idea for your household or the animal!

Mathematics

Middle/Junior High School

STATE GOAL 6: Demonstrate and apply a knowledge and sense of numbers, including numeration and operations (addition, subtraction, multiplication, division), patterns, ratios and proportions.

6.A.3   Represent fractions, decimals, percentages, exponents and scientific notation in equivalent forms.

Product numbers hunt

HOUSEHOLD PRODUCTS Together with your child, search the kitchen cabinets, refrigerator, and the bathroom cabinet for an array of products with weights and/or sizes listed in various forms (whole or mixed numbers, fractions, decimals, and so forth). Place them all on a

table. Ask your child to divide the items into groups with similar expressions (all the products listed in ounces together, all those in pounds together, and so forth). Then have your child line up the items in each group from the smallest to largest quantity. Hence, a .5 ounce bottle of perfume would be placed before a 2.5 ounce jar of hand cream. Then, ask your child to write the amount of each product in a different form, changing decimals to fractions, fractions to mixed numbers, and so forth. Thus, a 2.5 ounce jar of hand cream could be written as 2 $\frac{1}{2}$ ounces or 2 $\frac{5}{10}$ ounces, and so forth. Each time your child gets one of his equivalent format answers correct, he can take the product off the table, continuing until none is left. Play a second round with other household products that display different number formats and try to have your child "beat the clock," setting a timer that allows forty-five seconds for writing an answer for each product.

6.B.3a   Solve practical computation problems involving whole numbers, integers and rational numbers.

6.B.3b   Apply primes, factors, divisors, multiples, common factors and common multiples in solving problems.

6.B.3c   Identify and apply properties of real numbers including pi, squares, and square roots.

Orange mathematics

ORANGE, STRING, RULER, KNIFE, CARDBOARD Challenge your child to find the approximate <u>circumference</u> (the distance around a circle) of an orange using just string and a ruler. (Wrap the string around the orange once, mark its length, unfold, and then measure it against the ruler.) Now help your child find the orange's circumference using the formula circumference = π x diameter, to prove whether his estimated string measurement is correct. (If necessary, review that the <u>diameter</u> is a straight line passing through the center of the circle and meeting the circumference at each end.) Have your child find the diameter of the orange either by cutting the orange in half and measuring its diameter, or placing the cardboard flat across the top of the orange and measuring the distance from the table top to the cardboard. Then ask your child

to plug the diameter's number into the formula. Your child should now solve the formula, using 3.14 for π to test whether his string estimate is correct. As you share the orange, point out to your child that the circumference is always just a bit more than three times the size of the diameter. Together review information about circumference and test yourselves with a few online examples at http://www.ncsa.uiuc.edu/edu/RSE/RSE orange/application.html.

6.C.3a   Select computational procedures and solve problems with whole numbers, fractions, decimals, percents and proportions.

6.C.3b   Show evidence that computational results using whole numbers, fractions, decimals, percents and proportions are correct and/or that estimates are reasonable.

Catalogue delight

 ✍ WWW GIFT CATALOG, CALCULATOR Have your child imagine that she has just received a $1,000 check from a mysterious benefactor. The note with the check says your child can buy whatever she wants with the money, as long as she also buys gifts for others in the household. Also, she is required to make all of her purchases from one catalog. Have your child select her purchases (keeping a running estimate of her total) and then fill out the catalog order form. To complete the form, she should total the order and calculate the sales tax and shipping costs as indicated in the instructions. If her total after sales tax and shipping exceeds her $1,000 budget, ask her to revise her order. She should do all of her calculations first, and then use the calculator to check her work. For additional fun, together play the "Estimated Total Price with Sales Tax and Tip" game at http://www.aaamath.com/rat68-tip-estimate.html, which requires similar calculations.

6.D.3   Apply ratios and proportions to solve practical problems.

Sugar sip

✎ 🌐 *SODA OR JUICE BOTTLES/CANS Have your child find the amount of sugar in an individual serving of soda or juice on the product label. Have your child translate the grams of sugar in one serving from a ratio to fraction form. For example, x grams: 1 serving, which is the ratio form, becomes x grams/1 serving in fraction form. (If necessary, review information about ratios at http://www.mathleague.com/help/ratio/ratio.htm.) Now, have your child create and compute an equation that reveals how much sugar she drinks in a week's worth of juice or soda. (If your child drinks 1 can of soda or glass of juice a day, the equation would be: (x grams/1 serving) × (7 servings/1 week) = 7x grams/week. Have your child continue with this activity, looking for the sugar content in a single serving of cereal, cookies, ice cream, candy bars, and so forth to get an accurate sense of how many grams of sugar she takes in a week.*

STATE GOAL 7: Estimate, make and use measurements of objects, quantities and relationships and determine acceptable levels of accuracy.

7.A.3a Measure length, capacity, weight/mass and angles using sophisticated instruments (e.g., compass, protractor, trundle wheel).

Pie puzzle

✎ *COMPASS, SCISSORS, PROTRACTOR, CLOCK Have your child draw two large circles of different sizes using a protractor; then cut out the circles. Next, ask your child to draw five diameter lines within both circles. Each diameter should be a different distance from any of the others so that the "slices" aren't uniform in size. Now, have your child use the protractor to find the degree of the angle for each pie segment, writing down the corresponding number on its "slice." Have your child total the measurements to make sure the sum equals 360 degrees. Cut up the two pies into segments and mix them in a pile. Using the marked degree calculations on each slice, have your child reconfigure the two circles as quickly as possible, trying to beat his time in each successive round.*

7.A.3b Apply the concepts and attributes of length, capacity, weight/mass, perimeter, area, volume, time, temperature and angle measures in practical situations.

Brownie bake

✍ *TWO BAKING PANS (ONE SQUARE, ONE RECTANGULAR WITH ONE SIDE EQUAL TO THE SIDES OF THE SQUARE PAN) BROWNIE RECIPE AND INGREDIENTS, RULER Have your child help you prepare a brownie recipe (or other bar-type baking recipe), using the opportunity to practice measuring various volumes (ounces, cups, teaspoons, and so forth). Before baking, have your child pull out the two baking pans mentioned in the materials list. Have your child calculate the <u>perimeter</u> for each pan (2 × height + 2 × width = perimeter). Ask your child to predict the amount (volume) each pan will hold. Have your child fill the large pan with water and pour it into the smaller square pan. What happens? The extra water spills out, demonstrating why it's important to have the right size baking pan before pouring in the batter! Have your child prove that changes in perimeter affect volume through math as well, plugging the numbers from the two pans into the formula lwh = v (length × width × height = volume). Is the volume of the bigger pan larger than the smaller one? Finally, have your child pour the batter into the pan size called for in the recipe, or one with the same or slightly larger volume capacity. (If the recipe calls for a 9 × 13 × 1 inch pan, then you can use any pan that would have a volume capacity of at least 117.)*

7.B.3 Select and apply instruments including rulers and protractors and units of measure to the degree of accuracy required.

Recipe switch-aroo

wWw 📋 *RECIPE AND INGREDIENTS, MEASURING TOOLS, U.S. VOLUME UNIT CHART Together, review the breakdown of U.S. volume units for teaspoons, tablespoons, ounces, pints, quarts, etc. using a chart from a basic recipe book or one found online at http://www.aaamath.com/mea69-us-volume.html. (If you use the website, scroll down to the "Play" section for fun interactive games that test your volume memory.)*

Next, find a recipe to cook together. When measuring the ingredients, have your child put her knowledge of units of measure to work. Tell her that she needs to measure the ingredients accurately, but she cannot use the unit of measure called for in the recipe. So, for example, if the recipe calls for a tablespoon of an ingredient, she must use an equivalent measure (three teaspoons) instead. Tell your child that this is an "open book test," so she can consult the measurement chart as often as necessary. Enjoy the completed recipe together!

7.C.3a   Construct a simple scale drawing for a given situation.

Interior designer

✎ *TAPE MEASURE, CARDBOARD, SCISSORS* Ask your child to imagine that he is your newly hired interior designer. You will pretend to want to rearrange the furniture in each room at home, but first need to see a floor plan of what it will look like. Have your child/young interior designer use a tape measure to measure the dimensions of each room and then calculate the <u>area</u> for each (width × height). Your child also should note the dimensions and the perimeter for the main pieces of furniture (beds, tables, chairs), measuring the approximate amount of space each piece occupies on the floor. (If necessary, review the formula for <u>perimeter</u>, which is 2 (l +w), with your child.) Have your young designer draw a floor plan to scale on plain paper, draw each piece of furniture to scale on cardboard or thick paper, and then cut out the furniture shapes out and label them "bed," "couch," etc. Have him arrange the cardboard shapes on the floor plan to devise inventive ways of reorganizing your furniture without really having to move it!*

7.C.3b   Use concrete and graphic models and appropriate formulas to find perimeters, areas, surface areas and volumes of two- and three-dimensional regions.

Geo-jigsaw puzzle race

First, both you and your child will create abstract pieces for jigsaw puzzles. Draw lines on construction paper to create straight-edged geometric shapes—squares, triangles, and rectangles of *different dimensions so that no space remains. (Your respective pieces of paper should resemble a geometric jigsaw puzzle.) Then cut out the shapes to create your puzzle pieces. Now review the formulas for finding the <u>perimeter</u> (the sum of the lengths of the sides) and <u>area</u> (area = length x width) for these forms using an encyclopedia or math reference book, or by going online at http://pittsford.monroe.edu/jefferson/calfieri/geometry/geoframe.html or http://www.math.com/tables/index.html. With pencil and scrap paper for calculations in hand, start the game. Each player must find the perimeter and area for every piece in his or her puzzle. After doing so, the player can put the piece in its correct place to eventually reform the original rectangular puzzle composition. The player whose entire set of calculations is correct and whose puzzle is complete first, wins! Play successive rounds with new pieces of cut construction paper to hone your skills.*

STATE GOAL 8: Use algebraic and analytical methods to identify and describe patterns and relationships in data, solve problems and predict results.

8.A.3a Apply the basic properties of commutative, associative, distributive, transitive, inverse, identity, zero, equality and order of operations to solve problems.

8.A.3b Solve problems using linear expressions, equations and inequalities.

Popped equations

WWW *LARGE BOWL OF UNBUTTERED POPCORN, SMALL CUP, NOTE CARDS LABELED INDIVIDUALLY WITH SIGNS FOR =, +, −, ×, AND ÷ Begin by asking your child what clue exists within the word "equation" that provides a hint about this type of mathematical expression. The idea of "equal" is the key here. In a <u>linear</u> <u>equation</u>, the expression on the left side of the equal sign has the same value as the expression on the right side. Start simply. Place 3 popped corn kernels on the table. Place the + sign after them, and then put down 8 popped corn kernels and the = sign. Place the empty cup on the right side of the equal sign, explaining*

that this represents the unknown variable. Ask your child to solve the equation, putting the correct amount of popped corn kernels into the cup (11). Together, eat the correct "variable" while you create a harder popped-corn equation ($3x - 2 = 7$). Remind your child that to keep both sides of the equation equal, you must do exactly the same thing to each side. Here, add 2 popped corn kernels to each side ($3x - 2 + 2 = 7 + 2$). Have your child simplify the expression, giving you $3x = 9$. Finally, have your child divide each side by 3 (i.e., $\frac{3x}{3} = \frac{9}{3}$) and then simplify for the final value of the variable ($x = 3$). Continue snacking on the found "variables" while your child works on increasingly difficult equations. Find further explanations and expressions to solve at http://www.aaamath. com/equ725-equation6.html.

8.B.3 Use graphing technology and algebraic methods to analyze and predict linear relationships and make generalizations from linear patterns.

8.C.3 Apply the properties of numbers and operations including inverses in algebraic settings derived from economics, business and the sciences.

8.D.3a Solve problems using numeric, graphic or symbolic representations of variables, expressions, equations and inequalities.

Mayan math

 Together, explore the symbols the ancient Mayans developed to represent numbers by researching the topic using an Internet search engine or library resources, or exploring "Maya Mathematics" online at http://www.michielb.nl/maya/astro.html. Have your child use the symbols to express the individual ages of everyone in your household. Then play a game that requires scorekeeping, and have your child keep score using Mayan mathematic symbols.

8.D.3b Propose and solve problems using proportions, formulas and linear functions.

3 for $1.00

✍ *Visit the supermarket together and find sales where an item costs less if you buy it in bulk (e.g., 3 peaches for $1.00 or one peach for $.39) Have your child create a two-column chart listing "sale price per unit/item" and "regular price per unit/item." For each example you discover in the store, have your child use division to discover the unit price for the items if bought in bulk, and then compare this to how much each unit would cost if bought at the regular price. While on line or at home, have your child do the math for all the items you bought on sale to tell you exactly how much money you saved today!*

8.D.3c   Apply properties of powers, perfect squares and square roots.

Root it out

📶 📱 *CARROTS, KNIFE Explain that, whereas <u>exponents</u> indicate the number of times that the base number is multiplied by itself, <u>square roots</u> are the number which, when multiplied by itself, produces the base. For instance, the square root of 4 is 2 (2 x 2 = 4). Have your child demonstrate this square "root" by breaking a carrot (a "root" vegetable) into four equal pieces in length, and placing them in a pile. Next, ask your child to "write" a multiplication equation with the carrot pieces in which the same factor is multiplied by itself to give you the original number (e.g., 2 carrot bits x 2 carrot bits = 4 carrot bits). While you each snack on a "root" (2 carrot pieces), have your child find the roots for 9 (3), 16 (4), 25 (5), and 36 (6). To help your child, continue cutting and using the carrot bits to reinforce the idea of square roots. For further explanation and practice, use library materials or go to http://www. math.com/school/subject1/lessons/S1U1L9GL.html. Finally, together review the order of operations for equations that include numbers in exponent form. They should be tackled right after computing any operations inside parentheses or above and below a fraction bar. See this demonstrated by clicking on "order of operations" at http://www.harcourtschool.com/glossary/math/glossary8.html, or use library resources as an alternative. Finally, ask your child to express, in her own words, a succinct definition for square roots.*

STATE GOAL 9: Use geometric methods to analyze, categorize and draw conclusions about points, lines, planes and space.

9.A.3a Draw or construct two- and three- dimensional geometric figures including prisms, pyramids, cylinders and cones.

9.A.3b Draw transformation images of figures, with and without the use of technology.

Flip and turn

 Ask your child to imagine that a world famous clothing store has just hired him to design a tee shirt for kids. But the client has a specific request. The store wants a tee shirt with one image on the front that is transformed on the back. Have your child sketch a fairly simple design with basic geometric shapes on graph paper. Then view illustrations of translation, rotation, and reflection online at http://www.harcourtschool.com/glossary/math/glossary6.html. Have your young designer make a final sketch for the front of the tee shirt, and then apply one of the transformation concepts viewed on the website for the back of the tee shirt. Ask your child to present the design to the client (you and other household members), explaining specifically, using mathematical terms, how the image has been manipulated for an intriguing result.

9.A.3c Use concepts of symmetry, congruency, similarity, scale, perspective, and angles to describe and analyze two- and three-dimensional shapes found in practical applications (e.g., geodesic domes, A-frame houses, basketball courts, inclined planes, art forms, blueprints).

Architectural geometry I

 Explain to your child that an innovative technology company has come to her architectural firm for a design proposal for its new head-quarters. The company is open to any idea, as long as the building is not shaped like a standard cube. Before starting any sketches, your young architect needs to become familiar with existing buildings that have different geometric forms. For each example, your young architect should identify the geometric properties (planes, angles, area, and so forth) of

the shape of the building. Use library resources or the Internet to view I.M. Pei's famous pyramid-shaped entrance to the Louvre Museum in Paris. See the sharp points of the East Wing in the National Gallery of Art in Washington D.C., and also examine the tilt of Pisa's famed leaning cylindrical tower. Finally, study the ancient Egyptian pyramids. Then move to "Architectural geometry II" in Standard 9.C.3b.

9.B.3 Identify, describe, classify and compare two- and three- dimensional geometric figures and models according to their properties.

Picture perfect

 Have your child hone her identifying skills at the interactive site on polygons and solid shapes at http://pittsford.monroe.edu/jefferson/cal fieri/geometry/geoframe.html. Afterward, take the related online quizzes to test your skills.

9.C.3a Construct, develop and communicate logical arguments (informal proofs) about geometric figures and patterns.

π toss I

 CARDBOARD, COMPASS OR STRING Have your child tie a string around a pencil and then hold the loose end in place with one finger while drawing a circle (or use a compass). Ask your child to create at least three circles of different sizes. Together, review how to find the radius and diameter of a circle, and then help your child write the correct circumference and area directly on each example. (You can find information in a reference book or online at http://www.mathleague.com/help/geometry /polygons.htm#circle and http://www.mathleague.com/help/geome try/area.htm.) Ask your child to examine the "πs," and predict which one will travel the farthest if all of them are tossed with the same amount of force. Your child should support her statements by referring to the "πs" themselves, experience with a Frisbee, or any other relevant information. To test your child's prediction, find an outdoor space and move on to "π toss II" (Standard 10.A.3c).

9.C.3b Develop and solve problems using geometric relationships and models, with and without the use of technology.

Architectural geometry II

✎ STIFF PAPER Have your child review her findings in part I. Then, as a young architect, have her create at least two scale models of geometric buildings to show the client. Your child should write a brief description of why the properties of each of her proposed geometric buildings will meet the needs of the client. (For instance, how will the curved walls of a cylinder or the slanted walls or pointed roof of a pyramid work in terms of an office space?) Your architect should write and edit her work, using correct spelling, grammar, punctuation, persuasive tone, and evocative imagery to "sell" the client on her proposal. After the client (household members and/or friends) reads the material and examines the models, have your child follow up with an articulate, poised, and clear presentation to the client to reinforce her ideas and understanding of geometry as it applies to architecture.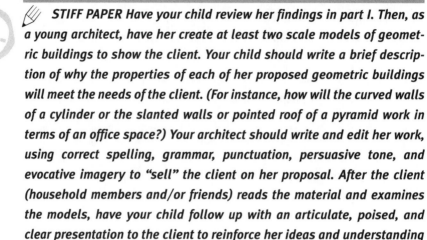

9.D.3 Compute distances, lengths and measures of angles using proportions, the Pythagorean theorem and its converse.

Constant right-angle triangles

✎ WWW 🗐 LONG RULER, TAPE MEASURE The Pythagorean theorem relates to triangles that contain a right angle. Together, learn about the theorem (triangle leg A^2 + triangle leg B^2 = hypotenuse^2, or $a^2 + b^2 = c^2$) using math reference books or an encyclopedia, or online at http://www.harcourtschool.com/glossary/math/glossary8.html. Then get online interactive practice at http://www.gomath.com/algebra /pythagorean.asp. Finally, create right angles with different length legs against your own walls. Kneel by a wall and place a ruler diagonally from a spot on the floor to a spot on the wall. The wall and floor are the legs and the ruler is the hypotenuse. Have your child use the tape measure to measure two of the variables (either both legs or one leg and the hypotenuse) and then complete the equation for the unknown quantity. Follow up by having your child research Pythagoras himself (using an Internet search engine or library materials). Afterward, ask your child to

write a letter to Pythagoras, describing what it is like to learn and use his theory today, more than two thousand years later. Your child should edit and revise his letter for correct spelling, punctuation, and grammar, and clearly communicate his understanding of the theorem.

STATE GOAL 10: Collect, organize and analyze data using statistical methods; predict results; and interpret uncertainty using concepts of probability.

10.A.3a Construct, read and interpret tables, graphs (including circle graphs) and charts to organize and represent data.

Home archaeology

TWO BLANKETS, TWO TAPE MEASURES, BALL OF STRING, SCISSORS, FIVE TO TEN SMALL OBJECTS Before asking your child to participate in this activity, set up the "dig" on the floor. First, spread a large blanket flat on the floor. Open both tape measures as far as possible and place them on the blankets from edge to edge so they cross at the center. The horizontal tape measure is the x axis and the vertical tape measure is the y axis. Now place five to ten items from your home in the different quadrants. Cover the "dig" with another blanket, serving as the top layer of "dirt." Bring your child in and ask her to imagine that she is an archaeologist of the future, who is uncovering this "find" from an ordinary twenty-first century home. Like all archaeologists, your child must carefully record any finds on paper, which she will do on graph paper, before removing them for further study. Your child should draw an x and y axis in the center of a piece of graph paper and then carefully dig (pull away the blanket) to see what she will uncover. Eureka! Your child has found many items in this small plot! Ask your child to carefully mark the items on the graph paper as they appear in the dig. Have your child use taut string to draw straight lines from the x and y axes to each object to help determine the correct points on which the objects sit. When transferring the information to the graph, your child should use the inch marks on the tape measure as the coordinates on the graph. Hence, if your child discovers a coin 5 inches to the left of the central point and 7 inches up, its

coordinates on the graph would be (x,y) = (–5, 7). Have your child carefully chart all the objects before removing them. Then, have your young archaeologist examine all the objects, and from the point of view of a future scientist, discuss what the materials reveal about this era of human civilization.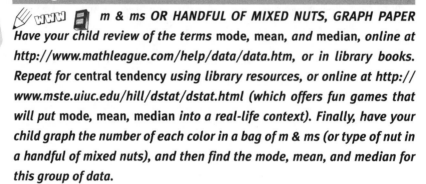

10.A.3b Compare the mean, median, mode and range, with and without the use of technology.

Average m & ms

m & ms OR HANDFUL OF MIXED NUTS, GRAPH PAPER Have your child review of the terms mode, mean, *and* median, *online at http://www.mathleague.com/help/data/data.htm, or in library books. Repeat for* central tendency *using library resources, or online at http:// www.mste.uiuc.edu/hill/dstat/dstat.html (which offers fun games that will put* mode, mean, median *into a real-life context). Finally, have your child graph the number of each color in a bag of m & ms (or type of nut in a handful of mixed nuts), and then find the mode, mean, and median for this group of data.*

10.A.3c Test the reasonableness of an argument based on data and communicate their findings.

π toss II

CIRCLES FROM "π TOSS I," MEASURING TAPE, GRAPH PAPER Have your child toss each different sized "π" separately, making sure to use the same amount of force. After every toss, your child should measure the distance the "π" travels, marking it on the circle itself next to the information for its circumference and area. Next have your child create a line or bar graph and record the accumulated data. (The distance traveled should run along the left side and the circumference/area should run along the bottom line.) What conclusions can your child draw from her experiment about the distance traveled by increasingly large circles given a constant force (how hard your child throws)? Ask your child to compare the results to her initial predictions. How did they match up? Was there a consideration your child might have missed when making the prediction that she can identify after the experiment?

10.B.3 Formulate questions (e.g., relationships between car age and mileage, average incomes and years of schooling), devise and conduct experiments or simulations, gather data, draw conclusions and communicate results to an audience using traditional methods and contemporary technologies.

10.C.3a Determine the probability and odds of events using fundamental counting principles.

Play to win

🌐 *Together, learn why the "house" usually wins at casinos because of the laws of probability at http://www.learner.org/exhibits/daily math/playing.html.*

10.C.3b Analyze problem situations (e.g., board games, grading scales) and make predictions about results.

Cheeseburger dependent

✎ 🌐 📖 *INGREDIENTS FOR HAMBURGERS OR TURKEY BURGERS, CHEDDAR CHEESE, MOZZARELLA CHEESE, OLIVE Together, first review information about dependent compound events using library resources, or online at http://www.mathgoodies.com/lessons/vol6/dependent_events.html. Then, have your child help you prepare hamburgers or turkey burgers. This is an excellent opportunity for him to practice measuring skills with the necessary ingredients. When forming the patties, insert a small piece of cheddar cheese, a small piece of mozzarella cheese, and half an olive. (Patties should be short and fat, and the items should be separated from one another.) After cooking, cut the burgers into bit-sized pieces and serve on a plate with the rest of the meal. Have your child randomly select the first "unit" to eat. Before actually biting into the piece, have your child mark the probability as a ratio of this first bite containing the cheddar cheese. (If the burger is cut into 16 pieces, then it would be a $\frac{1}{16}$ chance.) After eating, have your child mark the probability as a ratio of getting a piece of mozzarella (or any other item he hasn't eaten yet) in the next randomly selected bite. (This would be $\frac{1}{15}$.) Repeat with the olive ($\frac{1}{14}$), having your child write statistics with each diminishing bit of the burger.*

Science

Middle/Junior High School

11.A.3a Formulate hypotheses that can be tested by collecting data.

11.A.3b Conduct scientific experiments that control all but one variable.

11.A.3c Collect and record data accurately using consistent measuring and recording techniques and media.

Vanilla or chocolate statistics I

Explain to your child that he has just been hired by an ice cream manufacturer to discover people's choice for most popular basic flavor—vanilla or chocolate. (If Chunky Rocky Road is in a chocolate base, it would be considered chocolate; if Cookies 'n Cream is in a vanilla base, it would be listed under vanilla.) Before gathering information, have your junior analyst (child) hypothesize about the flavor he thinks will be the most popular. Then, your child needs to conduct field research. Have your child station himself in front of an ice cream store or in front of the correct isle in the supermarket for a pre-determined amount of time, say twenty minutes. Your child should make notations on paper about the age, gender, and ice cream flavor selection of all buyers. Move to step II.

11.A.3d Explain the existence of unexpected results in a data set.

11.A.3e Use data manipulation tools and quantitative (e.g., mean, mode, simple equations) and representational methods (e.g., simulations, image processing) to analyze measurements.

Vanilla or chocolate statistics II

OPTIONAL COMPUTER SOFTWARE After your child conducts his fieldwork, have him plug the information into tables, graphs, and/or charts, using computer software, if possible, and making sure to represent the different variables (gender, age). For example, your child might create a bar graph that represents different age groups and their corresponding flavor selections, or a table that breaks down chocolate and vanilla preferences by gender. Also, have your child discover the mean, mode, and median of the numbers for each variable. Continue with part III.

11.A.3f Interpret and represent results of analysis to produce findings.

Vanilla or chocolate statistics III

Ask your junior analyst to make inferences and draw conclusions about his research. Move to the final step.

11.A.3g Report and display the process and results of a scientific investigation.

Ask your young scientist to make a formal presentation to the ice cream manufacturing company owners (household members) in an articulate and well-supported manner, using the charts and graphs he created to display his results.

11.B.3a Identify an actual design problem and establish criteria for determining the success of a solution.

Product-design analyst

HOUSEHOLD MATERIALS Have your child identify a design problem in a household object such as a toy, electronic gadget, piece of furniture, kitchen implement, and so forth. Then, have your child establish criteria to determine the success of a solution. For instance, should the product work faster? Does it need to be less labor-intensive? Does the product need a supplemental piece attached? Discuss the criteria with your child and make sure she can articulate why she thinks they will help solve the problem. Then, see if the two of you can come up with additional criteria.

11.B.3b Sketch, propose and compare design solutions to the problem considering available materials, tools, cost effectiveness and safety.

Lung savers

Ask your child to imagine that she is a car designer who has been asked to invent a fabulous looking, energy saving, alternative fuel car. Before beginning her design process, your young designer should do some research about the history of cars and fuel, including the types of cars and fuel in use today. She can use library materials or type terms such as "alternative fuel," "new cars," and so forth into any major Internet search engine. Your child can also visit "Alternative Fuel Vehicles" at http://www.energy.ca.gov/education/AFVs/index.html to see an overview of alternative fueled vehicles of the future. After con-

ducting her research, your child should sketch and revise her design for a prototype, and then present the final car design, clearly labeled with its environmentally sensitive elements, to the client (you).

11.B.3c Select the most appropriate design and build a prototype or simulation.

Just Right I

TOOTHPASTE, TOOTHBRUSH, ORDINARY HOUSEHOLD ITEMS Challenge your child to invent a way to consistently place just the right amount of toothpaste on a toothbrush. Ask him to come up with several suggestions (perhaps using a ruler, paper clip, tape, or pencil) and decide which one he thinks is most likely to work; then have him use common household objects to create the prototype. Move to step II.

11.B.3d Test the prototype using available materials, instruments and technology and record the data.

Just Right II

PROTOTYPE MATERIALS Have your young designer test his prototype for a week and make notes about its success and/or drawbacks. Continue with part III.

11.B.3e Evaluate the test results based on established criteria, note sources of error and recommend improvements.

Just Right III

After a week of testing, have your young designer analyze his notes to identify significant errors and make improvements in the model. Move to the final step.

11.B.3f Using available technology, report the relative success of the design based on the test results and criteria.

OR COMPUTER WRITING PROGRAM Have your child draft and revise a detailed product-design report to potential backers (household members) of the improved "Just Right" toothpaste dispenser invention. The report, containing correct spelling, grammar, and punctuation, should outline the research, prototype testing, and revisions. Distribute the report to the potential backers to see if your young designer's invention receives approval for mass production.

STATE GOAL 12: Understand the fundamental concepts, principles and interconnections of the life, physical and earth/space sciences.

12.A.3a Explain how cells function as "building blocks" of organisms and describe the requirements for cells to live.

Eating green I

Can humans make their own food? What organism on earth can? Green plants can turn sunlight into a meal! Together, learn all about photosynthesis, its role in food/energy production, and the food chain either online using an Internet search engine, or from reference books. From the research, have your child draw images to illustrate each step along the way in the photosynthesis process.

Whose tosis?

LONG YELLOW STRING BEANS, LONG GREEN STRING BEANS, LARGE DINNER PLATE, TWO SMALL DESSERT PLATES First learn about mitosis, the process of cell division at http://esg-www.mit.edu:8001 /esgbio/cb/mitosis.html. To reinforce the concept visually, use string beans (representing chromosomes) and plates to recreate the diagram on the website. First, have your child place four green string beans and four yellow string beans on a large plate (representing the cell, as seen in the website diagram). Continue the mitosis process as illustrated. Pair up the string beans with similar colors (two yellow sets and two green sets),

then align them vertically down the center of the plate, and finally divide them up onto two smaller plates—with one set of green and one set of yellow on each. Each "daughter" cell should now look like the original.

12.A.3b Compare characteristics of organisms produced from a single parent with those of organisms produced by two parents.

12.A.3c Compare and contrast how different forms and structures reflect different functions (e.g., similarities and differences among animals that fly, walk or swim; structures of plant cells and animal cells).

The sun's taste

✍ www 🗐 OPTIONAL: SAMPLE OF CHLOROPHYLL FROM HEALTH FOOD STORE Using life science or biology reference books (or an encyclopedia), or searching online, explore the similarities and differences between plant and animal cells. Have your child create a chart, with "plant cells" and "animal cells" in columns across the top, and listing the characteristics that they have in common, and the ones that are particular to a certain kind of cell. For instance, in plant cells, chloroplasts, resembling incredibly tiny footballs, contain chlorophyll, which helps make food for the plant. To taste the dark green building block of life, buy an organic bottle of chlorophyll at your local health food store. Enhance half a glass of juice (or water) with a tablespoon a day. Besides its nutrients, chlorophyll helps freshen breath.

Edible cell comparison

www 🗐 MATERIALS FOR CELL MODEL Together, review the information in the "Sun's taste" activity. Then, have your child construct one model cell for an animal and one for a plant using Jell-O and other edible items, such miniature marshmallows, m&ms, licorice, and so forth to create the cell membrane, cell wall, nucleus, cytoplasm, chloroplasts, mitochondria, and vacuoles. Have your child identify as many of the differences and similarities between the two cells as possible.

12.B.3a Identify and classify biotic and abiotic factors in an environment that affect population density, habitat and placement of organisms in an energy pyramid.

Living/nonliving detective

Review the definition of <u>biotic</u> (of or relating to life) with your child. With this information, have your child determine the definition for <u>abiotic</u> (characterized by the absence of life or living organisms, such as water, temperature, soil, and so forth). Then, together walk around your neighborhood and have your child fill in a two-column chart listing living (plants, people, animals) and nonliving (buildings, rocks, pavements, traffic lights, signs) elements in the environment. Don't forget to look up high and down low. Later at home, have your child analyze each item on the list and identify to you how the factor may or may not affect population density, habitat, and location of organisms in an energy system. For instance, too many more buildings might wipe out the "live" greenery and animals. An overabundance of squirrels might overrun gardens or lawns. In the future, be on the lookout for environmental changes in your neighborhood and have your child continually update the biotic/abiotic chart.

It's a small world

LARGE, CLEAR PLASTIC SODA BOTTLE WITH TOP CUT OFF, GRAVEL, SMALL PLANTS, ROCKS, BRANCHES, MOSS, PLASTIC WRAP Explain to your child that he is going to create a small ecosystem at home. If possible, first visit a local plant store and examine various terrariums. Then, help your child create an example at home using either the simple online instructions at http://www.nsc.org/ehc/kids/terrariu.htm or a reference book on how to build terrariums (such as a children's book of science experiments). Have your child create an illustrated "viewer's information poster" to display by the container, adding information and observations about the ecosystem of the terrarium over time. The poster should address the living organisms as well as <u>abiotic</u> factors (those without life, such as water, temperature, soil, and so forth). Afterward, discuss what limitations the terrarium has in fully representing the natural environment. (Do animals, insects, and changes in weather interact in the terrarium as they do in a real environment?)

12.B.3b Compare and assess features of organisms for their adaptive, competitive and survival potential (e.g., appendages, reproductive rates, camouflage, defensive structures).

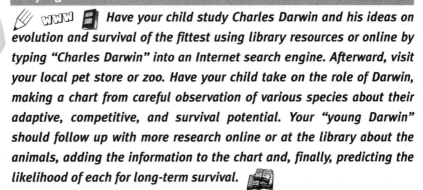

Have your child study Charles Darwin and his ideas on evolution and survival of the fittest using library resources or online by typing "Charles Darwin" into an Internet search engine. Afterward, visit your local pet store or zoo. Have your child take on the role of Darwin, making a chart from careful observation of various species about their adaptive, competitive, and survival potential. Your "young Darwin" should follow up with more research online or at the library about the animals, adding the information to the chart and, finally, predicting the likelihood of each for long-term survival.

12.C.3a Explain interactions of energy with matter including changes of state and conservation of mass and energy.

A cell's choppers

__Mitochondria__ convert the chemical energy contained in food into energy the cell uses to grow, divide, and function. Have your child investigate this cellular "digestion" using reference books or by typing "mitochondria" into an Internet search engine. Ask your child to give a "cell digestion" talk during dinner to household members, explaining the way this process occurs in cells. Your child's discussion should be clear and articulate and presented in a logical, easily understandable manner. Afterward, have your child solicit nicknames from diners for mitochondria, such as "tiny powerhouses" or "mini power plants," to make sure everyone understands the importance of mitochondria and their function.

Whistle away

TEA KETTLE THAT "WHISTLES" Boil water in a kettle that whistles. From a safe distance, have your child describe what happens as the water heats up. What form of energy makes the kettle whistle? (The heat boils the water—the heat energy makes it move, and the resulting steam makes the kettle "whistle.") Discuss with your child what happens when heat is taken away from the tea kettle (the water stops boiling and even-

tually returns to room temperature). Together invent silly lyrics for a song about heat as a form of energy, inserting the whistling kettle at appropriate moments for audible emphasis.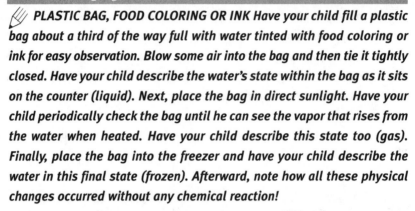

PLASTIC BAG, FOOD COLORING OR INK Have your child fill a plastic bag about a third of the way full with water tinted with food coloring or ink for easy observation. Blow some air into the bag and then tie it tightly closed. Have your child describe the water's state within the bag as it sits on the counter (liquid). Next, place the bag in direct sunlight. Have your child periodically check the bag until he can see the vapor that rises from the water when heated. Have your child describe this state too (gas). Finally, place the bag into the freezer and have your child describe the water in this final state (frozen). Afterward, note how all these physical changes occurred without any chemical reaction!

12.C.3b Model and describe the chemical and physical characteristics of matter (e.g., atoms, molecules, elements, compounds, mixtures).

GUMDROPS, TOOTHPICKS, MINIATURE MARSHMALLOWS Together, learn about protons, neutrons, and electrons in science reference books, or by taking a virtual tour of atoms at http://education.jlab.org/atomtour/. Then, help your child create an edible atomic model. Have your child select gumdrops to represent protons and neutrons (using a different color to represent each), connecting them with toothpicks into circular forms. Then add small, lightweight electrons, using miniature marshmallows.

MEASURING SPOON, SALT, WATER, SUGAR, SHORT CINNAMON STICK, LEMON PEEL, STERILIZED BOTTLE FOR LIQUID STORAGE Allow your child to help you make a natural sore-throat soother, keeping an eye out for chemical and physical changes. First, have your child predict if combining salt and hot water will produce a chemical or *physical change. After adding $\frac{1}{4}$ teaspoon of salt to a cup of hot water in a mug, what happens to the salt? It dissolves. But what happens chemically? The salt (NaCl) and water (H_2O) combine to create salt water: a chemical and physical reaction.*

The tiniest substance

WWW 🗐 *SUGAR, OPTIONAL MAGNIFYING GLASS, PERIODIC TABLE*
Have your child look at a single grain of sugar (with a magnifying glass, if possible). Ask if this is as small as the substance gets. One tiny sugar crystal is made up of millions of sugar molecules! A <u>molecule</u> is the smallest particle of a substance that retains all the properties of the substance. Molecules themselves are made of atoms. Learn more about molecules and atoms, elements and compounds at http://www.nyu.edu/pages/mathmol/textbook/compounds.html, or by researching the topic in a physical science book or encyclopedia. Then, have your child use a periodic table (online at http://pearl1.lanl.gov/periodic/) to identify the type of atoms and their number in a molecule of sugar when written as $C_{12}H_{22}O_{11}$. (12 carbon atoms, 22 hydrogen atoms, 11 oxygen atoms). Also, ask your child how many atoms are in a single molecule of sugar (45). ¹²₃

12.D.3a   Explain and demonstrate how forces affect motion (e.g., action/reaction, equilibrium conditions, free-falling objects).

Arm wrestle

Explain that you will arm wrestle with your child to explore a scientific idea about force. Both take a neutral arm wrestling position. Then, have your child exert a moderate force, which she should keep constant throughout the experiment. Explain that you will change the amount of your own force, from very little to a lot. First, exert just a tiny bit so that your child's hand tips yours over. Then slowly add more force so your hands come into balance, and then, finally, exert more force so your child's hand goes down. Repeat the experience switching roles and having your child speed up the process just a little, noting how much more quickly your clasped hands change location. 🚲

Go outdoors and tell your child you are going to test his baseball pitching arm by enhancing sensitivity to the mass of the ball. For this exercise though, your child won't be using balls. Have your child find three rocks of different masses—light, medium, and heavy. Next, mark the "pitcher's mound" where your child should stand. Then mark "home plate," drawing in the dirt or placing something on the ground that's easy to see (a bright sweater or jacket). Stand out of the way as your child tosses each rock toward the plate, repeating the activity until each rock makes it over home plate. After your child perfects his "pitching arm," ask what he learned about the amount of force needed to make each rock hit the same place. Your child should be able to articulate that the heavier the mass, the stronger the force needed in his pitching arm.

Air-blown race

JAR CAP OR SIMILAR SIZED OBJECT, ITEMS THAT CREATE AIR MOVEMENT SUCH AS A HAIR DRYER, PAPER FAN, BALLOON, OR TIRE PUMP Have your child place a jar cap, or similar sized and weighted object, on the floor. Experiment with sliding it across the floor by using different methods and amounts of force: blowing with her mouth, using a hair dryer at different settings, fanning with paper, letting the air out of a balloon, or even using a bicycle tire pump. Hold an "air-force" competition with two people using the same method of propulsion and marking off how far each different force pushed the cap.

12.D.3b Explain the factors that affect the gravitational forces on objects (e.g., changes in mass, distance).

Mass-weight "diet"

SCALE, CALCULATOR Together, explore the difference between mass and weight. First, have your child weigh himself on a scale and write down the number. Explain that <u>weight</u> is the pull of gravity on an object. If a person weighs 120 pounds, Earth's gravity pulls the person with a 120 force. Ask your child if he would weigh less on Earth or on the Moon. (If necessary, remind your child that the Moon is smaller and has

less gravity.) The Moon's gravitational pull is about $\frac{1}{6}$ as powerful Earth's. Have your child calculate his weight on the Moon, checking the answer with a calculator. Have your child create two sketches of himself— one on the Moon and one on Earth, labeling each figure with the appropriate weight. Now discuss mass—the amount of material in an object. Ask your child if his mass would be different on the Moon than it is on Earth. As a hint, have your child think about astronauts and space vehicles. Do they gain or loose material (or substance) once they leave Earth? If you child's sketches suggest a different mass (size) on the Moon than on Earth, make sure he revises them to reflect this understanding. Have your child use library resources or websites such as http:// www.exploratorium.edu/ronh/weight/ to learn about weight variations on different planets. Have your child ask five people of different ages and sizes if they would like to lose or gain weight, and then have him recommend a planet that would satisfy each person's desire.

12.E.3a   Analyze and explain large-scale dynamic forces, events and processes that affect the Earth's land, water and atmospheric systems (e.g., jetstream, hurricanes, plate tectonics).

Shake, rattle, and explode

WWW *INGREDIENTS FOR EXPLODING VOLCANO, MUSIC Using reference books or the Internet, together explore earthquakes and plate tectonics (online at http://wwwneic.cr.usgs.gov/neis/plate_tectonics /rift_man.html). Then read about volcanoes at http://library.thinkquest. org/17457/english.html. Ask your child to define the difference between volcanoes and earthquakes in his own words. Then build your own exploding volcano with simple kitchen ingredients as described at http://www.spartechsoftware.com/reeko/Experiments/volcano.htm. While working on the experiment, listen to music that parallels the energy of Earth's transformation, such as Russian composer Modest Moussorgsky's "A Night on Bald Mountain" (best known from the Disney movie Fantasia).*

12.E.3b   Describe interactions between solid earth, oceans, atmosphere and organisms that have resulted in ongoing changes of Earth (e.g., erosion, El Nino).

12.E.3c   Evaluate the biodegradability of renewable and nonrenewable natural resources.

12.F.3a   Simulate, analyze and explain the effects of gravitational force in the solar system (e.g., orbital shape and speed, tides, spherical shape of the planets and moons).

12.F.3b   Describe the organization and physical characteristics of the solar system (e.g., sun, planets, satellites, asteroids, comets).

Universal family

 WWW   *Have your child use family members or friends to set up the solar system, with each person playing a planet orbiting around the Sun/"son" (or daughter)! Take turns being different parts to get a sense of the entire solar system. See "Welcome to the Planets" at http://pds.jpl.nasa.gov/planets/ for images of the planets and their relationship to the Sun.*

STATE GOAL 13: Understand the relationships among science, technology and society in historical and contemporary contexts.

13.A.3a   Identify and reduce potential hazards in science activities (e.g., ventilation, handling chemicals).

Science safety

 Ask your child to describe why safety measures must be taken in science activities and have her come up with as many different safety measures as possible, such as wearing safety goggles, putting on gloves before handling chemicals, knowing the location of the fire extinguisher and how to activate it, never leaving an open flame, and so forth. Have your child create a science safety poster to describe what each safety measure accomplishes.

13.A.3b   Analyze historical and contemporary cases in which the work of science has been affected by both valid and biased scientific practices.

Explain to your child that scientific discoveries and practices aren't always accepted when first introduced. Then, using online resources (typing his name into any major Internet search engine) or library materials, have your child investigate the astronomer Galileo, his theories, and the serious trouble they caused him. Galileo's observations through his telescope proved that Copernicus's observations were true— the Sun, not Earth, was the center of the universe. The thinking of the day (in accordance with religious dogma) advocated that man, and thus Earth, was the center of the observable universe; so his ideas came under severe attack. Have your child write and revise a letter, with correct spelling, punctuation, and grammar, to Galileo, explaining why his work was so important from a twenty-first century point of view.

13.A.3c   Explain what is similar and different about observational and experimental investigations.

13.B.3a   Identify and explain ways that scientific knowledge and economics drive technological development.

13.B.3b   Identify important contributions to science and technology that have been made by individuals and groups from various cultures.

Tell your child to imagine that you are going to be the final judge for this year's "World Science and Technology Award," an award that spotlights important new inventions. In this imaginary scenario, it is your child's job to "nominate" potential candidates in writing. Your young nominator (child) should search the Internet or library resources for inventions created by individuals representing different genders, races, and ethnic groups. Have your child take detailed notes about each potential nominee's development and impact, addressing the following: 1) inventor 2) inventor's background 3) name of invention or

industry 4) brief history of its origins 5) its relationship to and impact on society 6) summary statement about why it should be elected as the award winner. As judge, explain to your young nominator that you intend to consider grammar, spelling, and punctuation when evaluating nominations, so it's important to revise and edit each submission carefully. Select one of your child's nominees to win the award, and describe what specifically in your child's writing persuaded you to make this choice. Have your child use what he has learned to create an illustrated award poster that articulates to others the nominee's strengths and background.

13.B.3c Describe how occupations use scientific and technological knowledge and skills.

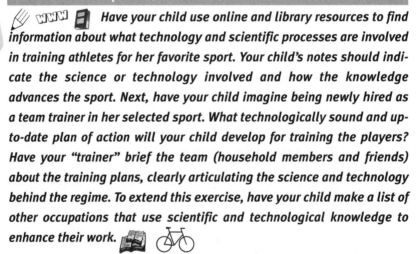

The science of sports

Have your child use online and library resources to find information about what technology and scientific processes are involved in training athletes for her favorite sport. Your child's notes should indicate the science or technology involved and how the knowledge advances the sport. Next, have your child imagine being newly hired as a team trainer in her selected sport. What technologically sound and up-to-date plan of action will your child develop for training the players? Have your "trainer" brief the team (household members and friends) about the training plans, clearly articulating the science and technology behind the regime. To extend this exercise, have your child make a list of other occupations that use scientific and technological knowledge to enhance their work.

13.B.3d Analyze the interaction of resource acquisition, technological development and ecosystem impact (e.g., diamond, coal or gold mining; deforestation).

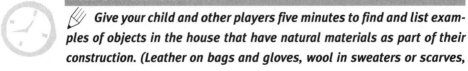

Natural materials hunt

Give your child and other players five minutes to find and list examples of objects in the house that have natural materials as part of their construction. (Leather on bags and gloves, wool in sweaters or scarves, wood in furniture, house plants as decoration, natural sponges, and food to make a meal are examples.) After five minutes are up, have the contestants come back and share their findings, checking one another to make sure the materials are natural. Next, ask everyone to identify for each listed example, the method of acquisition (e.g., sheep shearing for wool), technological needs (e.g., machines and tools for processing and manufacture of food), and impact on the ecosystem (e.g., deforestation for furniture). The player who correctly completes his or her list with the largest variety wins!

13.B.3e   Identify advantages and disadvantages of natural resource conservation and management programs.

13.B.3f   Apply classroom-developed criteria to determine the effects of policies on local science and technology issues (e.g., energy consumption, landfills, water quality).

Better it

Together at the library, research your local conservation laws regarding water use, energy, fuel, and so forth. Have your child take notes for each category. When you return home, have your child consider ways to improve on conservation in the community. (Restricting water use for lawns during dry periods, expanding recycling options or setting up a reward system for those participating in current ones to increase participation, are examples.) Have your child draft, write, and revise an articulate, well-defended letter (with correct spelling, punctuation and grammar) to your local representative stating his brilliant "green" ideas.

ILLINOIS

Social Science

Middle/Junior High School

14.A.3 Describe how responsibilities are shared and limited by the United States and Illinois Constitutions and significant court decisions.

Shared/limited card game I

WWW 📖 *Together, first become familiar with the history of federal versus state government either online at http://bensguide.gpo.gov/6-8/government/index.html or using library reference books. Additional information about state government can be found at http://bensguide. gpo.gov/6-8/government/state/index.html. Then, read through the Constitution of the United States (http://www.midnightbeach.com /jon/US-Constitution.htm) and the Illinois Constitution (http://www.*

legis.state.il.us/commission/lrb/conmain.htm). (These documents can. also be found in reference books at your local library.) Now move on to part II.

14.B.3 Identify and compare the basic political systems of Illinois and the United States as prescribed in their constitutions.

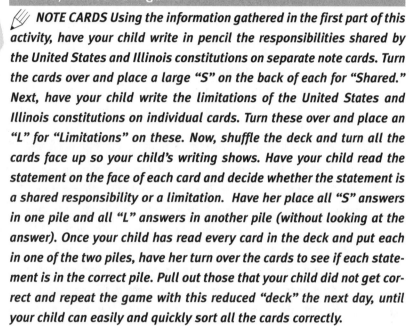

Shared/limited card game II

✍ NOTE CARDS Using the information gathered in the first part of this activity, have your child write in pencil the responsibilities shared by the United States and Illinois constitutions on separate note cards. Turn the cards over and place a large "S" on the back of each for "Shared." Next, have your child write the limitations of the United States and Illinois constitutions on individual cards. Turn these over and place an "L" for "Limitations" on these. Now, shuffle the deck and turn all the cards face up so your child's writing shows. Have your child read the statement on the face of each card and decide whether the statement is a shared responsibility or a limitation. Have her place all "S" answers in one pile and all "L" answers in another pile (without looking at the answer). Once your child has read every card in the deck and put each in one of the two piles, have her turn over the cards to see if each state-ment is in the correct pile. Pull out those that your child did not get cor-rect and repeat the game with this reduced "deck" the next day, until your child can easily and quickly sort all the cards correctly.

14.C.3 Compare historical issues involving rights, roles and status of indi-viduals in relation to municipalities, states and the nation.

Driving age

✍ WWW 📑 GRAPH PAPER Help your child understand that certain rights are determined by state government, not federal (e.g., driving age, highway speed limits). Have your child chart the age at which peo-ple can apply for their driver's license in ten states across the country on a bar graph. Draw a large box on graph paper. List ages sequentially, starting with the youngest age on the bottom and moving up along the left side. Across the bottom horizontal line, mark off ten columns for

the states your child has researched, drawing a vertical line from the bottom to the top of the graph. Label each column with a state. Then fill in a "bar" for each, stemming from the bottom line to the point on the graph that correctly indicates the state's driving age. As an extension, have your child chart the age allowance of all the states and then find the <u>median</u> (the middle value of a group of numbers arranged in order) for the age at which people can apply for their driver's license in the United States. Discuss with your child the reason why a law like the driving age might be left to the states, while other laws are created by the federal government.

14.D.3 Describe roles and influences of individuals, groups and media in shaping current Illinois and United States public policy (e.g., general public opinion, special interest groups, formal parties, media).

GMO debate

Together, explore the controversy over genetically modified food products, taking into account the different opinions of the involved parties, including farmers, food makers, and consumers concerned about the purity of what they consume. (Type "GMO" [Genetically Modified Organisms] into any major Internet search engine or read articles in newspapers or magazines. You also can find information online at http://www.agriculture.com.) With your child, follow the unfolding of the controversy over time, keeping an eye out for news headlines and articles in health magazines and online resources. Also, look for any organizations or policy groups that have played a role in this debate; for example, has a consumer advocacy group been created to fight the use of genetically modified foods? Are there government organizations involved in the debate? Have any of these groups helped shape public policy? Help your child understand the various economic, political, and health factors involved in the situation. Discuss how the GMO issue might touch your own lives, in terms of it affecting the foods you might or might not decide to eat.

14.E.3 Compare the basic principles of the United States and its international interests (e.g., territory, environment, trade, use of technology).

U.S. interests hunt

Have your child read and then summarize the day's newspaper headlines and first paragraphs of the major news stories involving the United States and other nations. Have your child clip each one and tape it to a sheet of paper. Ask your child to identify the reason for United States involvement in each case (territory, environment, trade, use of technology), marking it on the related sheet of paper. Continue the activity over the course of a week, helping your child understand the range and depth of concerns of the United States on the international level.

14.F.3a Analyze historical influences on the development of political ideas and practices as enumerated in the Declaration of Independence, the United States Constitution, the Bill of Rights and the Illinois Constitution.

Historical detective I

Explain to your child that he is going to be an historical detective, searching for the influences on the political ideas that helped shape the Declaration of Independence. Together, first read the Declaration of Independence at http://lcweb2.loc.gov/const/declar.html or find it in a reference book. Have your child summarize in his own words the key points, making a list with plenty of blank space in between each one (e.g., government by and for the people, inalienable rights of people, all men are created equal). Then, rent the movie of the highly entertaining musical 1776. (Helpful background information and questions for discussing the movie appear at http://www.teachwithmovies.org/guides/1776.html.) As you watch, have your young detective pause at any event depicted in the movie that he believes is related to the shaping of the Declaration of Independence. Your young detective should write down the event under the related key point. Ask your young detective to support his detective work with strong "clues." For example, your child could use a character's lines as support for the right to self-government or the end of tyranny. At the end of the movie, have your detective review his "clue" sheet to see how many ideas in the Declaration of Independence he can trace back to specific historical influences. Continue with "Historical detective II" (Standard 16.A.3c).

14.F.3b   Describe how United States political ideas and traditions were instituted in the Constitution and the Bill of Rights.

STATE GOAL 15: Understand economic systems, with an emphasis on the United States.

15.A.3a   Explain how market prices signal producers about what, how and how much to produce.

Be the producer

Review with your child the ideas of market price and supply and demand, either using reference books or the Internet. (Information can be found at http://pittsford.monroe.edu/jefferson/cal fieri/economics/SupDemand.html.) Then, have your child imagine that she runs a farm and is about to plant two new crops. Visit your local supermarket or fruit and vegetable store to conduct "market" research to see which items appear to be in the highest demand. Ask to speak to the store manager and have your child inquire, taking detailed notes, which fruits or vegetables have risen in price recently. Then, have your child ask which produce moves most quickly off the shelves. Afterward, have your child select two crops she will plant this season, supporting her decision and reasoning with specific information from the interviews. Make sure she considers how much competition there is, and how much she will have to charge to cover her costs and make a profit. To extend this activity, keep track of the market price and supply and demand of your young farmer's crops over the next few months.

15.A.3b   Explain the relationship between productivity and wages.

Equal pay for equal work

Have your child imagine running a professional swim team. As the coach, he pays everyone the same amount whenever they participate in relay races. Now your young coach is facing a management problem. One of the team members is not showing up to practice and isn't swimming at his best. The other players are getting annoyed because they are giving

it their all. Have your young coach call the problem player (you) into the office for a little talk, explaining the idea behind equal pay for equal work. What solutions might the coach come up with to solve the problem (e.g., reduce the pay until the player works with the same effort as teammates)? Then, have your child decide what he would do if the relay team won the league championship; would he give them a bonus for their enhanced performance? To extend the activity, have your child imagine that another member of the team approaches him about taking on more responsibility (such as swimming in an individual race in addition to the relay race). How would your child reward that swimmer for an increased performance?

15.A.3c   Describe the relationship between consumer purchases and businesses paying for productive resources.

Who's the consumer?

SMALL BOWLS FOR ICE CREAM, CARTON OF ICE CREAM WITH NUTS OR CHIPS Make the idea of businesses being both producers and consumers tangible for your child. At dessert time, have her imagine owning an ice cream store. Customers (household members) are coming in for ice cream. Stop and ask who is the producer and who is the consumer here? After serving the customers (household members), have them complain that this product is "defective." It has much less nuts (or chips) than usual. Your child realizes that this is right! What will she do to save the business and get the product she has paid for (the carton of ice cream)? Ask your child to outline, draft, edit, and revise a complaint letter, with correct spelling, punctuation, and grammar, to the ice cream supplier, explaining why she, as the consumer is unhappy with the product. Make sure she addresses the topic in the Standard. For example, does she willingly pay more for this ice cream than others on the market because it is a superior product? Are her consumers happier with this product than with other varieties that she has sold in the past? Is this product with less chips/nuts going to cause her to lose business?

15.A.3d   Describe the causes of unemployment (e.g., seasonal fluctuation in demand, changing jobs, changing skill requirements, national spending).

15.B.3a   Describe the "market clearing price" of a good or service.

Help your child understand the idea of the <u>market clearing price</u> of a good or service, in which the supply price leaves no surplus or shortage. Have your child describe a business he might like to run—lemonade stand, dog walker, newspaper delivery, and so forth. Before beginning the venture, your young entrepreneur will need to do some research. Help him begin by listing all the costs related to providing the good or service (tools, transportation, materials, etc.). Then, help your child decide how much profit he expects to make per unit of good or service. Using the research from cost and profit, help your child decide on a price to charge per service or product. Now, before opening for business, have your young entrepreneur survey at least five potential customers, asking if they would pay the price he has designated. Help your child adjust the price accordingly to find the correct market clearing price, so that the supply price leaves no shortages or surpluses. Finally, have your young entrepreneur design an evocative illustrated poster advertising (with correct spelling, punctuation and grammar) for his business, including the "just right" price, based on his research.

15.B.3b   Explain the effects of choice and competition on individuals and the economy as a whole.

Explore the concept of supply and demand on your next trip to the grocery store. Together, study the inventory at your local supermarket, paying special attention to categories where a lot of merchandise is displayed—peanut butter, breakfast cereal, ice cream, bread—and categories where very little merchandise is displayed—specialized gourmet foods. Ask your child what would happen if everyone in the neighborhood stopped eating peanut butter sandwiches and started eating anchovy paste sandwiches instead. What would happen to the store's inventory of these products? If your child was the store manager, would he change the number of supplies previously ordered for each of these goods? Ask the store manager if there has ever been a situation where

customer demand exceeded store supply—rock salt during a snowstorm; batteries and candles during an electrical blackout; charcoal briquettes during cookout season, etc. Now, ask your child to consider the opposite scenario: Would he stop shopping at this store and shop elsewhere if it no longer sold certain products?

15.C.3   Identify and explain the effects of various incentives to produce a good or service.

YELLOW PAGES Together with your child, use the Yellow Pages and newspaper employment ads to make a list down the side of a sheet of paper of as many businesses as possible that your child might want to operate. Then, next to each one, have your child explain the incentive for starting this business. For instance, the incentive to open a computer supply store might be because your child is interested in technology; for an ice cream shop, it could be because your child is an "expert" and can run the store easily; for a child care center, it could be because of the desire to provide a service to the community, and so forth. After running down the list and thinking of as many incentives as possible, have your child select just one business she would like to start. Ask your young entrepreneur to put together a simple business plan—outlining the materials, resources, personnel, and location necessary for starting such a venture.

15.D.3a   Explain the effects of increasing and declining imports and exports to an individual and to the nation's economy as a whole.

Pump fluctuation

Together, use the newspaper and Internet to investigate the cost of gasoline, its current state of shortage or abundance in the United States, and its relationship to imports and exports. Are we currently producing enough gasoline in the United States or is there a shortage? Have we had to import more? Do we need to find new sources of gasoline within the U.S.? Or, maybe we currently have a surplus – does that mean we're exporting more? Has the shortage or abundance impacted

the price? How will this affect the nation as a whole? How about individual purchasers of gasoline? Have your child use his research to design a script for a television talk show in which an economist, environmentalist, and politician discuss the subject, formulating written statements for each perspective. Each person's statement should use specific facts to support his or her view, and contain correct grammar, spelling, and punctuation. Afterward, read all three statements back to your child, asking him to critique how they sound. Are there ways your child can improve writing to make each person's case stronger? Have your child revise his work, and then together with a third actor, perform the talk show for friends and household members.

15.D.3b   Explain how comparative advantage forms the basis for specialization and trade among nations.

Best buy

EXAMPLES OF MUSTARDS FROM THE UNITED STATES, GERMANY, AND FRANCE Have your child imagine owning all the food concession stands that sell hot dogs in arenas, stadiums, and movie theaters in the United States. As the "top dog," your young entrepreneur needs to decide which mustard to buy for this huge national business. Taste test at least two mustards from different countries. Have your young owner determine which will sell the most hot dogs, supporting his decision with articulate reasoning (e.g., this one is too spicy, bland, or has a strange color; this one has an appealing smell and tang). Then, discuss how countries like France and Germany have come to specialize in mustard. Have your child identify the special products in the United States that are regularly sought by other countries for their quality. (e.g., Hollywood movies, sneakers, jeans).

15.D.3c   Explain how workers can affect their productivity through training and by using tools, machinery and technology.

Better batter soufflé

 WWW **MAC** **SOUFFLÉ (OR MERINGUE OR PIE) RECIPE AND INGREDIENTS, HAND EGGBEATER, ELECTRIC MIXER** *The kitchen is a perfect place for your child to learn how technology and training help productivity. Together, select an appetizing soufflé or meringue cookie or pie recipe (online or in a recipe book or magazine). Help your child prepare the dessert. When it comes time to beat the egg whites, have your child begin with the hand eggbeater. Once her arm becomes tired, switch to the electric mixer. Have your child note whether using the electric mixer makes the job easier or more difficult, as well as faster or slower. Then, have her consider how this tool would affect production if she was a chef for a bakery producing more than 100 soufflés, batches of meringue cookies, or pies a day. Repeat the exercise a few weeks later, or adapt it with a recipe involving whipping cream (by hand or electric beater), grating or slicing vegetables (by knife, grater, or food processor), and so forth, and have your child describe how her "training" (performing the task more than once) affects her productivity.*

15.E.3a Identify the types of taxes levied by differing levels of governments (e.g., income tax, sales tax, property tax).

Tax time

 WWW *TAX FORMS Together, visit the U.S. Department of the Treasury kids' site "Simplified Wage and Tax Reporting System" at http://www.employers.gov/stawrs/kids/ to learn about the tax responsibilities of starting a new business. Have your child discover what taxes are used for and the job of different government agencies. Then, have your child start his own virtual business from the three ventures offered at http://www.employers.gov/stawrs/kids/business.htm. The interactive experience will take your young entrepreneur through sales, hiring employees, and filing the correct forms. When tax season rolls around, show your child the different local, state, and federal forms that you use to determine income tax on earnings from salaries and investments.* **1 2 3**

15.E.3b Explain how laws and government policies (e.g., property rights, contract enforcement, standard weights/measurements) establish rules that help a market economy function effectively.

POPCORN, SMALL BOWLS Review examples of standard weights and measurements used in the United States (ounces, feet, acres, etc.). Now, demonstrate for your child why having a national standard of measurement is important. Place a large bowl of popcorn on a table. Explain that each of you can have one serving by taking as much as you can in just one hand. Ask your child to count the kernels in your serving and in hers. Are the serving sizes equal? What would it be like if every time you went to the movies your popcorn serving varied according to the size of the hands of the people behind the counter who were helping you? Would everyone be paying for the same amount of goods? Reinforce this idea with the use of standardized weights and measures on cereal boxes, canned goods, etc. Have your child explain how these standardized numbers allow you to compare one product to another and how rules like these help the economy function smoothly.

STATE GOAL 16: Understand events, trends, individuals and movements shaping the history of Illinois, the United States and other nations.

Historical eras

Local, State and United States History (US)

• Early history in the Americas to 1620

• Colonial history and settlement to 1763

• The American Revolution and early national period to 1820s

• National expansion from 1815 to 1850

• The Civil War and Reconstruction from 1850 to 1877

- Development of the industrial United States from 1865 to 1914

- The emergence of the United States as a world power from 1890 to 1920

- Prosperity, depression, the New Deal and World War II from 1920 to 1945

- Post World War II and the Cold War from 1945 to 1968

- Contemporary United States from 1968 to present

World History (W)

- Prehistory to 2000 BCE

- Early civilizations, nonwestern empires, and tropical civilizations

- The rise of pastoral peoples to 1000 BCE

- Classical civilizations from 1000 BCE to 500 CE

- Fragmentation and interaction of civilizations from 500 to 1100 CE

- Centralization of power in different regions from 1000 to 1500 CE

- Early modern world from 1450 to 1800

- Global unrest, change and revolution from 1750 to 1850

- Global encounters and imperialism and their effects from 1850 to 1914

- The twentieth century to 1945

- The contemporary world from 1945 to the present

16.A.3a   Describe how historians use models for organizing historical interpretation (e.g., biographies, political events, issues and conflicts).

History models

HISTORY TEXTBOOK Together, examine your child's history textbook to identify how the authors organized the information. Is the organization based on key individuals, events, or issues/conflicts (such as wars) throughout history? Ask your child to describe how, as a television producer of a series about world history, he would organize the historical information in a way that would grab viewers and facilitate their understanding of key events.

16.A.3b   Make inferences about historical events and eras using historical maps and other historical sources.

Historical visualizations

Visit your local historical society or library to view maps, drawings, and photographs of your community 100 years ago. Ask your child to be a visual detective and try to piece together the visual clues to tell you about the community. Were there any events of national significance occurring at the time that you can find clues about in the maps or photos? What about events in the community? Did people with the same ethnic or religious background tend to live in particular neighborhoods? Was the neighborhood growing or shrinking? Were train stations built? Have your child take notes about how the community was different in terms of physical environment, technology, population, and so forth. At home, have your child write and draw a "then and now" walking tour guide of your community. The map should lead people to places that demonstrate visual evidence of how things at different sites have changed, along with a brief explanation, containing correct spelling, punctuation, and grammar.

16.A.3c   Identify the differences between historical fact and interpretation.

Review the first part of this activity together (see Standard 14.F.3a). Next, have your child use textbooks, library materials, or the Internet to further research the events of the Second Continental Congress, on which the movie musical 1776 was based. Help your child differentiate fact from interpretation. For instance, we know that Thomas Jefferson drafted the Declaration, but his character in the movie interprets how he felt about the experience. Also, movies sometimes take creative license with historical events to make them more interesting or appealing; can your child find any evidence of this in the movie? Apply this same dissection technique to newspaper editorials about current events, asking your child to circle facts in one color and interpretation/opinion in another.

16.B.3a (US) Describe how different groups competed for power within the colonies and how that competition led to the development of political institutions during the early national period.

Let's party!

Ask your child to name the two major political parties in America today. Now, explore their origin together, learning about the Federalists, led by Alexander Hamilton, and Thomas Jefferson's Democratic-Republicans using reference books or online at http://gi.grolier.com/presidents/nbk/side/polparty.html (scroll down to the section "Parties Begin in the U.S."). Have your child use the information to identify the differences of opinion and approach to government between the two parties and then design campaign posters, using evocative images and text (with correct spelling, punctuation, and grammar) for both parties, defining and supporting the political stance of each. Finally, have your child imagine hosting a fundraiser (at which the posters will be hung) for the Federalists and one for the Democratic-Republicans. Given what your child has learned about the interests of each party, what types of people should your child invite to each party's bash to raise campaign funds? Which party would someone who wants strong state government likely support and why? How about someone concerned with the country staying out of foreign affairs?

211

16.B.3b (US) Explain how and why the colonies fought for their independence and how the colonists' ideas are reflected in the Declaration of Independence and the United States Constitution.

Declaration theater

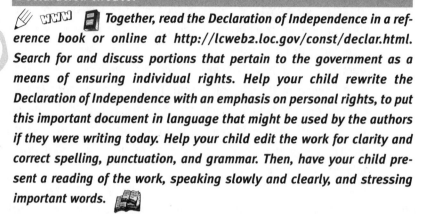

Together, read the Declaration of Independence in a reference book or online at http://lcweb2.loc.gov/const/declar.html. Search for and discuss portions that pertain to the government as a means of ensuring individual rights. Help your child rewrite the Declaration of Independence with an emphasis on personal rights, to put this important document in language that might be used by the authors if they were writing today. Help your child edit the work for clarity and correct spelling, punctuation, and grammar. Then, have your child present a reading of the work, speaking slowly and clearly, and stressing important words.

16.B.3c (US) Describe the way the Constitution has changed over time as a result of amendments and Supreme Court decisions.

Changing constitution

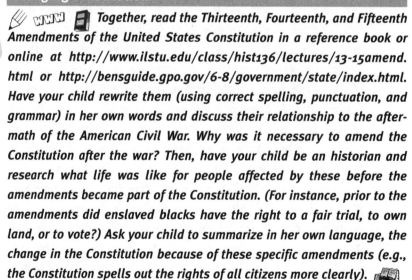

Together, read the Thirteenth, Fourteenth, and Fifteenth Amendments of the United States Constitution in a reference book or online at http://www.ilstu.edu/class/hist136/lectures/13-15amend.html or http://bensguide.gpo.gov/6-8/government/state/index.html. Have your child rewrite them (using correct spelling, punctuation, and grammar) in her own words and discuss their relationship to the aftermath of the American Civil War. Why was it necessary to amend the Constitution after the war? Then, have your child be an historian and research what life was like for people affected by these before the amendments became part of the Constitution. (For instance, prior to the amendments did enslaved blacks have the right to a fair trial, to own land, or to vote?) Ask your child to summarize in her own language, the change in the Constitution because of these specific amendments (e.g., the Constitution spells out the rights of all citizens more clearly).

16.B.3d (US) Describe ways in which the United States developed as a world political power.

16.B.3a (W) Compare the political characteristics of Greek and Roman civilizations with non-Western civilizations, including the early Han dynasty and Gupta empire, between 500 BCE and 500 CE.

Ancient East/West political power

First, together learn about the Republic of Rome at http://www.roman-empire.net/republic/rep-index.html (or by typing the term into any major Internet search engine); you can also find this information in reference books. Have your child take notes about its most important aspects, making a list on a piece of paper. Then, together learn about the politics and culture of China's Han dynasty with library resources or online at http://central.k12.ca.us/akers/dynasty. html #anchor1073558 and http://encyclopedia.com/articles/20584.html, also making a list. Afterward, together use the lists to compare the political and cultural characteristics of the ancient Greeks and ancient Chinese. You and your child should then each write a letter from the point of view of a citizen in one of the societies (one of you will be from ancient Greece, the other from ancient China), using your researched information to persuade the other that your form of government makes the most sense and why. Trade letters and respond to each other's remarks. The letters should include opening paragraphs presenting the main idea(s), and persuasive well-supported arguments in the subsequent paragraphs, as well as correct spelling, grammar, and punctuation.

16.B.3b (W) Identify causes and effects of the decline of the Roman empire and other major world political events (e.g., rise of the Islamic empire, rise and decline of the T'ang dynasty, establishment of the kingdom of Ghana) between 500 CE and 1500 CE.

16.B.3c (W) Identify causes and effects of European feudalism and the emergence of nation states between 500 CE and 1500 CE.

Together, explore the basics of feudalism using reference books or online at http://www.mc.maricopa.edu/academic/ cult_sci/anthro/lost_tribes/Feudalism.html and learn about each person's role in a feudal society. Have your child describe both the privileges and responsibilities of the monarch, noble, and serf within a feudal society, identifying and supporting which status he would have wished to have at the time. Further your child's understanding by taking on the roles of an older and younger vassal in the "Oath of Fealty," as described at http://www.mauigateway.com/~john/Feudalism/oath.htm. As an extension, together write your own oath, translating your rights and obligations to one another in contemporary terms. For instance, the "older vassal" will promise to feed, shelter, and care for the younger one. The "younger vassal" will pledge to attend to chores, keep his room neat, and be kind to siblings.

16.B.3d (W) Describe political effects of European exploration and expansion on the Americas, Asia, and Africa after 1500 CE.

16.C.3a (US) Describe economic motivations that attracted Europeans and others to the Americas, 1500-1750.

Investigate with your child some of the reasons that spurred Western European colonization in the Americas, including the Spanish Reconquista and other countries' colonizing efforts. Have your child imagine needing to recruit volunteers to join her on one of these colonizing ventures. She should create an illustrated advertisement that will persuade people to join the effort. What words and images will entice people to leave their homes and travel to a new, unknown land? Your young recruiter's poster, containing correct spelling, grammar, and punctuation, along with compelling visual images, should reflect an understanding of her research about the economic incentive for people who came to the Americas.

16.C.3b (US) Explain relationships among the American economy and slavery, immigration, industrialization, labor and urbanization, 1700-present.

Roots

WWW 📺 *Together, watch the videotaped version of the 1977 miniseries* **Roots**, *which details the life of a black family, starting in Gambia, Africa in 1750 through emancipation and reconstruction. Helpful background information and questions are available online at http://www.teachwithmovies.org/guides/roots-vol-i.html (with additional questions for each of the six episodes on related pages). Then, using your research and the tape as a basis, help your child identify the economic factors that brought slavery to North America in the first place. Have your child consider how economics, as related to slavery, also played a part in the division of the country into North and South during the American Civil War. (Southern plantation life and production depended heavily on slave labor.)*

16.C.3c (US) Describe how economic developments and government policies after 1865 affected the country's economic institutions including corporations, banks and organized labor.

16.C.3a (W) Describe major economic trends from 1000 to 1500 CE including long distance trade, banking, specialization of labor, commercialization, urbanization and technological and scientific progress.

Silk road journal

✍ 🖊 **WWW** 📓 *Explore the importance and lucrative allure of long-distance trade between the East and West. Together, read about and follow the "Silk Road" on the map at http://library.thinkquest.org/13406/sr/ or by typing the term into any major Internet search engine (you can also research this topic using library resources). Tell your child to imagine being a merchant traveling the 7,000-mile route, which spanned China, Central Asia, Northern India, and the Parthian and Roman Empires. Have your child research information (online or at the library) about each of the major countries he would have passed through. As you travel virtually from one location to another, have your child keep* *a detailed written and illustrated travel log about what he would sell or buy in each location. Your child's writing should contain correct grammar, punctuation, and spelling as well as capture the spirit of the trading journey during this time.*

16.C.3b (W) Describe the economic systems and trade patterns of North America, South America and Mesoamerica before the encounter with the First look at a map of the Americas before European Conquest.

16.C.3c (W) Describe the impact of technology (e.g., weaponry, transportation, printing press, microchips) in different parts of the world, 1500–present.

Printed word

Have your child hunt through your home and make a list of all the written material that has been produced with printing technology (books, newspapers, comics, magazines, junk mail, instruction manuals, food labels, CD and videotape covers, and so forth). Discuss how printing, something your child likely takes for granted, is essential to daily contemporary life. But printing did not always exist. Together, explore the history of its development either using reference books, or online at http://www.digital century.com/encyclo/update/print.html. Have your child describe what school would be like if there was no printing technology. Every book she reads would have had to be written and illustrated by hand! How might this affect the number of books available and their cost? (In earlier times, only the rich could afford handmade books, and only they could read.)

16.D.3a (US) Describe characteristics of different kinds of communities in various sections of America during the colonial/frontier periods and the 19th century.

French Illinois and Gold Rush California

Investigate the lives of people in two different communities during the nineteenth century. First, follow the engrossing individual stories of individuals in nineteenth century Illinois on the "At Home in the Heartland" website of the Illinois State Museum at http://www.muse-

um.state.il.us/exhibits/athome/1850/welcome.htm. Then, move westward together, clicking on "The People" at http://www.calg oldrush. com/ to learn about the various diverse communities in California during the Gold Rush. Have your child write lyrics for a song about the hardships of frontier life for people in both of these locations and periods. Your child might alternate verses for each location, or address particular themes (work, food, environment, etc.) per verse. Overall, your child's carefully revised musical composition should reflect an understanding of the differences and commonalities between the two areas and also contain correct spelling, punctuation, and grammar.

16.D.3b (US) Describe characteristics of different kinds of families in America during the colonial/frontier periods and the 19th century.

16.D.3 (W) Identify the origins and analyze consequences of events that have shaped world social history including famines, migrations, plagues, slave trading.

No potatoes

Together, view the illustrations and political cartoons of the times related to the infamous Irish potato famine at "Views of the Famine," hosted by Vassar College at http://vassun.vassar.edu/~sttaylor/ FAMINE/. Examine how these visual images convey different aspects of the crisis. Discuss how the famine was a major cause of emigration to the United States, as people came in the hopes of finding a better life. Where did they settle? What impact did this have on the culture of the existing cities? Were they welcomed, or did they struggle? Afterward, explore the countries of origin for the majority of new immigrants arriving in your own area (using library resources or the United States Census Bureau website at http://www.census.gov/ for information). Together, try to discern the reasons people leave their homes to come to this country today, interviewing immigrants in your community or speaking with community organizations. How do the reasons (political, economic, etc.) compare to those of the Irish in the nineteenth century?

16.E.3a (US) Describe how early settlers in Illinois and the United States adapted to, used and changed the environment prior to 1818.

Early pioneer environmental game

✍ **WWW** *Together, carefully look at the pictures and read the information about early pioneers in Illinois on the "Illinois Historic Preservation Agency" site at http://www.state.il.us/hpa/lib/edservices/Pioneers. htm. Both of you should individually "hunt" for evidence (in the picture and texts), making as long a list as possible of the ways the early settlers adapted, changed, and used the environment. Cutting trees, hunting, raising animals, farming, use of boats, and so forth are all examples. Afterward, each of you should describe how the items you noted interacted with the environment. Each person gets a point for correctly describing the relationship, say, "cutting trees for logs to make a house altered the environment" or "using boats for travel was adapting to it." Finally, either player gets a "bonus" point for noticing and listing something that the other player did not list. (For example, if only one of you noticed that a wagon meant roads had been built, and thus changed the environment.) The player with the most points wins!*

16.E.3b (US) Describe how the largely rural population of the United States adapted, used and changed the environment after 1818.

16.E.3c (US) Describe the impact of urbanization and suburbanization, 1850 - present, on the environment.

16.E.3a (W) Describe how the people of the Huang He, Tigris-Euphrates, Nile and Indus river valleys shaped their environments during the agricultural revolution, 4000 - 1000 BCE.

16.E.3b (W) Explain how expanded European and Asian contacts affected the environment of both continents, 1000 BCE - 1500 CE.

20-Minute Learning Connection

STATE GOAL 17: Understand world geography and the effects of geography on society, with an emphasis on the United States.

17.A.3a Explain how people use geographic markers and boundaries to analyze and navigate the Earth (e.g., hemispheres, meridians, continents, bodies of water).

International soccer

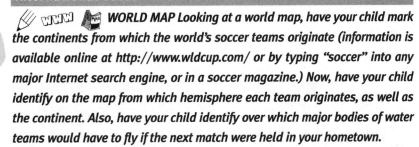

WORLD MAP Looking at a world map, have your child mark the continents from which the world's soccer teams originate (information is available online at http://www.wldcup.com/ or by typing "soccer" into any major Internet search engine, or in a soccer magazine.) Now, have your child identify on the map from which hemisphere each team originates, as well as the continent. Also, have your child identify over which major bodies of water teams would have to fly if the next match were held in your hometown.

17.A.3b Explain how to make and use geographic representations to provide and enhance spatial information including maps, graphs, charts, models, aerial photographs, satellite images.

Diorama identity

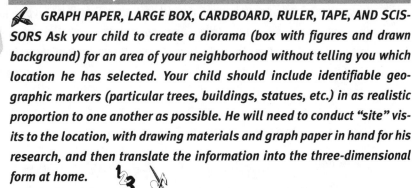

GRAPH PAPER, LARGE BOX, CARDBOARD, RULER, TAPE, AND SCISSORS Ask your child to create a diorama (box with figures and drawn background) for an area of your neighborhood without telling you which location he has selected. Your child should include identifiable geographic markers (particular trees, buildings, statues, etc.) in as realistic proportion to one another as possible. He will need to conduct "site" visits to the location, with drawing materials and graph paper in hand for his research, and then translate the information into the three-dimensional form at home.

17.B.3a Explain how physical processes including climate, plate tectonics, erosion, soil formation, water cycle, and circulation patterns in the ocean shape patterns in the environment and influence availability and quality of natural resources.

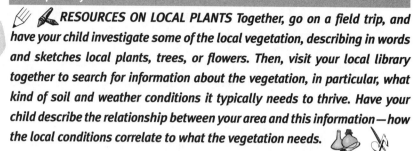

RESOURCES ON LOCAL PLANTS Together, go on a field trip, and have your child investigate some of the local vegetation, describing in words and sketches local plants, trees, or flowers. Then, visit your local library together to search for information about the vegetation, in particular, what kind of soil and weather conditions it typically needs to thrive. Have your child describe the relationship between your area and this information—how the local conditions correlate to what the vegetation needs.

17.B.3b Explain how changes in components of an ecosystem affect the system overall.

We're all connected

Help your child make a list, and describe the interrelationship, of all the elements of an ecosystem near you (vegetation, water, animals, including humans), using library materials or the Internet for research, if necessary. Then, reinforce the idea of interdependence in an ecosystem with the following physical activity: Gather a minimum of four people, each representing a different aspect of the ecosystem. Your child should assign everyone a role, explaining how he or she interacts with another element (person), eventually making sure that the group is linked up in a circle. Now, you should step out, asking everyone else to stay put (not close up the circle). Ask your child to describe how the hole left by your departure from the ecosystem affects each of the other components in turn. Use this activity as an introduction to the need for preservation and ecology.

17.C.3a Explain how human activity is affected by geographic factors.

Resort planning

On a walk together, discuss your neighborhood's physical environment. Have your child imagine that she is about to start a new business, opening a resort in your community. What activities will your child offer to take advantage of the natural environment? Will there be outdoor ice-skating, snow skiing, rock climbing, horseback riding, ten-

nis, or scuba diving? What outdoor activities are not feasible in the resort and which ones are appropriate, given its geographic location and seasonal weather patterns? Have your child make a detailed plan for her resort, with descriptions of the activities to be offered and the natural environment in which they will take place.

17.C.3b Explain how patterns of resources are used throughout the world.

Shopping detective

WORLD MAP At the supermarket, have your child find and make a list of the countries of origin of as many products as possible—fruits from the Caribbean islands, olive oil from Italy, coffee from Kenya, cheese from the Netherlands, yogurt from France, and so forth. When you return home, have your child mark a world map with the name of each resource on its respective country of origin. See if your child can add more items to the list on subsequent shopping trips and start drawing correlations between the types of products that each country produces (such as fruits and vegetables from the Caribbean, dairy products from the Netherlands, and so forth). Also, help your child find patterns between countries with similar characteristics (such as a warm climate or rich farmland) and the types of foods they produce.

17.C.3c Analyze how human processes influence settlement patterns including migration and population growth.

Industrial revolution/urban growth

Together, read about the Industrial Revolution in reference books or online at http://tqjunior.thinkquest.org/4132/info.htm. Then, explain that with the growth of factories during the American Industrial Revolution, increasing numbers of young people, including women, migrated to urban areas. Together, explore the life of a "Mill Girl" working in Lowell, Massachusetts at http://www.fordham.edu/halsall/mod/robinson-lowell.html. Have your child use information from the site to write a journal entry from the point of view of a young working girl in the mill, describing her typical day and feelings about it—

doing repetitive work, being far from home, but also having the new free-dom to live with other single females in an urban setting. Give your child feedback on the journal entry, and then have him revise it, responding to your comments and double-checking for correct spelling, punctuation, grammar, and evocative tone.

17.D.3a Explain how and why spatial patterns of settlement change over time.

Charting United States growth

www 📖 *Have your child explore the "U.S. Territorial Growth" maps from 1775–1920, selecting three examples from different time periods at http://www.lib.utexas.edu/Libs/PCL/Map_collection/histus.html. As you move chronologically forward, have your child describe the changes in settle-ment patterns in North America. Then, for each of the three time periods, have your child use the Internet or library materials to discover what was occurring in history that contributed to the country's expansion (e.g., the discovery of gold in California drew thousands to the area in the mid-1800s).*

17.D.3b Explain how interactions of geographic factors have shaped present conditions.

STATE GOAL 18: Understand social systems, with an emphasis on the United States.

18.A.3 Explain how language, literature, the arts, architecture and traditions contribute to the development and transmission of culture.

Multicultural festival

✎ www 📖 *WALL CALENDAR TO WRITE ON, JOURNAL Together, cre-ate your own multicultural calendar, looking for information about differ-ent holidays and celebrations around the world using library resources or online at http://www.kidlink.org/KIDPROJ/MCC/. Select several holi-days and mark the name of each on its corresponding date on your cal-endar. Identify which aspect of each you will celebrate on that particular day (food, music, story, dance, game). The night before the celebration day, have your child select and read aloud a myth for the culture represented, using library resources or the Internet (such as at http://www.fullwebinfo.com/Top/Arts/Literature/Myths_and_Folktales /Myths/). Keep an eye out for local cultural celebrations open to the public, having your child keep a journal describing in detail the differences and similarities between the experiences.*

18.B.3a   Analyze how individuals and groups interact with and within institutions (e.g., educational, military).

Lines of interaction

On a large piece of plain paper, have your child draw a big circle. Inside, have your child list everyone in the household, using one color pen. Within the circle, have your child list some examples of how and when household members interact with one another (e.g., at meals, doing chores, watching television, playing sports). Then have your child use a different color pen to make individual small circles outside of the single large circle, and list the names of other institutions or groups (e.g., school, extended family, friends). Have your child use a third colored pen to draw a line from the family circle to the smaller individual circles. On each line, ask your child to describe how your household interacts with these other groups. To extend the activity, have your child add circles around each of the small circles for those groups that they interact with, getting an increasingly complex visual picture of social interaction.

18.A.3b   Explain how social institutions contribute to the development and transmission of culture.

Cultural transmission

OBJECTS FROM HOME Discuss how a museum—be it art, history, or science—transmits and contributes to culture. Recall a museum trip you've taken, using it as an example of how you learned about earlier times in a history museum, or the life of an artist in a different country in an art exhibition. Next, have your child "curate" a small exhibition based on your household's heritage and culture. First, have your child think about what it is she would like others to understand about your house-hold. What might you communicate about your social activities, beliefs and morals, origins, educational experiences, etc.? Have your child search the house for objects that will communicate these themes. Look at photographs, clothes, artwork, special serving ware and utensils, deco-rated tools, holiday-related items, and so forth. Have your child select several items to represent her curatorial theme. Then, have your curator write (after outlining, drafting, editing, and revising) an explanatory label for each object. The legible label, with correct spelling, punctua-tion, and grammar, should share how the item fits into the household and illustrates an aspect of culture—your activities and beliefs. Invite others to view the exhibit, with your child acting as the museum guide, explain-ing the works and their intended meaning.

18.C.3a Describe ways in which a diverse U.S. population has developed and maintained common beliefs (e.g., life, liberty and the pursuit of hap-piness; the Constitution and the Bill of Rights).

July 4th sing along!

Discuss the rich variety of cultural, social, and religious beliefs in the United States with your child as reflected by the abundance of differ-ent cuisines, holiday observances, religious institutions, and the like. Next, ask your child to summarize the rights of United States citizens, reviewing the earlier "Declaration theater" activity, if necessary (see Standard 16.B.3b [US]). Ask your child to compose lyrics for a Fourth of July song that celebrates the ways the diverse United States populations also are threaded together by common beliefs, such as life, liberty and the pursuit of happiness.

18.C.3b Explain how diverse groups have contributed to U.S. social systems over time.

Democratic contributions

Together, read how the Haudenosaunee (Iroquois) and other Native American confederacies helped shape the ideas of democra-cy in the early United States online at http://www.fee.org/educa tion/lessons/9909/sturgis.html or using library resources. Learn about connections between United States political systems and rights, and those developed earlier by native people with whom the early founders of the United States had contact. Have your child draw a line down the middle of a sheet of paper and place "Native American Institution" as the header in the left column, and "United States Institution" in the right. Then, have your child note parallels between the two societies, such as The Great Law of Peace, which included a section similar to the U.S. Bill of Rights, both of which protect the individual's rights to the freedom of worship, speech, and assembly.